UNDER-STANDING LAUGHTER
the workings of wit & humor

UNDER-STANDING LAUGHTER

the workings of wit & humor

Charles R. Gruner

Nelson-Hall nh Chicago

Library of Congress Cataloging in Publication Data

Gruner, Charles R
    Understanding laughter.

    Bibliography: p.
    Includes index.
    1.   Laughter.   2.   Wit and humor—Psychology.
I.   Title.
BF575.L3G79   152.4   78-16759
ISBN 0-88229-186-6

Copyright © 1978 by Charles R. Gruner

Manufactured in the United States of America.

10   9   8   7   6   5   4   3   2   1

Contents

Preface

Two considerations prompted the writing of this book; first, the many disparate theories and minitheories of why people laugh cause confusion and, often, compel people to throw up their hands and declare that humor is absolutely unexplainable; second, anyone interested in empirical evidence of the communicative impact of wit and humor can find it only in scattered professional journal articles written in academic language. And, even if these journal articles could be found and interpreted, the reader would be unable to judge for himself the quality of the humorous material used in the study, unless he could find the original thesis or dissertation (which would provide the humorous material used in the appendix) or could obtain the material from the authors.

The target for this book is the more literate and educated adult reader. I have found in my writing and speaking about the psychology of humor that a great deal of interest is shown by our better educated citizens in "what makes humor funny." A number of people in academe, as in psychology, sociology, communication, language and literature, etc. might find this book interesting and useful in their work.

I feel that the benefits of the book are basically two-fold: it is educational, but also entertaining. While making all laughter and laughter-provoking stimuli understandable, and dispelling some "myths" about human laughter, the theoretical sections are generously illustrated with humorous material. In the last two chapters, each a summary of a body of research, again the material is liberally sprinkled with humor, that used in the actual studies. The book is a small treasury of humor, a theoretical argument, and a reference book.

This book covers much the same territory as Albert Rapp's *The Origin of Wit and Humor* (Professor Rapp gave kind permission to quote him liberally); however, *Understanding Laughter* goes beyond Rapp's work to show further proof for the theory's correctness by using such formulations as Jung's theory of personality. Further, this book demonstrates how the theory propounded can be used to explain the relationship (and differences) between "wit" and "humor," a distinction often grappled with in vain. In attempting to demonstrate that all humor and wit can be explained within the confines of a single theory, the book goes beyond such works as *The Psychology of Humor* edited by Jeffrey Goldstein and Paul McGhee (Academic Press, 1972) which will not theorize beyond what there is solid and verifiable evidence to support. They despair at contemplating a single and all-encompassing theory, preferring to stick with noncomprehensive minitheories.

This book is unique in that it summarizes all the available research on humorous stimuli *as communication* and, at the same time, presents the humorous material used in the research so that it can be judged as to quality. I would like to thank my fellow researchers for the time and trouble of getting to me the humorous stimuli used in their studies. Also a strong word of thanks must go to my wife and colleague, Marsha W. Gruner, who helped so much in the preparation and typing of this manuscript.

I

THEORETICAL CONSIDERATIONS:
The Causes of Laughter

1

Fuzzy Thinking about Laughter

Human societies treasure laughter and whatever can produce it. Without laughter everyday living becomes drab and lifeless; life would seem hardly human at all. Likewise, a sense of humor is generally considered a person's most admirable attribute. Indeed, few people would be willing to admit that they are deficient in this quality. It is perhaps this high value which humans place upon laughter, its stimuli, and the sense of humor which has caused so much fuzzy, chaotic, downright illogical thinking on the subject. Alexander Pope wrote in his *Moral Essays*:

> The ruling passion, be it what it will,
> The ruling passion conquers reason still.

I have remained a more or less serious student of laughter, its causes and effects, since 1955. My interest and study in the field have provided me fodder for several graduate school term papers, a Ph.D. dissertation on the persuasive effect of satire, and enough experimental/scholarly projects to remain relatively competitive in the publish-or-perish game played in our modern universities. This fairly constant study over the years has caused me to promise myself many times that I would write

1

a book in which the fuzzy thinking about laughter and its stimuli would be exposed, if not to ridicule, at least to common sense
analysis. The present volume is that promise carried to
completion.

To begin with, some people consider laughter so precious a
commodity they claim it solely for human beings. Just as some
Biblical dogma supposes that God provides only humans with
souls, human egotism has exclusively reserved the gift of laughter for Homo sapiens. Ernest Harms put it this way:

> A child is born with an urge to laughter as one of the most
> specific human attitudes; this urge is not found even in the
> highest representatives of the animal kingdom.[1]

His pronouncement is echoed by psychologist Martha
Wolfenstein:

> Humor is a distinctively human achievement: among liv-
> ing things only human beings laugh.[2]

Charles Greville has been quoted to the effect that

> Man is the only creature endowed with the power of
> laughter.[3]

And the German philosopher, Nietzsche, in *The Will to
Power*, said:

> Man alone suffers so excruciatingly in the world that he
> was compelled to invent laughter.[4]

Is it really true that only *people* laugh? Egotism and scattered expert testimony notwithstanding, the answer must be
"No." Although humans alone have the sophisticated language
ability for making up jokes, puns, riddles, conundrums, and so
on, they are not the only species that laughs. Careful observation and experimental studies show that higher primates produce a small share of the total world laughter.

Psychologists Edwin Weinstein and Morris Bender[5] experi-
mented with monkeys (macaca mulatta). They applied electrical stimulation to the brain stems of these creatures, and elicited
from them facial contortions, interruptions of normal breathing
patterns, vocalizations, and general muscular dissembling, all of
which combined into a pattern they felt they could label "laugh-

ing." One might possibly consider electrical stimulation of the brain stem a pretty underhanded way to get a laugh, or one might even feel outraged at such "inhumane" treatment as buzzing their brains, but it is difficult to read their report and doubt that the behavior they wrung from their Simian subjects was, indeed, laughter.

There seems little doubt that the ability, even the tendency, to laugh is something we are born with as babies; tickle even the youngest infant and you will get the muscular dissembling, vocalizations, interrupted breathing, and so on that we call laughter. But human babies are not the only creatures to demonstrate such behavior; it is not widely known that the dissembling behavior we call laughter can be elicited from baby chimpanzees by tickling them. Desmond Morris, author of *The Naked Ape* and *The Human Zoo*, reports that in his own research (*and* in that of his colleague Jan van Hooff in the Netherlands), the tickling of these most-like-man primates elicits behavior which is strikingly similar to that elicited from tickled infants.[6]

So apes and monkeys *can* laugh. But only from electrical or manual tickling? Do they ever laugh as a result of a "joke" or an event involving "joking behavior"? Yes, research shows, they do. Apes do not *tell* jokes, of course; they do not *tell* anything, in terms of formal language. But they *do* jokes—*practical* jokes. For instance, the chimps at the Yerkes Laboratories of Primate Biology, Orange Park, Florida, have been known to delight in reaching through their bars to knock off the hats of visitors.

> This gives the chimps a good laugh. They may further demonstrate their sense of humor by squirting a mouthful of water at a passer-by. The more upset he is, the more fun. This habit, along with throwing stones and dirt, has grown into a disorderly conduct problem at Orange Park that neither human nor ape seems able to remedy:[7]

It would seem that zoo visitors would be well advised to beware the monkey house.

I grew up near St. Louis, Missouri, where, as a boy, I heard a story that the St. Louis zoo's monkey house had been modified. Glass had been placed between the monkeys and the visitors to prevent the denizens of that impoundment from throwing dung at the visitors. I recently wrote the general curator, Charles H. Heossle, to check on the story. His answer indicated that the story had some foundation, but he denies both modification of the monkey house and the presence of "laughter."

> The monkey house has not been modified.
>
> However, occasionally one of the chimpanzees or gorillas will toss fecal material through the bars at spectators.
>
> Also, our male gorilla loves to splash water from his pool at the spectators.
>
> We are sure he does it for the response it brings, but no one has heard him chuckle.[8]

It might very well be that "no one has heard him chuckle" because of the possible differences between human and primate "chuckling," although Clarence Leuba declares that, "In response to tickling, young chimpanzees become excited and make sounds *similar to* the human chuckle [italics mine]."[9] Van Lawick-Goodall describes the chimp laugh somewhat differently.

> Young chimpanzees in the wild are quite as playful as those that are in captivity. . . . I once saw a youngster chasing J. B. around a tree for 20 minutes. Big fat J. B., normally so crusty, was making *the panting sounds of chimp laughter as he ran* [italics mine].[10]

It seems sure that higher primates do, indeed, laugh. The question now remains, do other *lower* animals laugh? Probably not, although there must be thousands (or more) of dog lovers throughout the world who would swear that their dogs, while perhaps not laughing, *do* engage in teeth-baring, lip-stretching, ear-drooping, tail-wagging *smiling* behavior. But the evidence is anecdotal and unconvincing, and I carry no official brief for laughing *or* smiling dogs. (Unofficially, however, my wife is convinced that our own "Noble" smiles regularly!) But that apes laugh and engage in behavior in order to laugh is sure. The myth that laughter is uniquely human must be discarded as an artifact of human chauvinism.

Human knowledge as we know it would hardly be possible without the principle of classification. Classification allows us to group phenomena according to their likenesses one to another, and to differentiate phenomena of one group from another according to their differences. The characteristics of a particular classification must be all-inclusive; that is, they must apply to all members of the class. Likewise, the critical characteristics must be mutually exclusive; that is, they cannot be shared with another classification. Thus all oranges share the characteristics of being classified, botanically, as berries, and grow on evergreen rutacious trees of the genus *Citrus*. These characteristics differentiate oranges from apples, which are red or yellow edible pome (fleshy) fruits growing on trees of the family *Malaciae*. As a result of classification, shoppers have little difficulty separating the oranges from the apples at the supermarket. They likewise experience little trouble separating foods into fruits, vegetables, and meats. Each classification of foods has characteristics which make the class mutually exclusive and all-inclusive.

Another concept of characteristics that determines whether they classify logically is the "necessary *vs.* sufficient" difference. To be classified as an "apple," it is *necessary* that the fruit grow on a tree, but the fact that it grows on a tree is not *sufficient* to distinguish it from an orange. However, the difference in their family trees (*Citrus vs. Malaciae*) is *sufficient* to differentiate these two tree-grown fruits.

Establishing categories for types of humor, when compared with the scientific classifying of flora and fauna, is by far a more difficult task. For instance, consider the following, a suggested list of categories that was compiled for an analysis of humorous juvenile literature from studies done by a number of investigators of children's humor:

Categories of Humor

1. *Exaggeration*, making use primarily of an obvious over- or understatement of such things as size, numbers, proportions, facts, feelings, deeds, experiences, etc.

2. *Incongruity*, associating two generally accepted incompatibles; it is the lack of a rational relation of objects, people, or ideas to each other or to the environment.

3. *Surprise*, exploiting the occurrence of the unexpected—whether fact, thought, feeling, or event; in its more sophisticated form it becomes *irony*.

4. *Slapstick*, the form of humor that depends for its effect on fast, boisterous, and zany physical activity and horseplay . . . often accompanied by broad obvious rowdy verbal humor.

5. *The absurd*, that which obviously lacks reason, which is foolish or ridiculous in its lack of good sense, includes *nonsense*, the nonsensical use of logic and language; the *preposterous*, arising from the incongruity of reality and fantasy; and *whimsy*, a fanciful or fantastic device, object, or creation especially in writing, art, or decoration.

6. *Human predicaments*, featuring situations in which a character appears foolish or bested, includes the humor of *superiority* and *degradation*, which is based on self-aggrandizement or the release of hostility through the discomfiture, failure, or misfortune of others, and *comic predicaments*, which is based on an attitude of sympathetic acceptance of the human predicament and can be seen in situations in which either oneself or someone else appears foolish or bested by life for the moment; in this case, however, no hostile feelings are intended to be aroused or expressed.

7. *Ridicule*, primarily the teasing and mockery of others or oneself, can be seen expressed, for example, in the mockery of adults, their bigness, power foibles, their world and its customs and institutions, etc. *Negative ridicule* finds its source in feelings of self-aggrandizement or the release of hostility through the mockery of others. *Playful ridicule*, on the other hand, is based on the sympathetic acceptance of human foibles. *Satire* is primarily a sophisticated artistic form of humor arising from both types of ridicule.

8. *Defiance*, primarily the release of hostility or aggression through rebellion, includes the violation of conventions, the perpetration of situations socially unacceptable to adults, the expression of forbidden ideas, and the violation of adult authority.

9. *Violence*, primarily the release of hostility or aggression through the expression of sudden or extreme violence.

10. *Verbal humor*, the manipulation of language through word play, puns, jokes, sarcasm, wit, name-calling, and the

like may contain either a positive or negative emotional content but differs from the other forms in being a verbal rather than a situational form of humor.[11]

It will now be profitable to consider just how logical all those categories and their descriptions are.

Let's first examine number 1, *exaggeration*. Certainly, some exaggeration causes laughter—but does *all* exaggeration? Of course not. To say, "If I've told you once, I've told you a double quadrillion times, . . ." is to exaggerate. But it is hardly funny. Also: perhaps that which is exaggerated in a joke is also number 2, *incongruity*? The incongruous heights of two movie stars were exaggerated in an old joke I remember from childhood. At a wild Hollywood party Mickey Rooney supposedly hauled off and slugged Gary Cooper in the ankle. Can it be said that this anecdote is funny because of *exaggeration*, or because of *incongruity*? One could pretty much take his pick.

And mustn't the punch line come as a *surprise* (number 3) in the incongruity/exaggeration joke, above, in order to produce laughter? Cannot the exaggeration take the physical form of number 4, *slapstick*? Is not number 5, *the absurd*, even a specific form of exaggeration? Does not the exaggeration/surprise/incongruity Rooney-Cooper joke involve exaggeration of number 6, *human predicaments*? Does not the exaggeration/ etc. story of Rooney's low blow involve *ridicule* (number 7) of Mickey's short stature and state of inebriation?

Consider "definition" number 2, *incongruity*. Must the juxtaposition of two or more phenomena which are not "suitable or concordant in nature or qualities" always be funny? I must argue that it must *not*. Custard pie in the face of an elaborately tuxedoed stuffed shirt might be a hilarious incongruity. But would a lovely, smiling child sitting unscathed in the ruins of her demolished hut in Vietnam? Such an incongruity would hardly elicit laughter.

Number 3, *surprise*, is quite necessary for most humor; but it is not *sufficient* for any. Take the following story:

> Old Luke won $50,000 in a lottery he had entered. His family was wary about telling him he had won this huge amount of money for fear the news would be too much for his bad heart. So they asked their minister, a master of

rhetoric, to break the news to him gently. "Luke," the
minister began, "do you ever enter lotteries?" "Sure do,"
Luke replied, "every once in a while." "What would you do,
Luke," the preacher asked, "if you were to win a large
amount of money—say $50,000?" "Why," said Luke, "I'd
give half of it to the church." The minister dropped dead of
a heart attack.

The surprise ending helps make the story funny. But the
minister was surprised, too. And he did not laugh. One could be
surprised at the news that he had gone bankrupt, lost a loved
one, or that a tree had fallen through his roof. Despite the surprise, a victim of these calamities could hardly get a laugh out of
any of them.

Other specific examples showing where these categories
overlap a great deal could be cited, but such an exercise would
become highly redundant. Consider another attempt to classify
humorous stimuli, this time by *form*.

It is obvious, of course, there are several different forms of
humorous stimuli. Sigmund Freud, in his early book *Wit and Its
Relation to the Unconscious*, postulated that there are two forms of
wit, *tendency wit* and *harmless wit*. Tendency wit, he argued,
depended for its laughter-provocation on its ridiculing, demeaning, or discomfiting of some person, institution, or group,
whereas harmless wit had no "tendency" and depended upon
form alone for its laughter production. For instance, Freud
would probably classify as "tendency wit" the story about the
psychologist who had twins—he had one baptized and kept the
other for a control. This one-liner ridicules the alleged pro-
pensity for members of the psychological profession slavishly to
base decisions (even family-rearing ones) on the results of
experimental studies. He might have labeled as "harmless wit"
the following definition: Psychologist: a man who pulls habits
out of rats. Notice the reversal pun on "rabbits out of hats."
This is at least akin to what Freud had in mind as harmless wit,
for it would involve "word play" as the principal laughter-
producing ingredient. Note also, however, that even in this
playful little reversal pun lies a grain of ridicule: psychologists
are, after all, doing their little maze-running learning theory
experiments with rats and then trying to generalize about how

human children should be taught. And lots of people are not entirely enamored of such a chain of inferential leaps. It is interesting to note, by the way, that Martin Grotjahn, in his book *Beyond Laughter*,[12] points out that Freud himself was patently *unable to supply a single example* of "harmless wit" which did not also have some "tendency."

This distinction of Freud's (between "tendency" and "harmless" wit) is the one usually drawn between "wit" and "humor." Classifying laughter-provoking stimuli as either "wit" *or* "humor" seems to indicate existence of definitive types or classifications; it suggests that wit and humor are separate, distinct, perhaps even opposite from one another. Chapter 5 will take up in detail this alleged distinction between classes, and attempt to persuade the reader that "wit" and "humor" are simply two ends of the same continuum, that they differ only in *degree* and not in *kind*.

Probably the most heroic effort to categorize humor by type or *form* is *The Humor of Humor*,[13] turned out by a truly fine scholar of the field, Evan Esar. Esar not only demonstrates a comprehensive grasp of the very broad field of humorous verbalisms, but, in addition, has taken the time and effort to study the historical background of types of humor and their evolution. He is one of the few, for instance, to acknowledge that the practical joke is a "lower form" of humor than the "pun," and that the pun evolved from the conundrum (or "punning riddle") which, in turn, evolved from the simple riddle. His book will be appreciated by any serious student of humor.

Through careful definition Esar is able to establish seven free-standing types of humor: the wisecrack, the epigram, the riddle, the conundrum, the gag, the joke, and the anecdote.

The wisecrack is a clever witticism, always directed at a particular individual:

> You should meet my wife, the gal with the whim of iron.

The epigram is much like a wisecrack, but differs in that it ridicules a group or class of persons or things:

> The major duty of suburban mothers is to deliver children—obstetrically once and by station wagon forever after.

This can be changed to a wisecrack:

> Janie is a typical suburban mother. Her major duty is to deliver children—etc.

Riddles, once a major form of verbal duels of wit among primitive peoples, are now chiefly the coin of exchange among small children who delight in stumping one another. Riddles, as children develop, turn into verbal wit in riddle form:

> Why did they bury Lincoln in Springfield, Illinois? Because he was dead.

> What happens to a rock when you throw it into the Red Sea? It gets wet.

A conundrum is a punning riddle, using the riddle form but containing a double-meaning word which makes the riddle unanswerable *as* a riddle.

> Why is excess weight like sugar in iced coffee? Because in time it will settle to the bottom.

Esar has some difficulty separating the *gag* from the *joke*. He even says that the gag in popular meaning *is* any kind of a joke. However, as he uses the term, it means a "definite form of comic dialogue. It differs from the wisecrack because it is conversation rather than monologue, and from the joke which involves no situation."

> He: You neither smoke nor drink?
> She: Right. And two out of three isn't bad.

> He: I am a self-made man.
> She: Now I know what is meant by "unskilled labor."

The *joke* is a short story, stripped of detail, with a definite setting and narrative form.

> A Martian landed in Times Square. He parked his flying saucer at the curb, in imitation of the motorists he saw. In further imitation he tried to slip a coin into the slot of his parking meter, but it would not fit. Turning to a passing pedestrian, he addressed him: "Excuse me, sir, but do you have change for a gridgeon?"

The anecdote is an interesting or striking event or incident. Other than suggesting that anecdotes differ from jokes in that they either (a) concern famous people or (b) involve some moral principle, Esar does not do much to differentiate the anecdote from the joke. He also mentions "the extended joke," but not as a particular type of humor.

As stated above, the seven-fold classification by Esar tends to hold water, logically. He tends to specify how one type differs from all others, but it is somewhat amazing that he does not call the *pun* a separate type of humor. Puns he classifies in Book 4 as one form of "wordplay" (along with the Wellerism, the transposer, the antonymism, the blendword, the repeatism, the macaronic).

He points out that he once determined to classify all the varieties of puns, but found it to be a potentially unending task because of the infinite variety of types of puns. This does not deter him, however, from classifying six kinds of "the fool" (Book 5), five types of "the slip" (Book 6), six types of "the blunder" (Book 7), seven kinds of "the wisecrack" (Book 8), seven types of "the gag" (Book 9), six versions of "the trick" (Book 10), five types of "the twist" (Book 11), six types of "caricature" (Book 12), five types of "satire" (*including* "satire") in Book 13, five types of "the epigram" (Book 14), five types of "the funny story" (Book 15), and five types of "nonsense" (Book 16).

Any time one attempts a classification system this far-reaching, some nonlogical choices are bound to occur. Esar himself admits here and there, usually in an indirect way, that much overlapping between supposed categories occurs. He says, for instance, that "Apart from wordplay and nonsense, practically all wit is satire of one kind or another." Several inconsistencies greet the reader, also. For instance, in Book 12, as types of "caricature" he furnishes the henpecked husband, the woman driver, the efficiency expert, the mother-in-law, the mad psychiatrist, and the chatterbox. One wonders why he did not place in this category also the absent-minded professor instead of grouping him with, among others, the little moron in Book 5, "The Fool." Surely the hazy-headed prof is as much a standard caricature in modern jokedom as the efficiency expert and the mad psychiatrist! It would also seem that his "the woman driver" belongs as easily with "the little moron" in the book entitled "The Fool."

Perhaps the above seems as niggling criticism serving only

to vent professional bias, but other misclassifications can be in-
ferred. For instance, Esar classifies as a "sentry dialogue" that of
the commanding officer who told the lady WAC sentry: "No!
No! Miss Johnson. When someone approaches your sentry post,
you say, 'Halt: Who goes there.' You don't say, 'Stop or I'll
scream!'" In Esar's classification, the "sentry dialogue" is
grouped with such as *repartee* and *hecklerisms* under "The Gag"
(Book 9). It is certainly just as reasonable to classify that story of
the wacky WAC in the "feminine logic" category in Book 16
("Nonsense").

Despite my feeling, which I will repeat again, that Evan
Esar's delightful and scholarly book is well worth reading, I
think that his classification system cannot be considered *logical*.
Part of the problem lies in the fact that some of the classifications are based upon the *content* of the joke or witticism (such
as women ridiculed in "feminine logic") and others are based
upon the *form*, as with the "limerick." Such classification is
pretty certain to lead to confusion. How do you classify a combination of the two?

> There once was a maiden of Siam
> Who said to her lover, young Kiam,
>   "If you kiss me, of course,
>   You will have to use force,
> But God knows you are stronger than I am."

The solution to the problem of classification lies in either
one of two directions. One would be the use of an infinitesimal
number of classifications based upon types of *form*, with a large
number of "hybrids" composed of one or more forms. The other
would be, I think, more useful: a classification based almost exclusively upon *content*, but with several broad categories of form.
Jokes would be classified, then, according to whom or what the
joke was on.

The last sentence above is important: Jokes and other witty
or humorous material would be classified as to whom or what
the joke is *on*—not just "about."

An illustration would, perhaps, be useful in showing the
above distinction. In recent years we have seen a "new" trend in
humor, "Negro humor." Recent racial history would dictate use
of the term "black" instead of "Negro," but "black humor" is

something else again. A once (at least) popular dispenser of "Negro humor" is Dick Gregory. Most of his lines are *about* blacks in this country, but they are directed *against* the white establishment. One of his cracks has to do with the end of segregation in the Birmingham busses. On the first day of integration a black gets on a bus and sits in a front seat. The driver is so angry he drives around town backwards.

This story exemplifies the frustrated anger of the Southern "redneck" and the stupidity which it leads to. The white is ridiculed, not the black.

Another example: Gregory explains why Negroes can afford big shiny cars. It's easy. Right away a black saves $45,000 by not having to buy a big house in the suburbs. He might save up to a couple thousand a year by not having to join the Country Club. He doesn't have to spend money on the fanciest restaurants in town, nor in the swankier hotels and motels, etc.

Are the blacks ridiculed here? Of course not. White bigotry, in terms of restrictive covenants and outright discrimination, is the target.

Changing the content of a joke or gag without changing the form often changes the joke or gag more than would changing its form. Consider an example which Esar would classify as a gag:

> *Englishman*: What do you get by crossing an Irishman with a gorilla? A retarded gorilla.

This, as can be seen from the content, is an anti-Irish gag. But change its content, retaining exactly its form:

> *Republican*: What do you get by crossing a Democrat with a gorilla?

Voila! A political (anti-Democrat) gag. Change again:

> *Black*: What do you get by crossing a Ku Klux Klanner with a gorilla?

> *Professor*: What do you get by crossing a typical college sophomore with a gorilla?

> *Student*: What do you get by crossing a College Dean with a gorilla?

Depending upon the audience, there are endless possibilities.

All the examples immediately above are classifiable by technique to a single, particular technique: that of *ridicule*. In fact, it is a major thesis of this book that *ridicule* is the basic component of all humorous material, and that, to *understand* a piece of humorous material it is necessary only to find out who is ridiculed, how, and why.

In the "gorilla" gags, immediately above, the object of ridicule, the butt of the gag, changes, thus changing the gag from an "Irish" to a "Democrat" to a "KKK" to a "student" gag, etc. If jokes and gags, ͟ ͟refore were classified according to who is ridiculed, accepting broadly the idea that the basic *form* of jesting is *ridicule* of someone or something, classification would be simplified.

Another illustration might help. There are some compilers of humorous material which think of "sex jokes" as a genre. Is this logical? Certainly, there are a number of jokes which are classifiable as "sex jokes" because their content deals explicitly or implicitly with certain sexual functions. But are they really very different from ordinary nonsexually oriented jests, in that someone if not demeaned, is found to be deficient, etc.? The answer must be no. Consider this "sex joke":

> During a coffee break, three secretaries decided to "confess" their nastiest tricks on their boss. The first said: "I deliberately switched the addresses on two letters he was sending out, Personal. One was to his bookie and the other was to his banker!" After the tittering subsided, the second said: "The meanest thing I ever did was one afternoon while searching for something in his desk I found some condoms; I took a pin and punched teeny holes in the end of each." The third secretary fainted.

We laugh at the secretary because she has been "caught." She is found out. If her crime had been embezzlement, and she had been found out so suddenly and "accidentally," the story might be about as funny as when her sin has been fornication. There are no "sex jokes"; there are only jokes which ridicule in the area of sexual function.

One more example of "sexual humor," this time one classifiable by Esar as a wisecrack:

> She's pregnant; she took seriously what I only poked at her in fun.

The object of the ridicule? Women. The basis of the wisecrack is that the male of the species indulges in sex primarily for physical pleasure; woman's role is more deep-seeded within her psychological and physical being for the perpetuation of the race. The verbal wisecrack makes fun of the different motivations in a way that reminds the female of the lightness with which the male enters into an act so fraught with meaning for her.

Recently a wave of "sick" jokes has rolled through our culture. Are "sex jokes" any different from "sick" jokes? They are, of course, in content, but, again, not in basic idea. In the "sick" joke, or "gruesome" or "Bloody Mary," as they have been called, the basic technique is *ridicule*. Someone is *hurt*; or someone is reminded of his low estate. The classic,

"Aside from that, Mrs. Lincoln, how did you like the play?"

gains its humor from the cool and unconcerned manner in which the inquirer callously ignores the uncommon grief of the President's so-recent widow.

For the most part, the so-called "sick" jokes have to do with such horrors as death, including widowhood, as above (and: "Mrs. Custer, would you care to contribute to Indian relief?"), and such gory and distasteful subjects as mutilation, amputation, and monsterhood.

"Mommy, can I go swimming."
"Don't be silly. Your hooks would get rusty."

"Can Jimmy come out and play baseball with us?"
"Of course not; you know he has no arms or legs."
"We know. We just want him to be first base."

"You can't come in. I'm in the bathtub."
"But your daughter was run over by a steam roller."
"Well, then, just slip her under the door."

"Daddy, I don't want to be a vampire."
"Shut up and drink your blood."

There are even jokes which are *both* "sick" *and* "sexual," although there is not so rich a lode of sexual material for the truly "sick" joke format. The reason is probably that there is little that is so thoroughly monstrous about sex as there is about death, widowhood, mutilation, amputation, etc. And there are fewer

well-known victims of, for instance, multiple rape than there
are well-known widows of cut-off-in-their-prime husbands. I,
however, did see a fairly "sick" sexually oriented bit of graffiti
on the wall of a men's washroom in Columbus, Ohio. It was a
drawing of a book's cover with the title and author:

Ideal Love, by the Marquis de Sade

And, then, even in so-modern America today there are some
sexual subjects that are highly repugnant enough to make for
"sick" sexual jokes. One of these repugnancies is the ancient
taboo of incest:

The fourteen-year-old backwoods boy was making love to
his twelve-year-old sister. "Man, Sis," he wheezes, "you're
almost as good as Maw!" "Yeh," she gasps back, "that's
what Paw says."

This incest joke requires some narrative to supplement the
dialogue, and thus does not strictly meet the "dialogue-only"
format requirements of the "gruesomes" so popular just a few
years ago, but the casualness of the language used to unfold
such an abhorrent situation must certainly qualify the joke as
pretty sick, according to most "middle Americans."

A later section will discuss the reasons why jokes of such
gruesome content, baiting freshly-widowed grievers and openly
ridiculing the mutilated, deformed, and maimed can be bantered
about in polite society without evoking social censure. But at
this point, while discussing the "gruesomes" fad of the late
1950's, it becomes quite appropriate to take up another area of
fuzzy thinking pertaining to this particular type of humor: the
lack of "a sense of history."

Each time a "new" humor form comes along, it is hailed by
some as just that: "new." And the sick jokes, or gruesomes, are
no exception. Thus it was not surprising that Gerald Walker,
writing in the December, 1957 *Esquire* magazine ("Sick Jokes"),
argued that the fad of "Bloody Mary's" erupted in response to
the unique social-political-ethnic atmosphere of America in the
1950's. Mr. Walker's article demonstrated much keen perception into the world of sick humor, but I disagreed then and
now with his thesis that sick humor was a unique product of
America's 1950's.

In fact, this writer frankly doubts that a particular fad of "joke type" can be unique to any time/place locale. A sense of history of the joking business convinces that "sick humor" has always been with us, and always will so long as humankind survives.

Let us consider the present; is "sick humor" still around? To answer, we must first consider what are the two *necessary* ingredients of sick humor. And we would have to answer that sick humor must have (1) brevity mixed with light, simple language combined with (2) otherwise uncivilized and "inhumane" content, such as mutilation, mangling, death, monsterism, or the like. The content, further, must be an expression of an idea that would be quickly rejected in "polite society" unless couched in the "joke form" so that it will be immediately and unerringly recognized *as* a joke. To illustrate, consider:

> One brother: "I just pushed Mom over the cliff."
> Other brother: "Don't make me laugh; my lips are chapped."

Imagine this joke told at a cocktail party today. Either the auditors would immediately recognize it as a "joke" (because of the form), or else they would be instantly horrified at the behavior and attitude of the two brothers, perhaps doubting their sanity or wondering what punishment could possibly be harsh enough for the monstrous cretins.

Given these criteria, then, what of "sick humor" today? I contend that it still exists, but in various forms. For instance, there is the "Polish joke." Of course, some "Polish jokes" are no more than fairly harmless conundrums, such as:

> "Ever hear of Alexander Graham Korwalski? He was the first Telephone Pole."

But some of them, most classifiable by Esar as "Stereotypes," would be vicious slanders against Americans of Polish descent if not "taken as jokes."

> "Know why you need only two pallbearers at a Polish funeral? A garbage can has only two handles."

> "The Polish neighborhood had a beauty contest, and you know who won? Nobody."

> "Hear about the Polish mob that kidnapped a son of a Polish businessman? They sent the son home to deliver the

ransom note. And the father paid it by sending his son back with the money!"

These are, to me, at least as "sick" as amputee jokes.

There are other jokes making the rounds these days, with as many elements of "sickness" as any 1957 gruesomes I have ever heard. Just lately I heard these jokes demeaning the bigotry of Southern law enforcement officials:

> The body of a Negro man was dragged from a river in Mississippi; almost sixty pounds of steel chain was wrapped around the body. These events occasioned the sheriff to remark: "Just like a colored man; steals more chain than he can swim the river with."

> The body of an Alabama Negro man was found with twenty-three bullet holes in him. The sheriff drawled, "Worst case of suicide I ever seen."

Again, note that these are not "Negro" jokes, in the sense that they ridicule people of the black race; they demean our *stereotype* of the Southern Sheriff. But their content definitely leans to the left of nausea. Another form of "sick joke" still alive and kicking (circa 1972) is the "Christ joke," generally making reference to His crucifixion:

> Look, Man, if you can't carry that cross, you'll have to get out of the parade.

> Hear about the new do-it-yourself Easter Kit? Two boards and four nails.

If these are not *sick* jokes, they can hardly be called "healthy."

So "sick humor" is still with us. How about the pre-1950s? One need not go back far to find jests to upset squeamish stomachs. The early 1940s produced a fad of Little Moron jokes. Many of these were simple playful nonsense, such as "Did you hear about the little moron that took a bale of hay to bed so he could feed his nightmares?" But others contained elements of masochism and sadism resulting from our hero's moronity.

> Did you hear about the little moron who:
> cut off his hands so he could play piano by ear?
> cut off his arms so he could wear sleeveless sweaters?
> cut off his fingers so he could write shorthand?
> murdered his parents and then pleaded for mercy on the grounds that he was an orphan?

jumped off the Empire State Building because he wanted
to be a hit on 5th Avenue?

Consider humor in the English-speaking world just before
the turn of the century. In 1899 a soldier in the English Cold-
stream Guards, Harry Graham, published a book entitled *Ruth-
less Rhymes for Heartless Homes*. These rhymes were usually qua-
trains, in light, tripping language, but with thoroughly
gruesome subject matter. Louis Untermeyer describes the
verses as "calmly savage,"[14] and offers these as perhaps two of
Graham's most famous five:

Aunt Eliza
In the drinking well
  Which the plumber built her,
Aunt Eliza fell.
  We must buy a filter.

Billy
Billy, in one of his nice new sashes,
Fell in the grate and was burnt to ashes.
Now, although the room grows chilly,
I haven't the heart to poke up Billy.

Perhaps inspired by the title, "Billy," poems of this type
became known quickly as "Little Willies." For a quarter of a
century newspapers all over the land printed "Little Willies"
sent in by readers, each of whom competed fiercely to "invent a
catastrophe more gory in event and more nonchalant in effect
than his predecessor."[15] Here are a few of the most popular:

Willie fell down the elevator—
Wasn't found till six days later.
Then the neighbors sniffed, "Gee Whizz!
What a spoiled child Willie is!"

Little Willie from the mirror
  Sucked the mercury all off,
Thinking, in his childish error,
  It would cure the whooping cough.
At the funeral his mother,
  Weeping, said to Mrs. Brown,
"'Twas a chilly day for Willie
  When the mercury went down!"

Willie saw some dynamite,
Couldn't understand it quite;

Curiosity never pays;
It rained Willie seven days.

Father heard his children scream,
So he threw them in the stream,
Saying, as he drowned the third,
"Children should be seen, not heard."

It would be most difficult to blame the popularity of these grisly gems on the similarity of America's 1950s and the "Gay Nineties" *cum* pre-WWI days when Europe and Asia were regarded roughly as distant from the U.S. as the moon.

But our trip back through history in search of sick humor need not stop with that nostalgic version of "the good old days." The sickly and the ghastly lived in humor long before barbershop quartet singing was supposed to have been so popular.

In 1739 an unsuccessful English poet named John Mottley published a slim volume of 247 jokes entitled *Joe Miller's Jests*. He subtitled it: "The Wits Vade-mecum. Being a Collection of the most Brilliant Jests; the Politest Repartees; the Most Elegant Bons Mots, and the Most pleasant short Stories in the English Language." The Joe Miller of the title was a recently deceased actor who had been quite popular. And, although 3 of the 247 jokes are attributed directly to Miller in the book, the late Joe had nothing at all to do with the book. Mottley merely swiped his name because he thought its popularity would help his book sell, which it most assuredly did. In fact, Mottley gave the dead actor's name to the English language perhaps permanently; we still call an old, crude joke a "joemiller" today.

Did Mottley's old joemillers demonstrate the characteristics of "sickness?" Consider number 33, about a chap with no nose:

> Sir *William Davenant*, the Poet, had no Nose, who going along the Meuse one Day, a Beggar-Woman followed him, crying, ah! God preserve your *Eye-Sight*; God preserve your *Eye-Sight*; Why, good Woman, said he, do you pray so much for my *Eye-Sight*? Ah! dear Sir, answered the Woman, if it should please God that you grow dim-sighted, you have no Place to hang your *Spectacles* on.

Number 199 jests about a common staple of the sick joke, death—and, in this case, violent death:

Two Brothers coming to be executed once for some enormous Crime; the Eldest first turn'd off [hanged] without saying one Word: The other mounting the Ladder, began to harangue the Crowd, whose Ears were attentively open to hear him, expecting some Confession from him, *Good People,* says he, *my Brother hangs before my Face, and you see what a lamentable* Spectacle *he makes; in a few moments I shall be turned off too, and then you'll see a Pair of Spectacles.*

Number 222 takes a swipe at *cripples* ("a crooked Fellow"):

One observing a crooked Fellow in close Argument with another, who would have dissuaded him from some inconsiderable Resolution; said to his Friend, *Prithee, let him alone, and say no more to him, you see he's bent upon it.*

Number 226 rubs salt into the psychological wound of a dying man:

A Gentleman lying on his Death-Bed, called to his Coachman, who had been an old Servant, and said, *Ah! Tom, I'm going a long and rugged Journey, worse than ever you drove me; Oh, dear Sir,* reply'd the Fellow, (he having been but an indifferent Master to him,) *ne'er let that discourage you, for it is all down Hill.*

It is probable that a thorough search of extant records of humor would show that "sick humor" was circulated during all the ages of man. The evidence cited here cannot prove such breadth, but should certainly lay to rest the upstart idea that sick humor is a product of the 1950s alone of all the ages. And it *suggests* that some sly scribe of ancient Rome, interviewing Julius Caesar's widow during the confusion of temporarily leaderless Rome, might have stuck in the question:

But aside from that, Calpurnia, what did you think of the opening day of the Senate?

In summary of the argument so far, let us list conclusions:

1. Man is *not* the only animal who laughs, although he is the only one who can tell jokes the least bit well.

2. Systems of classifying jokes suffer from classifications involving critical criteria not mutually exclusive to its class, not all-inclusive of members of the class, or criteria which are necessary but not sufficient to cause laughter.

3. Evan Eser has come up with perhaps the best seven-fold classification system, but logical loopholes appear when further delineation by *form* is attempted.

4. Jokes can be classified by who or what is ridiculed, not just what the joke is "about."

    a. "Sex jokes" ridicule people for some sexual phenomenon.

    b. "Sick jokes" ridicule victims of terrible human tragedy, such as widowhood, amputation, maiming, etc.

    c. "Negro jokes" usually ridicule white bigotry.

5. "Sick humor" is not limited to certain historical periods or geographical locations.

Chapter 2 begins the task of demonstrating that a single wide-ranging theory of laughter and humor, with the help of a few modern concepts from the fields of psychology and learning theory, can be used to understand all laughter, its causes, conditions, and effects.

2

From Many Theories Toward One

Now is the time to embark onto the treacherous ground of humor theory. The central question is, "Why is humor funny?" Involved also is the question, "Why do we laugh?"

The footing of this ground is treacherous because of the relatively large number of theorists who have trod the territory before. As shall be noted later in this chapter, an extraordinary number of different theories have been put forth; and I intend to illustrate why most of these theories hardly deserve the name *theory*. To begin, it is necessary first to consider what a theory *is*. For the summary beginning with the next paragraph, I am greatly indebted to Calvin Hall and Gardner Lindzey for their "relatively conventional summary of the thinking of methodologists or logicians of science."[1]

First of all, a theory is neither true nor false, but is, rather, relatively *useful* or relatively *not useful*. What does this mean? Useful or not useful for what? Primarily, a theory's usefulness is determined by two criteria: its *explanatory comprehensiveness* and its *verifiability*. It is necessary to consider these two criteria separately.

Explanatory comprehensiveness means simply that the theory is a set of logically consistent statements which satisfactorily explain *all* observable phenomena which the theory purports to cover. To the extent that it cannot explain certain phenomena related to the subject it purports to cover, to that extent is the theory's usefulness reduced. If some phenomena appear which do not "fit" the theory's statements, one might add on to the theory other statements that explain the phenomena. But any statements "added on" must interrelate to and integrate with the other statements of the theory; they cannot "stand apart" as minitheories of themselves, or conflict with the previous statements.

A theory is *verifiable* if it generates new knowledge that tends to confirm the veracity of the statements in the theory. New knowledge can be generated in two general ways: first, propositions can be tested by empirical research, which may or may not verify the proposition's "truthfulness"; second, other statements might be suggested that will stimulate other ideas or even disbelief and/or resistance (which is another way of furthering knowledge). This latter result is called a theory's "heuristic influence."

After a theory's explanatory comprehensiveness and verifiability have been established, one might consider simplicity, or "parsimony," as it is often called. That is, if two or more theories appear to be about equal in comprehensiveness and verifiability, the simpler (-est) is usually to be preferred.

Another attribute of a good theory is that it prevents "the observer from being dazzled by the full-blown complexity of natural or concrete events."[2] That is, it should keep the observer or researcher's attention focused upon the specific phenomena in question, and it should cause him to disregard phenomena not related to the theory, regardless of the fascinating nature of that irrelevant phenomena.

Although left unstated until this point, suffice it to conclude this theoretical summary by pointing out that the statements of a useful theory are composed of terms for which operational or empirical definitions can be determined.

To illustrate the rather abstract and theoretical discussion, above, of the attributes of a theory, let us apply it to theorizing about the cause of stuttering.

First, suppose we theorize that stuttering is caused by the anxious overconcern of parents about their child's "normal" nonfluencies; their overconcern and correcting of their child's speech creates anxiety in the child over the anticipated nonfluencies. Through conditioning, this anxiety becomes habitual, producing more nonfluencies, and blocking, again habitually. And the nonfluencies, circularly, cause anxieties, which cause nonfluencies, etc.

For this theory to be useful in comprehensively explaining all observable phenomena, it ought to explain why most stutterers, for instance, stutter when talking but not when singing; it ought to explain why more boys than girls become stutterers; it ought to explain why the stress of reciting or public speaking usually increases stuttering, etc.

The theory should generate research. For instance, it would suggest that researchers should look for common features in the childhood relationships of stutterers and their parents. It should suggest that electromyographic recordings ought to show increases in muscular tension in stutterers at the moment of the stuttered utterance. It ought to suggest that systematic desensitization of stutterers to critical stimuli would decrease their stuttering, etc.

If this theory is as verifiable and comprehensive as other, competing theories, it should be preferred if it is the simplest.

If one should follow this theory in the treating of a stutterer, he would disregard his patient's political party preference, his attitude toward water fluoridation, the star under which he was born, and his chosen religion. What *is* specified in the theory, or becomes, through extension, a logical and consistent part of the theory, *will* be considered.

Now that it is settled what a theory is supposed to be and do, attention can be turned to the theorizing that has been done as to what laughter is and does. In this area there has been no plethora of theories and partial theories.

W. E. Blatz, K. D. Allen, and D. A. Millichamps, in their study of laughter in nursery school children, are able to list a total of thirty-seven different theories of humor extant at the time.[3] That is quite a few, but these authors fall far short of the

total number compiled by J. Y. T. Greig. Thirteen years earlier
he was able to list in the appendix of his book[4] a total of eighty-
eight separate theories. However, Greig does admit that this
large accumulation of theories borrow heavily from and overlap one another extensively. The late psychiatrist, Edmund
Bergler, in a more recent book[5] has been able to list a total of
eighty separate theories, each of which he more or less contemptuously dismisses so that he can argue for the acceptance
of his own. Bergler claims, in a footnote, to be using irony when
he asserts:

> Moreover, I consider that *most* of the theories presented by
> my precursors in the field are of dubious value. Of course,
> this opinion is counterbalanced by my belief that my own
> theory is the only correct one. This, too, is stated in com-
> plete modesty, and for the sole purpose of sticking to
> tradition.

But I suspect that he is merely *pretending* irony; what he really
means is that he feels no modesty whatsoever.

And what of Bergler's theory? Why, according to him, do
people laugh at jokes? It must be confessed that it is not easy to
explain *briefly* what Dr. Bergler has in mind, since he takes an
entire book of almost three hundred pages—and an interminable string of Freudian, neo-Freudian, and Bergleresque
jargon—to explain himself on laughter. But analysis of a few
features of Bergler's formulation should be enough to discredit
it sufficiently.

First of all, consider what might be called the basis of his
theory, which makes up the title of his Chapter 3: "Laughter in
the Adult Sense: Internal Antidote Against Fear of One's Own
Psychic Masochism." To understand Bergler's explanation of
laughter, one *must* understand those final two words: "psychic
masochism." Bergler says that each of us transfers externally
perceived displeasure into internally perceived pleasure—that
we are all unconscious masochists. However, the superego, the
"Censor," will not allow that; the ego is not allowed even this
little "pleasure." So the unconscious ego develops a constant
readiness to respond to jokes with *pseudoaggression*. The resultant
laughter is a constantly used alibi to escape censure from the

superego. The unconscious ego argues: "How can I be accused of masochism? See how aggressive I am!"[6]

And why do people become masochistic? For one thing, Bergler alleges, each of us as babies suffered from extreme megalomania as well as extreme *fear*; in fact, we suffer from a "septet of baby fears" during infancy, these being: the fear of starvation, of being devoured, of being poisoned, of being choked, of being chopped to pieces, of being drained, and of being castrated. Bergler claims, further, that we learn to smile from the smile of Mother—her smile imparts to us the message, "Don't be afraid, I won't eat you." Because the infant divides things into "good" and "bad" on the basis of whether they emanate, respectively, from himself or from mother, he lays the ground for the eventual view that mother is a threatening witch.

The above observations are, admittedly, out of context because it is difficult to condense the extensive construction of this fascinating book. But as one reads Bergler's formulations, one can hardly resist the idea that his book is a massive joke, a gigantic pulling of the leg of the educated reading public. One constantly wonders, "Can he really be *serious?*" But let us examine some of the features of his theory in light of our criteria above of what a theory should do and be.

First, Bergler claims that laughter is an outward expression signaling only *pseudo*aggressions, not *real* aggression. Laughter clearly derives from play situations, and not from direct attempts to ridicule with aggressive intent. Now, according to our criterion of explanatory comprehensiveness, we should not be able to find, according to Bergler, laughter as a result of *real* aggression. So, *can* we find laughter that isn't really *pseudo*-aggression? I think so. Let us consider *satire*.

Several years ago syndicated editorial cartoonist Herbert L. Block (Herblock) turned out a caricature of conservative Barry Goldwater. Briefcase-toting Goldwater is depicted glowering down at a thin, ragged little family huddled miserably in a doorway; the caption: "If you had any gumption at all you'd get up from there and go out and inherit a department store." It is not possible to convince me that the people who enjoyed that little arrow of outrage were not doing so because it allowed them to share a massive spleen-venting with Herblock. The laughter derived from psyches fed up with the sanctimonious work ethic expounded by the heir to the Goldwater retail empire. The people who laughed at that one were not exactly playing games, and conservative *Time* magazine was not pleased in the least. *Time*, in fact, was incensed, and took page 1 to lambast Herblock's rancor and lack of taste; they claimed Block had "gone too far." *Time* felt that there was nothing pseudo about *that* aggression. Nor is there much harmless play in Mort Sahl when he observes of the American Medical Association: "The A.M.A. opposes chiropractors and witch doctors and any other cure that is quick." He is lashing out in revenge; a doctor once turned him away (and almost to his death) because he lacked $450 to pay the doctor's proposed fee. And the crowd at the hungry i or the Playboy Club who laugh at Sahl's observation have probably just found expression for their own experiences with medicine's concern over the business end of the profession.

So Bergler's statement that humor involves only *pseudo*-aggression automatically exempts his theory from the ranks of explanatorily comprehensive theories. And it would be extremely difficult to verify. How does one go about making empirical investigations of a theory which rests upon a labyrinth of unproven concepts of Freudian ancestry? How does one, systematically and rigorously ot serve an ego? An id? A superego? Once these "entities" are isolated, how does one examine their interrelationships and conflicts? How can we empirically explore the unconscious? How can we devise experiments to locate and measure each of the "septet of baby fears"? How can we measure the "complete megalomania of infants"? Obviously, we cannot do any of these things.

We can, of course, sit back in our armchairs and contemplate this theory, knock it about this way and that, find occasionally insightful glimpses into human nature, or even develop new thinking in resistance to Bergleresque formulations. In this way, fear of one's own "psychic masochism" can generate some "heuristic value." But that is about all the use you can get from it.

I hope to have effectively disposed of Dr. Bergler's explanation of laughter, regardless of the confession that I have had to oversimplify. Those who enjoy understanding the human condition only through the murky labyrinths of Freudian speculations should, by all means, go and read *Laughter and the Sense of Humor*; it is a fascinating book. But I wish to hear no more of infants being devoured except through the kind of joshing Swift got off in *A Modest Proposal*.

Now, what about those eighty-odd other theories?

It has already been pointed out that, although Greig quotes the largest number of theories (eighty-eight), he admits that they all borrow heavily from each other and often disagree on very small matters. We can probably simplify things even farther than that. Anthony Ludovici, in his book *Secret of Laughter*,[7] argues that all theories of humor can be classified into two categories: those that agree with the theory of seventeenth-century philosopher Thomas Hobbes, and those which do not; and Ludovici gave little credence to those theories which did *not* agree with Hobbes. A central thesis of this chapter is that Hobbes' theory is by far the most useful theory for explaining the nature of laughter. It is often called the "derision theory," and is exemplified dramatically in Sheridan's *The School for Scandal*, Act I, scene 1:

Maria: For my part, I own, madam, wit loses its respect with me, when I see it in company with malice. —What do you think, Mr. Surface?

Joseph Surface: Certainly, madam; to smile at the jest which plants a thorn in another's breast is to become a principal in the mischief.

Lady Sneerwell: Pshaw! There's no possibility of being witty without a little ill nature; the malice of a good thing is the barb that makes it stick.

Hobbes' actual definition of the "derision theory" comes to us in Chapter IX of his *Treatise on Human Nature*.

The passion of laughter is nothing else but *sudden glory* arising from a sudden conception of some *eminency in ourselves* by comparison with the infirmity of others, or with

our own formerly: for men laugh at the *follies* of themselves past, when they come suddenly to remembrance,
except they bring with them any present dishonour.

He reaffirms his position in the *Leviathan*:

> *Sudden glory* is the passion which maketh those *Grimaces*
> called LAUGHTER, and is caused either by some sudden
> act of their own, that pleaseth them; or by the appre-
> hension of some deformed thing in another, by com-
> parison whereof they suddenly applaud themselves. And it
> is incident most to them, that are conscious of the fewest
> abilities in themselves; who are forced to keep themselves
> in their own favour, by observing the imperfections of
> other men. And therefore much laughter at the defects of
> others, is a signe of Pusillanimity. . . . For of great minds,
> one of the proper workes is, to help and free others from
> scorn; and compare themselves onely with the most able.

I contend that the Hobbes' explanation is the most useful
for explaining the phenomenon of laughter. The two words,
"sudden" and "glory," make up the two elements necessary for
any evoking of laughter. Why does a pie in the face of a pom-
pous stuffed shirt make us laugh? We perceive the difference
between the victim and ourselves; he is deflated, defeated, and a
sloppy mess—and we are not. This perception makes us feel
"glorified." But this perception of "glory" must be *sudden*; the pie
must splash into his visage as a surprise to us. After the surprise wears off the "glory" is no longer "sudden." Suppose he
sits around for several minutes with pie all over himself. We
might even begin to feel sorry for the poor slob.

The next chapter will take up my explicit ideas of how
Homo sapiens evolved into a race that can be convulsed into
interrupted breathing, facial contortion, and incoherent vocalizations by sudden perceptions of glory (superiority). The present chapter will stick to the point of examining other evidence
of why Hobbes' position is to be preferred over all others.

William Hazlitt offers a long list of laughable stimuli, all of
which suggest "derision" or "sudden glory."

> We laugh at absurdity; we laugh at deformity. We laugh at
> a bottle-nose in a caricature; at a stuffed figure of an alder-
> man in a pantomime, and at the tale of Slaukenbergius. A
> dwarf standing by a giant makes a contemptible figure

enough. Rosinante and Dapple are laughable from contrast, as their masters from the same principle make two
for a pair. We laugh at the dress of foreigners, and they at
ours. Three chimneysweepers meeting three Chinese in
Lincoln's Inn Fields, they laughed at one another till they
were ready to drop down. Country people laugh at a person
because they never saw him before. Any one dressed in the
height of the fashion, or quite out of it, is equally an object
of ridicule. One rich source of the ludicrous is distress with
which we cannot sympathize from its absurdity or in-
significance. It is hard to hinder children from laughing at a
stammerer, at a negro, at a drunken man, or even at a mad-
man. We laugh at mischief. We laugh at what we do not
believe. We say that an argument or an assertion that is
very absurd, is quite ludicrous. We laugh to show our satisfaction with ourselves, or our contempt for those about us,
or to conceal our envy or our ignorance. We laugh at fools,
and at those who pretend to be wise—at extreme simplicity, awkwardness, hypocrisy, and affectation.[8]

In Chapter 1 we saw how Katharine Hull Kappas classified
the causes of laughter (exaggeration, surprise, etc.); what was
pointed out then must be reemphasized here. Each of these
"causes" may be a *necessary*, but not a *sufficient* cause of laughter.
What *is* necessary and sufficient to cause laughter is a combination of a loser, a victim of derision or ridicule, with *suddenness*
of loss. The victim must be embarrassed, discomfited, injured,
demeaned, or exposed, and our perception of his embarrassment, discomfiture, injury, demeaning, or exposure must occur
in a brief instant. Let us look at some contemporary examples.

Today's popular comedians gain their audiences' attention
(and even love and respect) by ridiculing and demeaning "safe
targets." They allow us to become suddenly aware of our
"glory" by producing stimuli that cause us to unconsciously
compare ourselves "with the infirmity of others"; these "others" are often the comedians themselves who "take it on the
chin."

The late Jack Benny, one of the most beloved of modern
comedians, was a walking one-man joke butt. He offered us
himself as the object of ridicule. He was stingy. He was vain. He
was often out of touch with reality. And he drew laughs by the
barrelful. He considered his ancient Maxwell automobile the
last word in motoring elegance; his wealth was hoarded in an

unbelievably feudal dungeon below his house; he was positive
that his scratchy, grating violin rendition of "Love in Bloom"
outdid Jascha Heifetz. On one program he was walking home
through a treacherous-appearing neighborhood when a gun-
man confronted Benny with the words: "Your money or your
life." During the long pause which follows we suddenly perceive that the miserly soul of Benny is actually anguishing over
the alternatives!

Self-deprecating Rodney Dangerfield, in his stand-up
monologues, almost out-Benny's Benny in self-deprecation. But
where Benny outwardly professed normalcy, Dangerfield daubs
himself with symbolic dung without apology:

> "I don't get no respect . . . Just the other day a doorman
> asked me to call a cab for him . . . Whenever I get on an
> elevator, the operator always asks, 'Basement' . . . At home
> my kid sends me to my room for talking back . . . And I
> never argue with the dog because my wife always takes his
> side."[9]

The great Red Skelton is a clown. He amuses us with his sudden
pratfalls, his ridiculous rubbery-faced mugging, and with his
array of characterizations: he plays the punch-drunk fighter
Willie Lump-Lump, the brainless country bumpkin Clem
Kadiddlehopper, the outrageously ill-mannered San Fernando
Red, and the scheming bum, Freddie the Freeloader, all potential
objects of ridicule.

The clever quips of Bob Hope puncture the little irritants of
life so effectively that we wish we'd said those things. When he
tells a bunch of army officer candidates: "You know what
Officer Candidate School is—that's a concentration camp on
our side!" the cadets suddenly perceive the aptness of this exaggerated comparison. And Hope is not at all reticent to put his
own head on the chopping block of ridicule. His dialogues with
cute girls abound in exchanges wherein Bob attempts to "make
it" with the chick, whereby the girl destroys him with a crack
about his age, his impotence, or his ski-nose. During his Christmas tour of army bases in 1970 he almost made a comedy star of
Cincinnati Reds' catcher Johnny Bench by giving Johnny all the
laugh lines, most of which were "on" Hope.

Don Rickles' famous "insult wit" is designed to do one

thing: to take people down a peg or two. But when his vituperation streams forth, we all know that he does not mean it; and the people he ridicules always take it with a smile. Even if he is "giving it" in all seriousness to some heckling Las Vegas drunk, we are happy enough to see the brash tippler get his comeuppance.

What do editorial satirist/humorists like Art Buchwald and Art Hoppe (the "Art Buchwald West") do to make us laugh? They just kid the socks off of any and every absurdity in life, whether it be capital punishment as a deterrent to murder, the unionization of professional football players, our myopic policy toward recognizing Red China, the telephonic addiction of Martha Mitchell, or the attempt of Richard Nixon to bury his old "hatchet man" image. (See examples in later chapters.)

What is so funny about the cartoon character Mr. Magoo? He gets into constant scrapes because he is nearly blind. How do the cat/mouse cartoon characters Tom and Jerry amuse us? By knocking out one another's teeth, bashing in one another's heads, and setting off bombs under one another. The Road Runner amuses us by never getting caught and constantly turning the tables on the hapless coyote who, in his efforts to make a meal of our hero, winds up being bashed around the mountainous landscape with crashing regularity. Charlie Brown's cupidity in trusting the fussbudget Lucy to hold the football for him to kick is persistent and comical; we always know that she is going to draw back the ball at the last minute, but we never know until the last panel the depths to which it will plunge poor Charlie. We laugh at the suddenly revealed stupidity of Walt Kelly's *Pogo* characters, as when, after a lengthy talk about (Christopher) Columbus, Churchy LaFemme asks Pogo "just who is this Columbus, and what's his last name?" Pogo laconically replies, "Ohio. He was an Irish Hawaiian." To the lampooners staffing *Mad* magazine no one person, group, or idea is exempt from their caricaturing.

Remove the "loser" from all these comic situations, and the humor evaporates. Remove the "suddenness" from the "losing," and the same thing happens. No more laughter.

Many people object to this description of humor. Laughing, after all, is one of the more pleasant of human activities, a signal for joy, well-being, happiness. How can it be a signal for "sudden glory"? Isn't it terribly impolite, even uncivilized, to enjoy the embarrassment, discomfiture, or injury of other human beings? Of course, most people recognize that there *is* something that can be called "derisive laughter" or "deliberate ridicule," as when children tease their less fortunate chums. But don't we separate that from "kidding," from laughing at "harmless" jokes and cartoons, from enjoying a good story with the gang? And don't we strive constantly to "civilize" (i.e., "educate") children so that they will cease their teasing and laughing at cripples, stutterers, and misfits?

And one must agree that there is a lot of distance between the ridicule in these two items:

> Mort Sahl on publication of the Yalta Papers: "They should come in a loose-leaf binder so you can add new betrayals as they come along."

> Did you hear about the little moron who stayed up all night studying for a blood test?

We might laugh derisively with Sahl's description of the American authors of the Yalta agreements, knowing that he is probably bitterly anxious to expose treason where he finds it. We know here that the laugh is intended to be *against* someone, probably FDR and his staff. But the little moron story; is it completely bland and "harmless"? In a way, it is; but in order to enjoy this caricature of the "fool," we must imagine some human being who is so stupid that he thinks a blood test is something you *do* study for. And we laugh at this stupidity. Fortunately, we do not know many "little morons" personally, so the subject of the joke is quite "safe." The little near-idiot is even so overdrawn and exaggerated (what, specifically, could he even *study?*) that the joke has not the slightest air of reality to it. So we can laugh comfortably, *without even thinking of it as a story ridiculing some person's intelligence.*

This last is an important point. We do not consciously analyze each joke we hear, deliberately thinking through until we find just why there is cause for us to feel grandiosely and deliberately superior to somebody or to "ourself formerly." Even the most "hostile" of humor, the most "derisive" of laughter can delight without a single conscious perception of "glory." An interesting experiment by H. F. Gollob and J. Levine[10] is pertinent to this issue. They had a group of female subjects rate the funniness of some cartoons before and again after they had their attention focused directly on the content of the cartoons. They rated the funniness of these cartoons (some "highly aggressive," some "low aggressive," and some "non-aggressive") before and after they were asked to explain "what made the cartoons funny to them." Their second ratings were significantly lower for *only* the "highly aggressive" cartoons. It seems that, once the subjects understood that the cartoons were funny because of their aggressive content, they became significantly less funny. Social custom will allow us to enjoy cartoons with little aggressive content, but will frown upon our enjoying greatly high aggression. As long as aggressiveness is sufficiently disguised in the joke-form, it is socially acceptable.

And joke-forms (and other humorous devices) permit a great deal of emotional expression that would otherwise have to remain unexpressed and "bottled up inside" us or else released in less socially accepted ways. If I feel oppressed by women in general and my wife in particular, I can express this oppression in one of several ways. I can stay away from women altogether; I can beat my wife; I can become a secret killer of women a la Jack the Ripper; I can compose villainous tracts calling for the "putting of women in their place," taking back their right to vote, etc.; or I can tell and enjoy jokes ridiculing women:

> "How long did it take your wife to learn to drive?"
> "It will be twelve years next April."

> A woman sideswiped a car driven by a man. The woman climbed out and apologized for the accident. The man demurred: "That's O.K. lady, it was all my fault. I could see it was a woman driving your car from half a mile away, and I had lots of time to drive off into a field and avoid all this."

> A baseball fan leaped to his feet, whooping wildly as the center fielder made a brilliant diving one-handed catch of a screaming line drive. "Why get so excited?" asked his wife. "Didn't you see that man catch the ball?" the husband replied, incredulously. "Of course," the lady replied, "but isn't that what he's out there for?"

Enjoyment of these jests is socially acceptable and allows an unconscious "getting back at" the fair sex.

The results of one more experiment are applicable here. D.L. Singer, Gollob, and Levine[11] hypothesized that appreciation of aggressive humor could be blunted through inhibition—by first presenting subjects with graphic nonhumorous brutality and sadism. Experimental subjects viewed brutal and sadistic works of Goya, while control subjects viewed benign works by that artist. Then each group rated the funniness of "aggressive" and "nonaggressive" cartoons. The experimental subjects (previously exposed to sadism) rated the aggressive cartoons much lower in "funniness" than did the controls (who saw no sadism). The authors summarize:

> These results [Gollob and Levine, *ibid.*] and findings of the present experiment are . . . that impulse expression plays an important role in aggressive humor, and that intensification of inhibitions surrounding aggression interferes with the appreciation of such humor.[12]

"Impulse expression" is likely to be inhibited by temporary or more lasting variables, also. Consider the Little Moron joke— almost everyone might consider it whimsically ridiculous and, therefore, funny. But the special education teacher who regularly struggles with the task of trying to train eight or ten educable mentally retarded children (little morons) might find little mirth in that direction.

The point here is that we can find aggressiveness, perhaps even the outer edge of downright tragedy, in even the most "whimsical" and "harmless" joke. Remember that Chapter 1 pointed out that Freud postulated the existence of completely "harmless" wit without the least bit of "tendency," but that he could produce not a single example of it.

Carolyn Wells claims that some jokes can best be understood as exemplifying the "Disappointment Theory," defined as "that of frustrating a carefully built up expectation." She offers as examples, among others, the following:

> "Is your wife entertaining this winter?"
> "Not very."

> "I have to go to Brooklyn—" says a perplexed-looking old lady to a traffic policeman. "Are you asking directions, ma'am," replies the cop, "or just telling me your troubles?"

Disappointment there might be here, but I would consider the first example a slap at the wife, the second a slap at Brooklyn. Take the sting from these slaps, or remove the slaps altogether, and the humor vanishes. George Rosenwald puts it succinctly:

> As a general rule, aggression is probably mixed into any joke or cartoon insofar as it makes a *dig* at authority, *robs* a character of his pretensions, *pokes* fun at an aspect of the human condition, or hits one with a *punch* line. The distinction between hostile and neutral cartoons is therefore always a matter of degree.[13]

The matter has been put poetically by Mrs. C. A. Robbins of Findlay, Ohio:

> We laugh, but our laughter is vain!
> That someone's unhappy, is plain—
>   At others' sad plight
>   We scream with delight!
> Getting pleasure from other folks' pain![14]

Beginning in the next chapter, we shall look at the long road our ancestors have trod in becoming as Mrs. Robbins portrays us.

3

Humor's
Ancestry

The book of Genesis of the King James Version of the Bible opens with, "In the beginning. . . ." It is realistic to think that most things had a beginning. I do not wish here to become embroiled in a philosophical discussion as to whether the cosmos has always existed and therefore had no beginning, or whether there was at one time *nothing* at all in the universe. But there is no doubt that practically everything we have today began from something, somewhere, at some time. We have not always had the Empire State Building, the internal combustion engine, or jet aircraft. Humanity did not suddenly spring forth from the soil of the previously lifeless isle of Britain prattling in the English of Shakespeare, Bacon, and Pope; that language had to develop over many centuries. Scholars in my own field (speech communication) know that systematic training in speaking as a discipline has not existed always, but had its beginning in ancient Greece, generations before Aristotle.

The question presently before the house is: Where and how and why did laughter begin?

It may be quite impossible to determine whether laughter actually *did* have a beginning. Perhaps man, *qua* man, has always had the capacity to laugh; the question then becomes, when did "man" *become* man? At what moment in the evolutionary development did the heavily browed, long-limbed, hairy, apelike creatures, the likenesses of which stare brutishly at us from the pages of anthropology texts, become, like the macaques mentioned in Chapter 1, able to laugh? But such questions merely divert from the practical to the philosophically preposterous.

Regardless of when man *began* to laugh, it had to be before he told jokes. And we do know that there was a time when man did not tell jokes. For there was a time when man did not talk. He had no language. It's that simple. No language, no puns—and no gags, punch lines, spoonerisms, malapropisms, bon mots, witticisms, etc.

An extremely important question about laughter's beginning must now be raised. And that is *how many*? How many beginnings must we look for? How many ancestors of "humor" can be found?

This business of "how many" is no idle conjecture. It is a well-known generalization that the kind of answers one gets is more dependent upon the kind of questions he asks than upon the method of investigation. If we go out looking, therefore, for a number of separate and distinct beginnings, we will have to find many; if we begin by seeking *one*, we may be able to achieve unanimity. In the case of humor, one might begin with a search for *many* beginnings, since the varieties or "types" of humorous stimuli at least *seems* extremely wide, and the richness of our English language provides almost endless descriptions of "different" kinds of laughter.

We have already seen, for instance, how Evan Esar can classify humorous stimuli into wisecracks, epigrams, riddles, conundrums, gags, jokes, anecdotes, tangletalk, spoonerisms, fuddletalk, tongue twisters; into Wellerisms, transposers, macaronics, malapropisms, boners, bulls, Freudian slips, double blunders, biograms, caricatures, repartee, hecklerisms, Parkerisms, tricks (including practical jokes), satire, irony, parody, sarcasm, burlesque, shaggy dog stories, nonsensisms, etc. The question we must then ask, "Does each of these varieties have a separate, distinct, unique beginning, or can they be said to have sprung from a common source?"

And how about the "different" kinds of laughter we can find described with our language. There is the laughter of rejoicing, exultation, exultancy, delight, joy, elation, gladness, triumph, jubilation. There is laughter which is a signal of mirth or merrymaking or congratulation. There are giggles (all varieties), titters, smirks, grins, sniggerings, chuckles, guffaws, cachinnations. Laughter comes in bursts, fits, peals, shouts, and roars. There are laughs that can gladden, cheer, delight, please, blithen, transport, exhilarate. One may cackle with laughter, burst out with it, or split one's sides with it. With laughter one can amuse, entertain, divert, beguile, charm, occupy, excite, or convulse people. Laughter might bring one cheer, rejoicing, solace, or sport. There is sardonic laughter, wry laughter, gay laughter, morose laughter, infectious laughter, and derisive laughter. We are driven to laughter by wittiness, cleverness, brightness, atticisms, piquancy, and whimsey. We laugh at banter, raillery, chaff, joshing, badinage, buffoonery, fooling, harlequinade, clownery, tomfoolery, farce, jocularity, jocoseness, facetiousness, waggishness, drollery, jesting, jocosity, and comicality. (If that's not enough "variety," check your *own* thesaurus.)

It should be obvious by now that, if we are to look for more than one origin of laughter, we will have to keep a sharp eye out as we move back through time; for the origins will be popping up in droves. We will have in our notebook at search's end a list of origins duplicating in number of entries those in the New York telephone directory.

Man was once a very simple creature, sans civilization, language, upward mobility, or the Peter Principle. It seems likely, then, that laughter began as something quite simple to early man, something closely related to his simple regimen of keeping body and soul together. Laughter's beginning probably had to have a strong relevance to the daily tasks of finding (and keeping) food, shelter, and mate.

The great "variety" of laughter "types" and laughter-provoking stimuli *might* indicate that a wide variety of beginnings must be sought. But it makes a great deal more sense to me that all laughter had a single, common ancestor. It boggles the imagination to attempt to conceive of all the different "varieties" springing to life full-grown and all fleshed out; spontaneous generation cannot have been the birthright of each form of humor. The central thesis of this chapter is: all humor forms are closely related, and belong to the same family tree; but that family tree grows from a single trunk, or stem. Let us look at that trunk, maintaining at all times that "sense of history" that was found to be useful in Chapter 1.

I wish to point out, first, that I feel that the basic reason for laughter is the Hobbes' "sudden glory" as explained earlier. In deciding *how* "sudden glory" or *derision* came about *as* the basis for all laughter, I am greatly indebted to the writings of Albert Rapp.[1] His phylogenetic theory, which has received (it seems to me) surprisingly little attention from other writers, and which forms the basis for this and the next chapter, seems eminently sensible and logical. Add to it, I think, a few of the well-tested concepts from modern psychology (mainly generalization due to stimulus- and response-substitution and "displacement" and "secondary reinforcements"), and you have an ideal theory of laughter—a theory that is comprehensive, verifiable, and parsimonious, and which prevents the observer from becoming "dazzled" by the "full-blown complexity" of specious but incomplete explanations of humor.

What is it that our simple primordial ancestor, primitive man, had to laugh about? From whence cometh his "glory"? In what ways could he suddenly perceive in himself some "eminency" in comparison to others? How could he suddenly discover his present superiority over his "former" self? By solving a difficult verbal riddle? No, of course not; no language, remember. By mastering some athletic achievement, such as the four-minute mile or the seven-foot high jump? Almost certainly not. No language, no rules for "games". By discovering, suddenly, that he was more handsome than his fellows, or that his latest self-grooming had turned him from rejected creep into potential movie idol? Nonsense. Some intellectual eureka such as the discovery of fire or the principle of the bow and arrow? That might do it, but that would come generations later, after laughter had had its start.

What, then? What touched off his nonverbal grunting, facial contortions, muscular dissembling, and breathing irregularities that presaged our modern "laughter"? Why, one thing that was available to each of our bestial ancestors: *victory*.

Success in combat. Usually success in combat with a fellow man. *Sudden* victory. The sudden realization that one has triumphed, that the prize is his, that his opponent is defeated!

Imagine this primordial scene: two of our ancient ancestors come together in a clearing of the primitive forest. At issue is some item of worth: perhaps a woman, or territorial or hunting rights to the area, or a promising cave in the hillside. But whatever is at issue is something important to each man. How do these grizzly relics of our past resolve their difference? Compulsory arbitration? Small claims court? No. They fight. Tooth and nail.

During the battle, a great deal of tension is built up in our cretinish combatants, especially if the battle is evenly matched for a considerable time. Adrenalin (or whatever they naturally hyped themselves up with in those days) flowed freely, energizing muscles for the emergency tasks required of them. A high emotional state is generated in each fighter (can we call it "fear" or "anger" at this early period?). After some moments, minutes, or hours, the fight ends in the usual way. It becomes clear that there has been a winner and a loser.

The winner now experiences the typical, automatic, autonomic prerogative. He must dispel the extraordinary tension developed during his battle; the central nervous system drives toward homeostasis.

So our winner bares his teeth, pumps his shoulders, and chops up his breath into grunts and moans, with appropriate grimaces. It is a crude kind of a horselaugh, this victory shout, but it has psychological and physiological uses. It permits a rapid return to homeostasis, and incidentally signals to anyone listening that victory is his.

What of our loser? Assuming that he is still alive, and conscious, he probably has the same strong drive for homeostasis charging out from *his* central nervous system. But he dare not imitate his victor. However, a mechanism is quite available to him: he contorts his openmouthed face, pumps his shoulders, chops up his breath into grunts and moans, with appropriate grimaces. He weeps.

The often striking similarity of laughter to crying has a

strong basis in physiology and phylogeny. Men have, for countless generations, used each for the same purpose—the dispelling
of tension and the return to homeostasis after a struggle. The
only difference is between winning and losing; and it is often
difficult to know whether one has clearly won or lost.

We now see the "glory" available to primordial man. But let
us deal now with the concept of the "sudden".

The amount of victory roar bellowed out is going to be
quite closely linked to the amount of tension generated in the
eventual winner. And the amount of tension generated in our
winner is going to depend greatly on the closeness of the combat. If our winner sees from the outset that he is to have an easy
time of it over his (check one: smaller, older, younger, less experienced, crippled, etc.) opponent, he develops little tension, and
thus spews forth little or no bellow at the foregone conclusion
to the scrap. His victory response is more likely to be, "Ho-
hum".

But, if, as he grapples with his enemy, he perceives that he
could very well lose this fight, and the girl, or the land (or
maybe even his *life!*), he loses, in the modern vernacular, a great
deal of cool. He calls upon every fighting resource at his
command, struggling mightily in the desperate battle. His heart
pumps the adrenalin and the glycogen around, energizing his
skeletal muscles for the rigors of the fray. And then: his Sunday
punch *connects* and his opponent crumples up like a pole-axed
sheep. Victory! And hoo-haws by the long ton! Sudden glory,
indeed!

Now: How can we be sure that it happened like this? The
answer is simple: we cannot be sure. Unfortunately, no *National
Geographic* photographers were on hand to record the anthro-
pological evidence. We can only use our best thinking, and try to
find vestiges of it remaining today. And we need look about us
only superficially to find those vestiges.

Who are the most primitive people available for our observation? I don't mean the near-stone-age nomadic savages of
New Guinea or Australia; I mean available daily, easily, right
here in middle-class-conscious twentieth-century technocracy?
Who among us have not yet acquired the veneer of civilization,
who might be expected to emit occasional victory roars? The
answer is frightfully simple: children.

Anyone who has not witnessed a struggle between two small combative urchins which resulted in squeals of victory from one and tears of mortification and/or pain from the other has spent precious little time around small children. But, of course, one need not be a *small* child—in fact, need not be a child at all—in order to shriek victoriously at the sudden successful conclusion of a vigorous contest.

Today, of course, older children and adults engage in few actual contests involving fighting. We have learned good substitutes for our aggressive instincts. We play games. And when the contest is fiercely contended on both sides, when the outcome is in doubt until the final gun, what a fierce roar of enthusiasm goes up from the winners (and, their fans, if present). When the home football team is beating Tech 52–0 in the third quarter, the conclusion of the contest hardly is likely to generate many screams of victory. But let the home team, perhaps even the underdog according to the bookies, pull the game out 16–14 by a field goal with only two seconds left on the clock! Pandemonium colossal for the home crowd! And for the losers: tears more bitter than wormwood (from the cheerleaders and players, at least).

Outpourings of victory screams can even become highly ritualized. Few readers of this book do not know of at least one school or college that rings a bell for a specified period following an athletic victory. We are all acquainted with elaborate victory chants or songs performed by groups of fans. In my high school days in Pinckneyville, Illinois, our basketball team perennially was a prep powerhouse. In honor of the many winning occasions, our squad of hard-working, routine-minded cheerleaders developed a little "victory number" consisting of a chanted song and precision acrobatic dance. This number was performed during a full one-minute time-out in the fourth quarter, when victory was assured beyond a doubt. When the home team was enjoying a generous lead in the fourth quarter, the fans looked forward eagerly to the victory time-out when the number would be performed. When the choreographed victory celebration would begin, it drew whistles, smiles, and generally uproariously volatile good will from the fans. The opposition, however, usually lacked the "sportsmanship" to enjoy having their faces ground into the hardwood.

Fatherhood has brought me into protracted contact with the violent world of the small American boy. As I write this I can look back upon ten years as an adult leader in Boy Scouts and three years in Little League baseball. And this world, so rife with conflicts, both mini and maxi, has shown itself to abound in frequent, often ritualized, triumphant roars. The current ritualized signal of victory among ten- and twelve-year-olds of my area is a high-pitched and loudly shrilled, "Hey-HEY!" It is usually accompanied by appropriate gestures, such as a clenched fist raised on high (boy power?), a tilting back of the head, and perhaps even a leap into the air. I notice this signal all-too-often from my son, Mark; in fact, nearly every time I miss my "long" shot in a tight game of basketball "longs and shorts".

Aggressiveness is no longer a life-or-death requirement for existence in the world of small boys, although it certainly does help in establishing their social and physical pecking order. But with primordial man it was life if he had it and death if he didn't. In the natural order of things so well documented by Darwin and later so well supported by his "bulldog" Huxley, the man lacking sufficient aggressiveness did not live long enough to pass along to the race his particular combination of genetics. Life was tough when our ancestors lived in trees and, later, in caves. It is no wonder that man evolved as a highly motivated competitor. And it is no wonder that man has had to develop so myriad a group of activities in which to exercise his "natural" competitiveness (read: aggressiveness). For, with the growth of "civilization", every individual learned his "place" in the power structure. The need for physical combat lessened; why fight your neighbor Glog if you already know that he can whip Gork, and you know from experience that Gork can tromp you? To fight Glog becomes an act of masochism (*conscious, not psychic*).

Still, you have this inborn necessity to compete, perchance to win and then to rend the air with your scream of victory. You still yearn for this "sudden glory" of victory in combat, this yen inbred into you over countless generations; you still feel what will later become known as part of "the human condition". You are eager for the tang of competition; you look forward hungrily for the "thrill of victory" (hoping to avoid the "agony of defeat"). So what do you do? You invent competitive contests that substitute for the life-or-death primordial combat: whist, poker, chess, checkers; footraces, relays, high jumps; football, basketball, soccer, tennis, baseball. And you keep some ritualized contests which do not completely substitute for the original primordial duel, only change and formalize it: boxing, the bullfight, hunting, capital punishment, war.

Primordial aggression substitute activities such as cards, chess, or athletics have been a great leap forward into "civilizing" the behavior of our ancestors. How much more polite (and less dangerous) to challenge one's neighbor to a game of checkers or a race around the block than to challenge him to twelve-pound clubs at close range! In the next chapter we shall begin to see further channeling of the "victory roar" into more "civilized" outlets of more concern to the subject within these covers.

4

From
Primordial Battle
to Joke:
Three Civilizing Routes

Any theory of laughter, as noted earlier, in order to be *complete*, must demonstrate *comprehensiveness*; that is, it must explain all cases, all kinds of laughter. And lack of such comprehensiveness has remained a fatal flaw in so many attempts to explain laughter and its causes. Max Eastman even proposed that there were two distinct types of laughter, each with its own neural machinery and, supposedly, each with its own origin.[1] I must reject quickly and sternly that there exists a "teeth-baring" laughter of derision which differs fundamentally and ancestrally from that of humor and pleasantry. However, taking such a position requires that one provide plausible links to connect the raucous laugh of ridicule caused by seeing someone slip on a banana peel and the sympathetic chuckle of a mother at her toddler's tumbles on his first hesitant attempts to walk. One must be able to reconcile the sardonic laughter evoked by a Swift or a Pope, a Mort Sahl or a Juvenal, with the smile aroused by the nonsensical conundrum about the way elephants make love under water (they take off their trunks). Relationship, even kinship, must be clearly detectable between the fit of giggles brought on by a TV announcer's malapropism ("News of the Russians once again crapped up in the news.") and the smile of

49

recognition which might greet a witticism such as Daniel Webster's "Falsehoods not only disagree with truths, but usually quarrel among themselves."

This chapter takes up this task of reconciling all laughter-provoking incidents as compatible members of the same family. It shows how, starting with primordial man's roar of triumph, explained in the last chapter, laughter became a civilized and civilizing activity. I agree with Rapp that the developmental process advanced in three "directions." Thus, each of these directions are detailed, and support for each of these historical developments is offered.

But first, a word on definitions—definitions of those concepts, mentioned in Chapter 3, which were the *agents* of the developments.

An unfortunate fact of record is that there exists still today considerable numbers of people naive enough to believe that man was created from scratch as a blue-eyed, nearly hairless biped; that he was imbued from the instant of his creation with a full vocabulary of some Near-Eastern language, although no one to talk to; that, to give him a companion for conversation (and for other, nonlinguistic activities), his mate was created out of his rib during a nap. In other words, there are still a lot of folks around who do not believe in evolution (sometimes called "*evi*lution"). Such ignorance and stubbornness should not surprise us, however, when one considers the fact, uncovered by both national surveys and sidewalk interviews on the main drag of Athens, Georgia, alike, that in 1974 just about one third of the American people still were not convinced that we have actually landed men on the moon.

To such people this chapter, nay even this book, will not make sense. For those to whom sense can be made, I next take up the concept of Carl Jung's "shadow archetype."

Jung knew that man developed from lower forms of life. He saw it everywhere he looked in the human soul and psyche. And he made it an integral part of his comprehensive theory of human personality.

An archetype, according to Jung, is "a universal thought form (idea) which contains a large element of emotion. This thought form creates images or visions that correspond in normal waking life to some aspect of the conscious situation."[2]

How does an archetype originate? "It is a permanent deposit in the mind of an experience that has been constantly repeated for many generations. . . . [for instance] man has been exposed throughout his existence to innumerable instances of great natural forces—earthquakes, waterfalls, flood, hurricanes, lightning, forest fires, and so forth. Out of these experiences there has developed an archetype of energy, a predisposition to perceive and be fascinated by power and a desire to create and control power. The child's delight in firecrackers, the young person's preoccupation with 'hot-rod' cars, and the adult's interest in releasing the hidden energies of atoms have their roots in the archetype of energy. Man is *driven* by this archetype to seek new sources of energies."[3]

This is how archetypes, in general, form. Members of the race experience, over countless generations, the same phenomena with some regularity. This experience gradually "wears a groove" in the collective unconscious of the race, becoming almost like an instinctual part of the general human psychological makeup.

I choose the analogy of "wearing a groove" deliberately, because Jung made much the same comparison:

> Archetypes are like riverbeds which dry up when the water deserts them, but which it can find again at any time. An archetype is like an old watercourse along which the water of life has flowed for centuries digging a deep channel for itself. The longer it has flowed in this channel the more likely it is that sooner or later the water will return to its old bed.[4]

Jung eloquently explains the strength of the basic animal heritage which each human being carries deep within his psyche—and sometimes not so deep at all. His words:

> It is not only primitive man whose psychology is archaic. It is the psychology also of modern, civilized man, and not merely individual "throw-backs" in modern society. On the contrary, every civilized human being, however high his conscious development, is still an archaic man at the deeper levels of his psyche. Just as the human body connects us

with the mammals and displays numerous vestiges of
earlier evolutionary stages going back even to the reptilian
age, so the human psyche is a product of evolution which,
when followed back to its origins, shows countless archaic
traits.

Just as a man has a body which is no different in principle from that of an animal, so also his psychology has a
whole series of lower storeys in which the spectres from
humanity's past epochs still dwell, when the animal souls
from the age of Pithecanthropus and the hominids, then
the "psyche" of the coldblooded saurians, and, deepest
down of all, the transcendental mystery and paradox of the
sympathetic and parasympathetic psychoid systems.[5]

Of course the idea is not original nor unique to Jung, this
idea that man is basically an animal who, because of a larger
brain and the consequent ability to conceptualize abstractly
through language, has covered his basic animalism with a thin
veneer of civilization. Lately, Walter Meyden, director of the
Footlighters Child Guidance Clinic in Hollywood's Presby-
terian Hospital has put it this way:

The veneer of civilization is at most 10,000 years. Behind that are a million years of jungle living lived pretty
much on an animal level with an animal-type of social
organization.[6]

My belief is that the many generations of men who responded to their sudden victories in violent encounters with
roars of triumph, over hundreds of thousands of years, wore a
groove, a riverbed, into the collective human unconscious. This
tendency to pant and vocalize uproariously at perceptions of
"sudden glory," of *victory*, can be thought of as being part of
what Jung called the "shadow archetype." This archetype

consists of the animal instincts which man inherited in his
evolution from lower forms of life. Consequently, the shadow to begin with typifies the animal side of man's nature.[7]

Thus man developed an inherent capacity for and tendency to
laugh.

Acceptance of this idea of a "humor" factor in the "shadow
archetype" is bolstered by evidence from child development
studies. George Thompson has been led to conclude that, "It

would appear that smiling *appears through maturation without special experience*, but that many of the circumstances which elicit smiling are learned, even during the first year of life [italics mine]."[8] Further, in "A Study of the Smiling and Laughing of Infants in the First Year of Life," Ruth Washburn found that the number of laughter responses did not change during that first year while the number of smiling responses increased markedly. She concluded: "This, coupled with the fact that the laughing behavior pattern is more stereotyped, suggests that laughing remains *a primitive form of behavior expressive of affective states*, while smiling, in certain instances assumes the character of a communicative, adaptive response rather than a purely expressive one [italics mine]."

And so, both the testimony from that eminent scholar and thinker, Carl Jung, and the data of developmental psychologists support the idea that our capacity and mechanism for laughter is *inborn*. We need not *learn* to laugh or smile, as we must learn to talk, to write, to drive an automobile. Also remember: as evidence cited in Chapter 1 attests, lower animals also possess these mechanisms and capacities. It can only make the finest of good sense, therefore, to assume that our base for laughter, the ancient roar of triumph, might very well have made its imprint upon the collective racial psyche of the higher primates, including man. At least I hope the reader will concede this point temporarily, so that we may look at some other well-established psychological concepts which will help explain how a combatant's victory roar can be father to the chuckle over the cocktail party repartee.

First, let us consider the psychological concept of "generalization." Analytically speaking, there are two kinds of generalization: there is generalization through response substitution and generalization through stimulus substitution. Although we are more concerned with the stimulus substitution, let us exemplify response substitution.

Generalization through response substitution occurs when a person "learns to emit a certain response to a given stimulus, [and] that stimulus becomes effective in eliciting 'similar' responses."[9] For example, let's say you try caviar but hate it; but you persist, and finally "develop a taste" for it. But caviar is expensive, you learn; so you do not buy it often, despite the fact that it tempts your palate. Now, each time you pass through the gourmet section of your food store and spy some caviar, you respond with a desire to buy and eat some. But other responses are likely to occur. You may wish you made more money; you may wish your wife was less extravagant on clothes so that you could buy caviar more often; you may feel anger at your boss for refusing your last request for a raise (and thereby denying you caviar); you may fantasy an instant daydream in which an attractive member of the opposite sex languorously feeds you mountains of caviar, etc. You may even resolve to demonstrate more ambition and aggressiveness in your job or profession, in order to be able to buy caviar more often. This is response-substitution.

But in tracing the various paths from victory roar to snicker over the men's room graffiti, we are concerned mostly with what is called generalization through stimulus substitution; for we are interested in the question, "How did the stimulus of the modern joke or witticism come to elicit the 'same' kind of response as did the sudden success in combat?" Stimulus substitution is defined as what occurs when a person "learns to make a certain response to a certain stimulus [and] certain other previously ineffective stimuli will also elicit the conditioned response."[10] The definition continues:

> If the stimuli are preceptually "similar," it is said to be PRIMARY STIMULUS GENERALIZATION. The greater the similarity of the related stimulus to the conditioned stimulus, the more frequently it will elicit the response.[11]

Reread and remember the last sentence of the above quotation, for its importance will soon be noted.

Can we exemplify generalization through stimulus response? Of course. It is through this activity that we form our stereotypes. We become acquainted, let us say with a gentleman whose national origin is Outer Silurvian; we react negatively to him because he demonstrates very miserly behavior. Sometime later we encounter an immigrant from Inner Silurvia. He too pinches pennies without mercy. We are apt to conclude that inhabitants of Silurvia and their descendants are an exceptionally thrifty lot; we may even generalize that *foreigners* are stingy, and react to all accordingly.

Such stereotypy works favorably, of course, also. For instance, my wife and I have had many fine experiences through meeting, at universities where I have taught, military personnel assigned to ROTC units. We number among our best friends acquired at colleges several such military people; we therefore *expect* pleasant social experiences when we meet new ROTC personnel.

We must define two more concepts useful in the discussion to follow, "displacement" and "secondary reinforcement."

The definition from Horace B. English and Ava C. English which explains for us "displacement" is that numbered 3:

> 3. A substitute activity, from a different activity system, resorted to when the usual consummatory response to a situation is prevented.[12]

"Displacement" is aptly illustrated by the so-called Kick-the-Dog Psychology. The husband has a tough day at work with his boss, whom he cannot tell off. So he comes home keyed up and angry, and blows his stack at his wife. The wife, angered yet afraid of the huffy husband, vents her spleen on six-year-old Johnny, their son. The upset child dares not "sass" his mom back, so he takes out his anger with a boot to the tail of Rover.

"Secondary reinforcement" or "secondary reward" is defined as "a reward that has become a source of satisfaction through learning, usually (perhaps always) from association with another object or stimulus situation that is satisfactory."[13] Eating a filet mignon in a nice restaurant will satisfy your primary drive for food (primary reinforcement) but may also give you a feeling of general well-being, will almost certainly please your palate, and may even make you feel "rich" or "extravagant" (secondary reinforcements).

Definitions are now finished and, there is hope the lesson is learned. Now, let us get back to that roar of triumph.

A. The Ridicule Road

In Chapter 1 we saw how Katharine Hull Kappas defined "ridicule." Let us now look at a more common definition:

> ri-di-cule (rĭd'ĭ-kul) *n* [F., adj & n., fr. L. *ridiculus* ridiculous, neut. *ridiculum* a jest, fr. *ridere* to laugh.] 1. Act or practice of causing laughter by poking fun at another person; remarks or actions intended to make people laugh at some

person. 2. A laughingstock; a butt of jokes. —*v.t.* To laugh
at or make fun of mockingly or contemptuously. *Syn.* Ridicule, deride, mock, taunt, quiz, chaff.

As I have indicated earlier, especially in Chapter 2, there is always some element of ridicule in a humorous situation. Sometimes the ridicule is highly recognizable as such. For instance,
devotees of nightclubs are familiar with the hired comic's retort to noisy drunks, the hecklerism:

> Look buddy, everyone has the right to be stupid, but you
> abuse the privilege.
>
> Pal, after meeting you I can really see why a lot of people
> are in favor of birth control.

But ridicule is also present in the silliest of whimsey stories:

> A drunk staggered into the street and was knocked down
> by a car driven by a woman. She stopped, leaned out the
> window, and said, "You'd better watch out, young man."
> The drunk propped himself up on one elbow and asked:
> "Why? You gonna back up?"

And, subtly, women drivers of the world are held up to ridicule
en masse.

So how did this kind of thing, ridicule, evolve from our triumph roar? Generalization through stimulus substitution. The
way it must have come about is detailed in the next few
paragraphs.

In the first place, our earliest ancestors must certainly have
come to recognize the roar of triumph for what it was when
they made it or when they heard someone else bellow it. They
must have come to associate this bellow of victory with the picture of the loser, the other guy. For the loser of a physical battle
will bear the signs of the vanquished: battered, bruised, hair and
teeth perhaps missing; maybe limping and/or nursing a pain-
fully wrenched shoulder; no doubt bleeding a bit here and there;
and quite likely weeping, perhaps in great, wracking sobs. Our
progenitors must certainly have become conditioned to know
what a defeated, thus *inferior* combatant looked like. For fighting
in order to demonstrate dominance is a well-documented animal function. Thus our ancestors required only the slightest of
generalization by way of stimulus substitution to accept the

mere *sight* of a battered, losing contestant for the actual battle itself. The psychological reaction—immediate, sudden, and usually unconscious—is a favorable comparison of one's own safe, comfortable self with the low estate of the unfortunate loser. This we might call *superiority laughter*, plain and simple.

This superiority laughter, this outward manifestation of inner recognition of defeat and ignominy, this reaction only one small step from the roar of triumph in actual battle, can certainly be considered "cruel;" it can be called "inhuman," it can be termed "callous" or "uncivilized." It is the kind of behavior we wish our "nice" children to extinguish as quickly as possible, at least in public, lest our friends and acquaintances determine for themselves that we are raising "little monsters."

And yet: is the laugh of derision not, at the same time, a more civilized, a more couth form of behavior than its progenitor? Is not the exercising of the archetypical tendency to strive for superiority (and its culminating, satisfying bellow) through laughter at the less fortunate more civilized, more sophisticated, and less savage than its physical counterpart?

Remember that, as noted in the last chapter, our ancient forbears at some time found it more comfortable and economical to live and hunt in groups, with established pecking orders of superiority. John E. Pfieffer suggests that this time came after man invented sharp hunting tools and developed greatly in brain size, thus making cooperative group hunting efforts more feasible than "going it alone."[14] With this pecking order of superiority established, the amount of fighting was reduced considerably. But the need-to-laugh groove was by this time well-worn into the "shadow archetype" of the collective human unconscious.

So, just let a member of the village, tribe, or clan wind up with a black eye or a broken nose as a result of picking a fight with the wrong guy—and he will wind up a laughingstock to his brethren, who will demonstrate their *un*battered superiority with horselaughs.

It is just one more small generalization through stimulus substitution from laughing at someone inferior-because-of-getting-throttled to laughing at *anyone, anywhere,* who appears in *any way* inferior at all. Thus the tribe's permanent cripple, or the village idiot, or the inept spear thrower becomes the perfect object of laughter; so does the female so ugly she cannot secure a mate; so does the cavewife who cannot cook filet of tapir without burning it; and ditto for the male suitor spurned by all eligible maids. And woe be unto the unfortunate in the tribe born with nose too long, or eyes too crossed, with hands and feet too large or without the proper number of digits.

Gradually, through generalization, man learned to exercise his laughter archetype any time he encountered anyone substantially different, and therefore "inferior," to himself. It is not hard to imagine the reactions when a roving band of pygmies encounters a hunting party of Watusi-sized seven-footers; the pygmies would probably squeal with glee as they derisively point fingers of scorn and ridicule at the gangling string-beans. And the giants would loudly cackle at the shrimpish stature of the small-fry. And the groove would wear deeper in the archetype.

If superiority laughter is an immediate and direct descendant of primordial man's roar of triumph in battle, we should expect to find it around today—and we can, quite easily. The tendency to laugh at the unexpectedly demeaned or defeated (thus, inferior) person is far too general to require much documentation. I simply ask you to recall how many times in the last week you have laughed at someone who made an error of judgment or speech, dropped food in his lap, or dribbled Coca Cola down his chin. How many antics of slapstick comedy have you enjoyed? Have you perhaps gotten off a horselaugh at a team (or player on a team) just defeated by your own "home" team? Did you perhaps guffaw at any mistakes made by your opponents in that game? How many slurs demeaning a race or nationality have evoked chuckles from you? Our natural tendency to laugh at the misfit, the inferior, is evident in the way entertainers capitalize upon it. Thus Martha Ray has made a good living off her larger-than-average mouth, Buster Keaton built a career on a frozen, bug-eyed face, Jimmy Durante made it on little more than a bulbous nose, and Roscoe Ates, comedian of another era, made his way to fame and fortune with a well-developed stutter.

So our forebears generalized from victory roar to the superiority laughter of ridicule. Then what?

Well, somewhere along the line, we are not sure when, man (or what we think evolved into man) developed language. We don't know exactly *how* he developed language—there are a dozen or so theories of that alone. But we can certainly figure out *why* he developed language, and we can be pretty sure of some of the consequences of his new ability to talk.

He learned to talk, after sufficient brain development, because it was a more economical way to do a lot of things. And, as one result of his new symbol-using ability, he was able to time-bind. That is, he became able to consider, not just the here and now, but also the past and the future, and the far away. And he could use this time-binding ability to diversify his ridicule immensely. Now he can dredge up to consciousness ridiculous events of the past, the future, the far away; he need not wait for the ridiculous to occur within his immediate range of perception. With language he can serve up ridicule *on demand*; he can engage in direct ridicule.

Let us exemplify: One day Snof sees Gligf drop his crude stone axe on his toes; Snof giggles gleefully at the stream of epithets and oaths which erupt from the pained Gligf. Superiority laughter, pure and simple. But several days later, while the tribal males are enjoying an evening aperitif of basted bison blood or some such, around the communal campfire, Snof describes in detail Gligf's accident and the welter of cussing he has sprayed upward to the Gods, all to the hearty amusement of the assemblage.

Language made man able, not only to recall past events, but able to discuss and predict future events—and to ridicule his fellow man for the what-can-be.

> "You're gonna marry Gerta? You'll be sorry. Marriage is an investment, certainly, but you can be sure Gerta's mother will put in her two cents worth."

> "You're so *stupid*. If you were going to a bridal shower you'd probably want to take the soap."

Lastly, language allows faults to be immensely magnified and intensified; and the faults of those ridiculed need not be physically present, but can be geographically far removed, even abstract enough to be unnamed.

> He is so stupid he has to go out of his mind to get an idea.

> She's so fat you can't see her double chin because her lip hides it.
>
> Is she skinny? I've seen more meat on a butcher's apron.
>
> He is such a grouch that even his shadow won't accompany him.
>
> She is so plain that she would have to go topless just to become a wallflower.

The development of language (and other symbol systems) thus allows primeval man to engage in *deliberate ridicule*. He need not wait for the accident of fate to deliver to him some inferior, thus laughable, companion. He needs no jester, clown, or dwarf constantly present. He can use language to remember, to predict, or to exaggerate, at any time, a peer's shortcomings, injuries, mistakes, and peculiarities. He needs no longer to be in direct proximity, in time or space, to someone less fortunate than he. He can verbally call up an inferior at will. Or, if he is mentally unable to verbally produce his own objects of derision, he can seek out that man (or, less often, woman) who has the facility for doing so. And so we have a built-in cultural need for a tribe wit; the role of the jester is born. Today we call him a comedian or a humorist or a satirist. Needing the medicine of laughter, wishing to bare our teeth and chuckle at the deliberate ridicule of others, we go to our newspaper, magazine, television set, or nightclub. And we find in these channels deliberate ridicule heaped upon a large nu mber of persons, places, actions, organizations, institutions, and so on.

Of course, as mentioned earlier, generalizations resulting in stereotypy are a result of stimulus substitution. This activity is made possible by language, alone, too—and results in a great deal of deliberate ridicule of one group by another. In one of his daily newspaper columns Sydney Harris[15] points out that man has always, apparently, ridiculed his neighboring groups by using them as symbols for stupidity, laziness, guile, or dishonesty. He mentions that, where he vacations, Polish jokes existed long before they became popular nationwide—but that up there in Wisconsin they were *Belgian* jokes "by virtue of a large immigrant Belgian community which provided the butt of this rustic humor." He adds:

> Thus has it ever been. There is no record of any culture anywhere that did not release its hostilities and exhibit its

invincible sense of superiority by deriding or down-grading some convenient out-group.

Harris cites many examples from the world's languages, using as his source Mario Pei's *The Story of Language*. Among them:

> The earliest Slavs called the neighboring Germans "Nemets," which means "mute" or "dumb." On the other hand, the word "slaves" comes from Slavs who were captured in battle.

> In France syphilis is called "the English disease;" in England it is called "the French disease."

> The English invented the term "to Welsh," a term meaning to renege on an obligation and thus an insult to the Welsh people.

> The English expressions "Dutch treat" and "Dutch courage" suggest that the Hollanders are tight with money and fond of alcohol. The expression "to Jew down" favors Christian charity, at the expense of Jewish greed.

> Both the French and Italians call a "confidence game" "the American swindle."

> The French call the driver of a getaway car *l'Americain*.

> In German, the term "Russian" also means "barbarous"; "English education" means "flogging."

The supposition that deliberate ridicule must have occurred very early in the evolution of humor in the race of man is suggested by its place in the evolution of the child's sense of humor. Ernest Harms has studied the child's developing sense of humor and presents a case for deliberate ridicule as a very early development in the child.[16]

The very first stage, in children up to about three, is not very important, according to Harms. It involves laughter "in direct response to any pleasing approach," or "humor as pleasure." This could be construed to mean something very akin to superiority laughter. But let us go on to the second stage found by Harms: Humor as Funniness or Curiosity.

Harms' basic method is to get the preschool (age three to seven) child to "draw something funny." He reports that children this age eagerly fall to the task and draw what, to them, is funny. What is it they draw?

> We frequently find it curious to see what is funny to the

child. Practically anything *unusual* has the effect of amusing
him. What he calls a "funny face" or a "funny man" is often quite the opposite to us. The shaking hands of an old
man, the feeble walk of an old woman, the abnormal size of
a nose or limb, or the grimace of pain—*cause for pity in
adults—are causes for merriment in the very young* [italics mine].

Harms elaborates by giving some examples:

> From a study of a large number of such funny drawings
> made by the three-to-seven-year-old group, we learn that
> humor is aroused in them by practically anything *strange and
> unusual* . . . . There appears a picture of the maid who has a
> toothache, the mother who is "mad," a man who has a nose
> "like an elephant," . . . A child calls himself funny when he
> has a black eye or a bandage because of a sore on the head.
> A dog drawn with too long a neck is as funny as a bird with
> four legs . . . it is funny to take a penny from the mother's
> purse, or to break a dinner plate because one does not want
> to eat the meal [italics mine].

And so, when asked to symbolize, through pictures, what is
funny, the children three to seven almost invariably draw something that could be interpreted as deliberate ridicule.

The tendency to deliberately ridicule must be an absolutely
inherent factor in the makeup of small children. And one more
of its symbolizations will be noted, one that will be instantly
recognizable to any observant person who has spent any amount of
time around small kids. I refer to a little song, nay, a chant, into
which one or more children will burst the moment he or they
perceive that one of their companions is in need of ridicule. There
is a great deal of rancor in it, and it is often accompanied with
facial grimaces, nods of the head, and appropriate gestures. It
invariably is delivered in an unpleasant, nasal voice, and goes:

ya
Yah ya   Yah
yah   Yaah!

One might be tempted to conclude that this derisive chant is native only to a particular area, such as the United States. But a
friend of mine, a professor of Germanic and Slavic languages

and a native of Germany, tells me that he has noted the chant emanating from ridiculing children in each of the large number of European countries he has visited.

What about later developments?

Harms' study of the humor in drawings of children after they mature to school age shows that their humor becomes more situation-bound. The dominant element is still deliberate ridicule, but it becomes situational instead of merely expressionistic.

> Our experiments confirm . . . that we may generalize and say that there is no longer any laughing about a fat woman as such; it is rather about comical situations in which she may be involved, as in passing through a small gate or trying to protect herself with an umbrella too small for her. It is not so much a stupid expression on the face of a country boy that is laughed at, as some incongruous sight of him—as seeing him in his farm clothes walking barefoot down Fifth Avenue in New York City. Or it is the father dressed up like a baby, an ugly man studying his own face in a mirror, a conventional waiter forced to serve a cow, a woman with a dog's head leading on a leash a dog with her head . . . . *Rarely do we find in this period traces of humor of verbal character* [italics mine].

The last sentence above is deliberately italicized. It is to again remind that the expression of this preadolescent ridicule is pictorial and quite nonverbal. It is not until later, at the onset of adolescence, that Harms' subjects still drew pictures of "funny" situations, but generally would add a line or two of caption to underline the ridiculous point.

> A few examples may be given. There is the usual family group of adults, pictured fighting like a wild gang, and a caption is added: "Children must play." A frail little boy stands before the platform with an old-maid teacher asking him, "Johnny, what is your father?" and Johnny answers, "He *was* a teacher, but now he works really."

Purely verbal humor develops later.

> With the middle of the second decade of life, the tendency toward pictorial expression of humor becomes weaker. The third- and fourth-year high-school students have developed intellectually to such an extent that they

prefer to read humorous stories and to tell instead of paint them.

Let us pull together some strands of thought by way of a summary.

It is hypothesized here that man's many generations of enjoyment of victory roars wore into the collective unconscious of man an archetype, a groove predilecting him to seek feelings of superiority. This archetype led him to generalize from actual victory over an actual opponent to unconscious victory over any fellow defeated by anyone else. This unconscious feeling of victoriousness generalized to fruition in any perception of any kind of difference in others (ugliness, lameness, stupidity, etc.). As man developed language and other forms of verbalizations, he found that he could *deliberately* ridicule his fellows.

Such a progression can also be found in the child. He begins with only a built-in tendency (the archetype) to smile and laugh at physical pleasure (superiority to a former, non-pleasure state) from contacts and approaches. As he matures to three years of age, the ugly and unusual become funny (inferior) to him. He is able to deliberately pictorialize the abnormalities he finds "funny." Later he prefers his ridicule in verbal form. It would seem that "ontogeny *does* recapitulate phylogeny,"[17] at least where the development of the sense of humor is concerned.

Before we venture down (The "What Is . . ." Way), two more steps must be covered down the Ridicule Road. The first of these is the development of "affectionate ridicule."

The child who chants our "Yah ya ya ya yah yah" at his playmate is not being very "affectionate." He wants the butt of the chant to feel sorely the humiliation of defeat or defect. He is taking his superiority feelings straight. He has not yet learned the more gentle, more civilized art of affectionate ridicule, of "kidding."

What is the trick of "kidding," the technique, the rationale? Really very simple. The "kidder" wishes to demonstrate temporary superiority, of course, and to feel and enjoy it. But he wishes *not* to enrage or overly humiliate his object; he wishes the butt of his jibes to remain in good spirits, to "brush off" the ridicule, to show he can "take it," to be a "good sport." It will help the "kidder" to achieve his goal if he, himself, will good-naturedly smile. "Smile when you say that, Podner," translated, means: "Prove with your face that you don't really mean it." Thus a black woman can smilingly admonish her husband, "You big black Nigger," and get maybe a kiss from her spouse; but Whitey undoubtedly would get an entirely different response from saying the same thing, especially if said with a straight face. Dick Gregory can jokingly claim that he chose the title of his book, *Nigger*, deliberately, since he could then send one to the President of the United States and claim he had achieved a lifelong ambition of seeing "a 'Nigger' in the White House!" The fraternity man can have fun (feel superiority) by joshing his buddy about the homeliness of his latest blind date without losing that chum's friendship.

And what happens if the "kiddee" becomes angry at the "kidder"? Kidding, after all, does backfire sometimes. Kidding can go too far, or can be misunderstood. What if the one being kidded explodes in anger? Why, the "kidder" dons the mask of innocence, smiles, displays the openhanded gesture of helplessness, and replies, "Oh, come on, can't you see I'm only *kidding*?" He might add: "Can't you take a little joke?" Or: "Come on—I thought you were a better sport than *that*!"

So, most of us learn to kid and to be kidded. We recognize the smile of the kidder, we notice his playful demeanor as he warms up on us. And we know that we need to "play along," to remain "good sports," to not take offense. We learn the social, playful, "harmless" nature of kidding. We learn the myriad lists of discrepancies and faults and *faux pas* that can cause us to get kidded, and we learn to try to avoid these. For, we may not mind being kidded occasionally, but a steady diet of it grows irksome. We thus learn the customs, mores, and taboos of our culture—which is another way of saying that we become "civilized."

From the victorious bellow of superiority over zonking an opponent into unconsciousness to the polite kidding that goes on at bridge table and cocktail party is a very long road, indeed. For mankind it has been a road of many thousands of generations, and for an individual man it spans the immense physical and psychological distance from the cradle to social maturity.

It is only natural, of course, for "kidding" to have become so

much a part of the short prose narrative we call the modern
"joke." For when two or more folks huddle to "enjoy a good
one" together, they take on the smile, the conspiratory playfulness, the friendly closeness of the kidder and the kiddee. The
only difference is who it is that gets kidded—for it is usually
some third party not present.

To illustrate: you walk up to your colleague while at work.
"Did you hear the one about the guy who came home to his
nagging wife after playing poker all night?" you say. Your colleague smiles, glances quickly around, and perhaps leans slightly
toward you in the classic pose of the coconspirator. His facial
expression of playful eagerness to hear the joke plainly means
he has not heard it. "Well," you say, "the minute he walks in the
door, she takes after him with the nagging. He holds up his
hand, says, 'That'll be enough of that. Pack your bags. I just lost
you in a poker game.' Stunned, she blurts, 'How could you *do*
such a thing?!' 'It wasn't easy,' he replies. 'I had to fold with a
royal flush!' " Shared laughter.

But why the shared laughter? The two of you laugh *with*
the poker-playing husband (the kidder) and *at* the deflated wife
(the kiddee). In order to enjoy this little episode the mantle of
reality must be suspended, temporarily. Men just do *not* put up
their wives as stakes in poker games; and, even if they did, what
poker player would *accept* a nagging, unpleasant woman as
stakes to play *for*? Thus the conspiratorial playfulness is a pre-
requisite. The stereotypical "nagging housewife" has gotten her
comeuppance within the socially acceptable framework of playful banter. How much more civilized than punching your own
better half in the mouth!

So we have seen how our triumphal scream of victory in
battle has evolved, phylogenetically as well as ontogenetically,
to the "harmless" kidding of social repartee and the joke. Let us
now turn to a second evolutionary road which that victory howl
has journeyed.

B. The "What is . . . ." Way

As the most primitive of human societies began to take
shape, and the amount of "victory roaring" was decimated by
the recognition by everyone of "his place" in the pyramidical

hierarchy based upon strength, the inherent need to exercise the "laughing groove" worn into the collective unconscious by generations of triumphant bellows was satisfied in a way significantly different from that of the Ridicule Road. Signs of apparent defeat and accident, and physical and social abnormalities continued to evoke laughter in the increasingly civilized creatures we assume were our ancestors. But another kind of laughter, one based upon actual conflict and its successful resolution, must surely have emerged as our bettle-browed ancestors grew larger and larger brain cavities, and filled them with larger and larger masses of cortical matter.

It may not have happened just this way, but then again, it just might have. Two members of the tribe, a little brighter but considerably weaker physically (and perhaps less brave, psychologically) than their fellows, decide to compete with one another, the one with the chance to win (and therefore laugh in victory), and the other to taste the bitter dregs of defeat (the penalty for grabbing for the brass ring of victory and missing). But: they do not intend to *fight*; they will compete with their *wits*! They will match intellects.

As in the primordial *physical* battle, the basic pattern with the exact same factors prevails. Each contestant places great store on the contest and its outcome. Each strives mightily to win, for to lose is painful. Glock poses a question to Glunk. Glunk sweats and ponders in his attempt to come up with the answer to Glock's question, while Glock anxiously hopes that his supposedly mental inferior has no chance to dredge up the answer.

When he feels assured of victory, Glock perhaps even poses the inevitable, "Give up, do you Glunk?" Glunk wearily nods, whereupon Glock triumphantly announces the answer and guffaws his superiority for anyone in earshot to perceive. The defeated Glunk boils inwardly in his gall; any cohorts of his hang their heads in sympathy at the defeat, but Glock's friends join *him* in victorious laughter. Again, we have had, as with the roar of triumph in the actual, physical combat, the two factors: (*a*) an intense duel, with great tension developing in each combatant, and (*b*) a *sudden* victory of one over the other resulting in glee for the winner and gloom for the loser.

How can we be sure it happened this way, or even in some way remotely like this? We cannot, of course. But we can assume, from historical evidence, that men *did* take contests involving duels of wit quite seriously, and that these duels, in the form of the *riddle*, were quite ancient. As reported in *Encyclopedia Britannica*:

> Riddle stories too began in time out of mind, for the enjoyment of puzzles is as old as humanity itself. But there is a practical utility in puzzle solving, also, that no doubt was recognized by the ancients; regular exercise is as necessary for the brain as for the body.[18]

The oldest known record of the riddle in literature comes to us from the Bible (Judg. 14: 12–18), in which Samson wagers thirty sheets and thirty changes of garments that the Philistines cannot answer the riddle, "Out of the eater came forth meat, and out of the strong came forth sweetness." When the Philistines were able to get Samson's wife to wheedle from him the answer (involving a swarm of bees and honey within the lion's carcass), it so angered Samson to be so defeated that he slew thirty men to allay his anger (and to secure thirty changes of clothing lost in the gambit).

Although this riddle is the oldest extant, it is probably not the oldest absolutely.

> The riddle of Samson, propounded in the Bible (Judg. 14: 12–18), is the most famous early example; but, although Samson has been called the father of riddles, it may be that older and better ones were even then buried in antiquity.
>
> Among the Egyptians, puzzling was a religious rite, and the Sphinx was their goddess. Such was the esoteric religion of the Egyptians that all the priests were riddlers and their religion one vast enigma. The classic riddle of the Sphinx, however, belongs to Grecian mythology. Its date is not authenticated, but it is of antiquity, for Sophocles wrote about it in the 4th century, B.C.[19]

This example of the Sphinx, incidentally, is the one which Rapp uses to substantiate the claim that the wit-duel inherent in the riddle was both taken as a very serious matter and that its history is ancient.[20] In case you have forgotten, the Sphinx was a legendary monster who sat upon a rock on the roadway to Thebes; to every wayfarer she posed the riddle:

> It goes on four legs in the morning, two legs at noon, and three legs in the evening. What is it?

All contenders lost and were subsequently murdered by the Sphinx, until the famous King Oedipus correctly answered the riddle (Man: he walks on all fours in the morning of his life, upright in the noontime of life, and with the aid of a cane, or third leg in the evening time of life). Defeat at the hands of Oedipus so enraged the Sphinx that she committed suicide by hurling herself from the rock. Each of these most serious consequences of losing in a riddle contest (murder and/or suicide), says Rapp, may be "indirect evidence of the day when these wit contests were taken as seriously as physical struggles."[21] I must concur that such reactions to losing at riddling are somewhat extreme.

It seems quite plausible and likely to me that duels of wits in ancient times probably were staged for audiences. I can conceive a situation in which the official top intellect of Tribe A challenges his like number from Tribe B to a contest of grey matter, the loser to forfeit, say, a pig or a goat. The time and place are set; announcements are made throughout the ranks of both tribes; perhaps even side bets are laid between the more sporting of the tribesmen. When the event begins, the fans from Tribe A sit on the side of their hero, while those of Tribe B glare across at them from behind their champion. As each combatant scores a "point," his laughter is accompanied by that of his following. At the conclusion of the contest, the contestant with the most points walks off with his opponent's pig, or goat, smiling and laughing, accepting the congratulatory whoops of his supporters. It is not even difficult to imagine one side's becoming so bitter in defeat that they begin an actual knock-down, drag-out brawl in order to wipe the victorious smirks from the faces of their vanquishers.

Well, then, let us agree that the riddle was (and is, among the young) a contest taken very seriously and one which probably sprang from the deep-seated yearning for combat in order to exercise the laughter response. Generations of such riddling and riddle contests must have preceded the next development;

but, as man developed a more and more complicated and sophisticated language, the next development was sure to eventually occur. One of our hoary ancestors must have combined the riddle form with a word with double meaning, thus inventing the *conundrum* or punning riddle.

> What's the best way to keep a fish from smelling?
> Cut off his nose!

Rapp suggests, and I concur, that the first wily riddler to crack a conundrum such as that above probably got a bust in the mouth from his defeated opponent. Why? Because the victim of this "riddle" had not only been "defeated," but he had been tricked and duped, as well. He thought he had been asked the question end of a "real" riddle. What *is* the best way to keep a fish from smelling, he ponders. He struggles at reviewing all he has learned about fish and their smells during his lifetime; he considers various proposals, such as salting it, cooking it, soaking it in brine, and drying it in the sun. During the time allotted to his answering the "riddle" he may even offer one of these suggestions, which are turned down by the "riddler." Finally, he gives up. "What *is* the best way to keep a fish from smelling?" he asks, realizing that, at least, if *he* has the answer, he can pull the riddle on his dumb cousin. The riddler bares his teeth, rises to his full height, and answers: "Cut off his nose!"

This answer does not immediately solve the problem for our puzzled loser of the riddle contest. For a brief instant he thinks, "cutting off a fish's nose does not stop it from— smelling? Hmmmm." Deep thought. "*Smelling. Doing* it, not *causing* it. By damn, I have been *tricked*!" And the riddler gets a shot to the proboscis. (Punch in the nose.)

But physical abuse could not stop the wave of potential conundrum artists. The desire to demonstrate man's versatility with his more and more complicated linguistic repertoire had to outweigh the danger of physical retaliation upon one for the "crime" of conundrumming. What linguistically gifted savage could resist the urge to demonstrate his verbal agility with a repertoire of conundrums as:

> How does a married man differ from a widower? One kisses the Mrs. and the other misses the kisses.

How does a flea differ from an elephant? An elephant can have fleas, but a flea cannot have elephants.

Who was the first man to bear arms? Adam.

What has four legs and flies? A dead horse.

When is a horse not a horse? When he turns into a barn.

Shortly after the conundrum appeared on the scene, however, its victims probably grew to recognize its relatively harmless nature. Certainly, there is still a protagonist (the riddler) and an antagonist (the loser in the contest). But losing to a conundrum is not the same as losing to a straight riddle. To be sure, the loser has been outsmarted, but *double meaning* was used! He could not really be expected to know that the riddler had intended *that* meaning of the word. Thus we have a most important change in the evolution of human humor. There has been a great dampening of the direct animosity, the aggressive competition, between the protagonist and the antagonist. The contest nature of the riddle has been lessened, has become more indirect. The riddle has turned from a "real" contest of brains to a "play" contest more like a game than a fight. The "winner" is not the more wise and the "loser" the more dense; it is simply that the "winner" was aware of the double meaning and the "loser" was not. The "duel" turns not upon wisdom and knowledge of the real world, but upon nonsensical symbolic manipulation of the "unreal."

We must note here three other highly important features of the conundrum which differentiate it from the "real" riddle; these three features further detract from the "contest" nature of the riddle and add to the "game" nature of "adult" and "civilized" humor.

First, the language of the opening gambit of the conundrum usually identifies it immediately *as* a conundrum, that is, as a *game* and not a real *contest* of gray matter. The wording of the question end of the conundrum places a "play frame" around the wit-producing incident, which, human beings quickly learn, marks it as "harmless" conundrumming and not as a serious challenge to the intellect. Note the following examples:

Why is a woman in the bathtub like a devout Christian?

When is a cow not a cow?

What happens when you throw a rock into the Red Sea?

What is lonely, sexy, and hums?

How could any reasonably intelligent person mistake these questions as asking for anything but relatively nonsensical plays upon words?

Second, the antagonist becomes a willing "victim" of the conundrum when, recognizing the "play frame" of the opening question, he realizes that, once he has endured this minor and insignificant "defeat," he can play the verbal superior over the next chum he meets who has not "heard this one" before. He hears his friend ask, "When is a cow not a cow?" Aha! A conundrum is coming, he perceives, and his interest perks. He asks, "When?", vaguely realizing but accepting the fact that he is going to suffer an infinitesimal loss of self-esteem but, at the same moment, realizing he may remember this "good one" to pull on the gang at the office later. The momentary and infinitesimal drop in self-esteem, upon hearing the punch line ("When she's turned into a pasture") is what produces his usual response to the conundrum: an audible *groan*, not a laugh, often accompanied by deprecatory facial expressions and gestures. But now he can hardly wait to find a colleague who has not heard "when a cow is not a cow."

The third feature differentiating the conundrum from the "real" riddle is the emotional reaction upon hearing and comprehending the answer. In the "real" riddle, the emotion is likely to be negative: inadequacy, defeatism, a sense of loss. But in the conundrum, the emotion is likely to be positive, one of success, or victory. There is a brief instant of incomprehensibility, of mystery. There is the feeling that "that can't be right." One must briefly mull over the answer, sorting through his verbal repertoire and his past experience to see how the answer "fits." Then it dawns upon him; he has "figured it out." He has been able to "win" *over himself* while being mildly "defeated" by his protagonist. And if he cannot "figure out" the conundrum, if he cannot experience this "victory" over his original puzzlement, he is unable to appreciate the conundrum or to feel the slight pang of momentary defeat which produces the "groan of recognition" which usually follows conundrums.

To illustrate this last feature (and the other two above it), let us take the example of Mr. A asking Mr. B: "Why is a mirror like a philosopher?" Immediately Mr. B recognizes some sort of figurative analogy based upon wordplay is coming ("What real physical likeness can exist between a flesh-and-blood person like a philosopher and a cold, hard glass object called a mirror?"), and he gets set for "play." Mr. B., never having thought of such a comparison before, now perhaps considers these two objects briefly, trying to see if he can come up with an actual or nonsensically analogous similarity between them. He does not bother his head long, however, because he knows it is some sort of absurdity that is to be the answer. He "gives up," now eager for the answer so that he can pull this one on his wife or on Uncle Charley. He gets the answer: "Because it reflects." Almost immediately he recognizes the schizophrenic character of the word *reflect* (1. To give back an image or likeness of; mirror 2. Careful thought; deliberation). He recognizes that mirrors and philosophers reflect, each in an individual way. He groans at his small, absurd "defeat," but hopes he can remember this little gem until he gets home or to the office. Of course, if Mr. B does *not* experience his little victory, if he does not do the successful remembering and connecting of the two meanings of "reflect," the humor of the situation is lost. He is likely to respond with, "What do you mean, A, that it reflects? A mirror can't think at all, much less think *carefully*!"

From the conundrum, or punning riddle, of course, it is only the smallest of steps to the *pun*. For it is no more than a punning riddle, or conundrum, turned into a one-liner. One example which Esar provides, for instance, is, "The first thing that strikes a stranger in New York is a big car." In riddle form it would be, "What is the first thing that strikes a stranger in New York? A big car." "Many a blonde dyes by her own hand," can be converted to, "How does many a blonde die? Of her own hand." "If you are too busy to laugh, you are too busy," can become, "What are you if you are too busy to laugh," etc.

The pun is merely a clever verbalism, and the punster is

demonstrating his verbal cleverness (superiority). Who is the antagonist, the "butt" of the pun? The *listener*—the person or persons to whom the punster is demonstrating this cleverness. And what is the appropriate response to the pun? As with the punning riddle, a *groan*, not a laugh, is expected.

In the pun, the contest nature of the event diminishes further; the listener was not "set up" for defeat by a question—instead, the speaker simply made a clever statement which employs at least one word that can have two or more meanings (he usually intends the less usual meaning). To the listener, the statement makes little sense; he ponders, however briefly, over the seemingly irrelevant remark, perhaps marveling at the expression of self-pleasure on the face of the punster. Then he "gets it," feels the eureka! response of success (which is pleasurable), but at the very same time realizes that he has been the victim of verbal trickery by a (temporarily) linguistic superior. Yech!

This development through our generations of ancestors from roar of triumph to duels of wits through riddles through punning riddles to the pun is not as important a development to our modern wit and humor as is the development of ridicule. I repeat here that there is *some* ridicule in every humorous incident, whether it be affectionate or not; but there is not always the punning element. However, the modern "joke" is a highly complicated affair, and might contain several elements of both ridicule *and* punning.

> The matron at the concert whispers to her husband, "My, doesn't that contralto have a large repertoire?"
> "Yes," her husband agrees, "and that dress she's wearing just makes it look worse."

The above joke, brief though it is, contains several possible causes for laughter. First, we may be amused at our superiority over the husband, for he certainly has not only demonstrated his *stupidity*, but has revealed a mind dwelling on something other than High Culture. We probably respond to the chagrin his wife feels to hear her oaf of a husband make such a stupid and low-life mistake; we may even be able to imagine her being embarrassed at the thought that others seated around them have just discovered what a gutter-minded loser she picked for a husband. And then, the acceptance of the unfamiliar word," repertoire," as a probable euphemism for a portion of the anattomy has a punning quality to it, a play on words. And this mistaken acceptance causes "sex to rear its ugly (and incongruous) head" in the midst of this refined cultural event, a laughable incident in itself.

Well, what proof is there that our victory roar evolved into the pun via this route? Admittedly, there is very little. We have only our good sense to guide us. It may be much more difficult to believe that the triumphal roar evolved first into the riddle, and thence to the punning riddle; but the pun must certainly have come from the conundrum. And we can look to the evidence of ontogeny for proof that the punning or "joking" riddle is the very earliest of verbal humor that children engage in.

Martha Wolfenstein has made a detailed study of the humor preferences of small children of various ages.[22] She is a keen observer, and a patient and thorough interviewer. Let us see how she describes the verbal humor preferences she observes in the six- to eleven-year-old child:

> The joking riddle is the favorite form of joke for children between the ages of six and eleven. The child who asks the riddle shows how smart he is, for when the other cannot guess, he gives the answer himself . . . . Children at this age are peculiarly preoccupied with the issue of who is smart and who is dumb. They are especially sensitive to being put in the wrong or not knowing what someone else knows. When a child has been outwitted or outdone by another, one hears the heartfelt cry: "You think you're smart!" Any advantage is apt to be felt as smartness, any disadvantage as dumbness. This preoccupation is reflected in the favored jokes of children of this age. The riddle form stresses the issue of who knows and who doesn't . . . .
>
> With striking punctuality children seem to acquire a store of joking riddles at the age of six.

Children younger than six are not "ready" for punning riddles; but as noted earlier in the Harms study, they go for the humor they can find in grotesqueness (ridicule) as Wolfenstein shows:

> When I tried to teach joking riddles to five-year-old children, they seemed to find them meaningless. I asked Nora, the five-year-old girl who had made up the funny story about the cat that got thrown out the window: "Do you

> know why the moron threw the butter out the window?"
> As she said she didn't know, I told her: "To see the butter-
> fly." She smiled slightly but, I felt, without comprehension.
> I explained that it was a joke. Nora said: "My brother
> knows those but I don't." (Nora's brother is eleven.) When I
> asked if she knew any other jokes like that, she said: "I'll
> show you on a piece of paper." She proceeded to draw and
> told me: "See, a man got so funny he fell in the water and a
> whale swallowed him. . . . Here's the man and here's the
> whale." Pointing to the whale: "Here's eyes and two noses.
> No, here's an eye and a nose and an eye and a nose. No,
> one eye." She laughed. . . .

Note the similarity of delight in the grotesque, above, with
Harms', findings, reported earlier.

Unfortunately, although Wolfenstein's credentials as an
observer and an interviewer seem nearly faultless, her analysis of *why* small children find joking riddles to be funny is badly
flawed by her psychoanalytic training—she is misled by large
dollops of Freudian rot.

She insists, for instance, that the answer to the harmless
riddle, "What has four legs and can't walk?" (A table) represents "a couple in intercourse" (Rabelais' "beast with two
backs"). Let us consider her analysis of the two riddles,

> Q. What has holes but holds water?
> A. A sponge.
>
> Q. What is a lady always looking for but hoping not to
> find?
> A. A hole in her stocking.

She claims that the first of the above suggests that, even
though the female has a vagina instead of a penis, she is nevertheless able to control her water; the second, she says, ex-
presses that a woman always hopes to find that she has a penis,
but finds a vagina (hole) instead.

One more example of her Freudian (sexual) interpretation
of all joking:

> Q. Why did the moron jump off the Empire State
> Building?
> A. Because he wanted to make a smash hit on Broadway.

How does she explain liking for that one?

> The huge phallic shape is the father's penis, the sight of

which impels the child to competitive exhibition. He hopes to have a sensational success, but also fears a catastrophic defeat. Unable to abandon his ambitions, he pays in advance.

The reader by now must assume that I hold no brief for such Freudian analysis of humor. Wolfenstein's book is recommended reading, nevertheless. But expect a murky psychoanalytic interpretation for every little superiority tendency.

Wolfenstein does not go to great lengths to typify the kind of humor preferred by older youths, although she points out that they tend to "outgrow" conundrums—with one exception: when adolescents get into a "silly mood" they apparently delight in returning to these childish ways. However, we have seen in the Harms' study, above, that the high school youngster graduates to the point where he much prefers verbal humor, presumably with at least some "plays on words." Wolfenstein, in this regard, stresses that the humorous jokes of adolescents differ only in degree, not in kind, from those of adults.

This last conclusion of Wolfenstein, supported by the Harms' study of laughter development in children, finds a remarkable parallel in a study of laughter of children in another country, Spain.[23] This Spanish study also tends to confirm the general kind of humor development in children as is suggested here in humor development in the race of man. An English translation in abstract form[24] adequately summarizes the study:

> Examines the development of laughter in children from 0-14 yr. old and concludes that, contrary to psychoanalytic theories, a child is able to laugh at a very early age (2 mo.). As the child develops, the stimuli for laughter gradually multiply until, at the age of 10, he acquires an understanding of that which is comical. His laugh reaches full maturity at 14, at which point he is able to appreciate humor. Any type of laugh that can be observed thereafter in an adult will have already appeared in the child. This does not mean that those situations which cause a child to laugh will produce the same effect in an adult. It is suggested that the best stimuli for laughs are always those situations that are particular to the age and last functional or intellectual achievement of the moment. Thus any stimulus that brings about a child's laugh has its parallel in an adult. It is proposed that such parallel situations be searched and out-

lined whereby the causes and types and laughs can be studied.

A study conducted in England on the sense of humor in children seven to ten, eleven to thirteen, and fourteen to eighteen revealed remarkably similar results.

> Development of the sense of humour was found to run parallel with general intellectual and emotional development. Deviations from the normal and conventional were outstanding causes of laughter in the youngest group. Incidents involving someone's discomfiture (which were also popular in the youngest group) were those most frequently referred to by the children in the second group. The humour of both these groups was predominantly visual; verbal wit was little appreciated. Distinguishing features of the adolescents in the third group were: (a) the marked individual differences in their sense of humour—although many no longer tolerated slapstick farce and preferred witty and realistic comedy, others enjoyed both, and others, again, gave as their best jokes fatuities that were popular among children in the youngest group; similarly, although several relegated the laugh of Hobbes' "sudden glory" to an inferior category, many gave first place to humour of this type; (b) their much greater appreciation of verbal wit; (c) the tendency of the majority to reflect on why they laugh, and of a minority (especially among the girls) to deprecate laughter that is unfeeling.[25]

Rapp and I may both err in describing what I call "The What Is . . ." Way, the evolution of triumphal roar to pun by way of several steps; but it is clear that something of the sort must have actually occurred. Unless punning developed from an ancestor common with that of ridicule, our roar of triumph, then it becomes necessary to imagine *two* (at least) phylogenetic developments, one for "humor" (ridicule) and one for "wit" (punning). Such a possibility must be rejected as highly improbable.

C. The "Constrain Yourself" Course

We now come to the third and last important developmental factor in our quest to understand laughter's evolution. Rapp called this development "suppression laughter" and granted it the status of a separate developmental direction or "leg." By granting the "Constrain Yourself" Course a separate section in this chapter, I seem to follow his logic, although I must demur from actual agreement with him. Let us see how Rapp describes "suppression laughter:"

> This . . . we may call *suppressive laughter*, or, more fully, the laughter of victory over one's repressor.
>
> That this exists, as an added and therefore separate factor, may be suspected from the following items. If a boy is watching the skaters at a rink and someone falls, that is usually funny to him. But if it should happen to be his Latin teacher that is much funnier. If a stranger's hat should blow off as he is crossing the street, many uninhibited persons would be amused. But if it were the local policeman, they would find it hilarious. At army maneuvers, even if your buddy should trip and land face down in the mud, you would laugh. But if it could only be your sergeant!
>
> In all the preceding examples there is provoked the laughter of ridicule; but in some there is a definite additional layer of laughter which requires investigation . . . . This suppressive laughter also appears in cases where it seems directed not against constraining persons, but against legal, religious, and social institutions.[26]

There can be absolutely no doubt that the enjoyment of ridicule is heightened when the object of the ridicule is some person or institution toward which we have had to constrain our true feelings. Rapp's examples above can be multiplied over and over. In wartime Germany, for instance, it was pretty dangerous to tell jokes ridiculing Hitler or any of his henchmen; but jokes about them flourished in an underground sort of way— and there can be no doubt that they were enjoyed hugely in lieu of the constraint placed upon outright anti-Nazi criticism.

Herman Goering's taste for gaudy medal-bedecked uniforms was well-known; this led to some wag's coining of a word, the "Goer"—this was defined as the maximum amount of tin a man could carry on his chest without falling flat on his face. Goebbels, Hitler's propaganda chief, gave rise to the coining of the "Goeb"; this was the least unit of energy needed to cause listeners to switch off 100,000 radio receivers. Goebbels' nickname became "Mahatma Propagandhi." As the war turned sour for Germany, *conditions* were ridiculed. A would-be suicide buys rope with which to hang himself, but it is of such poor quality that it breaks. He tries to drown himself in the

river, but the wood fibers in his ersatz clothing keep him afloat.
He gives up trying to kill himself, and starves to death after four
weeks on normal rations.[27]

In the fifties the following was reported to be popular in
Hungary:

> A schoolteacher asked ten-year-old Istvan to compose a
> sentence containing a dependent clause. "Our cat had ten
> kittens," said Istvan, "Of which all were Communists."
>
> "Excellent," said the teacher. "Exactly right. Be sure you
> do as well next week when the Government supervisors
> come."
>
> The following week she asked the prize student the same
> question. "Our cat," said Istvan, "had ten kittens, of which
> all were Social Democrats."
>
> "Why, Istvan," cried the teacher, "that's absurd. That's
> not what you said last week. Last week your kittens were
> all Communists."
>
> "I know," said Istvan, "but since then their eyes have
> opened."[28]

How can one doubt that constraint born of suppression would
increase one's enjoyment of such jokes. As Richard Hanser
puts it:

> If the joke packs its little charge of dynamite, if it delivers a
> sufficient blast at the prevailing system, if it jabs sharply
> enough under the skin of bureaucrat or *Gauleiter* or com-
> missar, it will be repeated with relish and listened to with
> satisfaction regardless of age or previous condition of
> servitude.[29]

The principle underlying suppression laughter is probably
greatly responsible for the fact that we find jokes on our
enemies to be more highly enjoyable than jokes upon ourselves, our friends, or our own reference groups. There are at
least two psychological studies that show that Republicans enjoy anti-Democrat jokes better than anti-Republican jokes, and
Democrats enjoy more highly anti-Republican jokes than
anti-Democrat jokes.[30] Of course, the fact that Republicans can
enjoy anti-Republican jokes and Democrats can enjoy anti-
Democrat jokes at all is a sign that we can become quite civilized
about not taking reference group membership "too seriously."
Fanatical members of a group or adherents of a belief, of course,
can find nothing at all funny about the organization or belief in

which they vest their fanaticism. Thus they reveal their mental imbalance. As Sydney Harris puts it:

> The rarest creature on earth is a fanatic with a sense of humor; fanatics repel us not so much by their passionate devotion to a cause as by their incapacity ever to laugh at themselves or at their *idees fixe*, which is a deadly flaw in the human animal.[31]

Rapp concludes that suppression laughter makes up one of three separate "families" of laughter, the others being ridicule and wit. On this point I tend to disagree with him; my position is that there can be none of what he calls suppression laughter without first the presence of wit and/or ridicule. That laughter is *heightened* by the fact that the person or institution ridiculed or defeated in the witwork is one toward which the one laughing has had to constrain hostile emotions does not, to me, make suppression laughter a separate *family*. The authoritarian position of the institution or person "defeated" merely spices up the laughter that would be produced without the authoritarian status. This is actually a small point of difference in opinion, but one worth noting.

Now then. Do children, in their development of a "sense of humor," show signs of what Rapp calls "suppression laughter." No one who has spent much time around small children can doubt that, at least after a certain age, children absolutely delight in catching adults in mistakes. What reader of this book cannot remember, as a child, listening to and retelling the most outlandish stories about his parents and/or teachers, or perhaps grade school principal? Who does not remember the childishly immature but devastatingly satiric names made up for the more repressive of his grade school teachers?

The many taboos which we begin to place upon the growing child cause resentment and constraint, also, which are released often in laughter of suppression. As Katharine Kappas puts it:

> The humor of these children [nine-year-olds] may also reveal some hostility and aggression, for, not only do they enjoy behavior or situations of which adults disapprove and sometimes delight in the misfortunes of others, but they also find amusement in deviations from the normal and conventional. The expression of taboo subjects in-

creasingly finds an outlet in humor as the child matures, and the joking forms of the nine-year-old show this.[32]

Now, before going to a graphical representation of the theory which the last two chapters have explained, let us once again look at the modern "joke" or funny story. Many can be seen to contain each of the three elements of our phylogenetic theory: ridicule, wit (plays on words), and suppression laughter. The *Reader's Digest* quotes Louis Azariel's story about Charles Coburn, the actor, as it appeared in the Baltimore *News-Post*. Coburn's story:

> As a boy, I fell in love with the theater and started seeing plays whenever possible. "One thing, Son, you must never do," my father warned. "Don't go to burlesque houses."
>
> I, of course, asked why.
>
> "Because you would see things you shouldn't," Father replied.
>
> That settled it. The next time I managed to get the price of admission, I went straight to a burlesque house.
>
> Father was right. I saw something I shouldn't have seen—my father.

Let us analyze. Father has been caught in an indiscretion. Ridicule. The oppressive father-figure, the "Censor," is overturned. Our rejoicing with the triumphant son is heightened by the authority of the deposed. Suppression laughter. And there is the double meaning of "something you shouldn't see" (meaning female anatomy) and "something you shouldn't see" (your father at the peep show).

Not all three elements are present in all modern jokes, but the point here is that these three elements *often* do combine to produce a highly "complicated" funny story. Now, by way of summary, let us look at a schematic block diagram of how humor developed.

As pointed out early in Chapter 2, a theory, such as a theory of humor and laughter, need not be *true* or *false*; a theory, instead is usually considered relatively *useful* or *not useful*. We cannot leave the theory of laughter presented in this and the last chapter without considering its *usefulness* as compared with that of other, competing theories.

As also stated early in Chapter 2, a theory's usefulness is assessed relative to its *explanatory comprehensiveness*; that is, on how

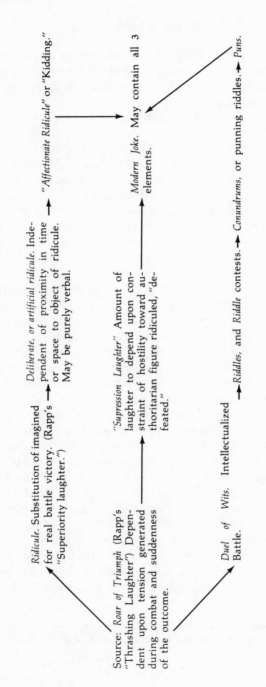

Ridicule. Substitution of imagined for real battle victory. (Rapp's "Superiority laughter.") → *Deliberate, or artificial ridicule.* Independent of proximity in time or space to object of ridicule. May be purely verbal. → "*Affectionate Ridicule*" or "*Kidding.*"

Modern Joke. May contain all 3 elements.

"*Supression Laughter*" Amount of laughter to depend upon constraint of hostility toward authoritarian figure ridiculed, "defeated."

Source: *Roar of Triumph* (Rapp's "Thrashing Laughter") Dependent upon tension generated during combat and suddenness of the outcome.

Duel of Wits. Intellectualized Battle. → *Riddles*, and *Riddle* contests. → *Conundrums*, or punning riddles. → *Puns.*

Schematic Diagram of Phylogenetic Theory

well it succeeds in providing an explanation for all the phenomena it purports to explain. In the case of a theory of laughter and
humor, it ought to be useful for explaining *all* laughter and
laughter-provoking situations.

Since 1955 I have heard countless thousands of jokes, read
countless thousands more, and seen innumerable cartoons,
whimsical and heavily political alike; I have consumed large
numbers of satirical pieces by Art Buchwald, Art Hoppe, Dick
West, *Mad*, and *National Lampoon*. I have laughed long and often
at such as Grin and Bear It, Pogo, Peanuts, and Li'l Abner. I have
even gone to the trouble to perform formal content analysis on
magazine cartoons for graduate-level term papers while pur-
suing the Ph.D. degree. And I have yet to find a laughter-provoking event that cannot be explained by application of the
theory expounded in the preceding pages.

Many people find uncomfortable a belief that laughter and
humor, such pleasant, desirable aspects of a full life, must rest
upon a solid basis of *superiority*. As a result of my research, I occasionally get invited to speak to various groups on the nature
of humor. During the question period following my explanation of what I consider to be the basis of humor, there are always argumentative questions. Disappointed audience members tell their favorite jokes and ask how these can possibly be
based upon *superiority*. As a result of a syndicated newspaper
article on my views I have become engaged in debates via mail
with such disparate individuals as a *proctologist* in Wichita Falls,
Texas, and a housewife in Green Bay, Wisconsin. In each case I
have been able to stifle objections with the force of logic and
dogged willingness to persist in expending the hot air or
keeping the electric typewriter going until resistance disap-
pears. But I suspect that the disappearance of resistance very often has signified fatigue and not acceptance of this "superior-
ity-evolutionary" theory. People are just not *happy* with such an
explanation. The problem and its solution are aptly put by Har-
vey Mindness, whose delightful book *Laughter and Liberation*[33]
should be required reading:

> The spirit of humor demands that we acknowledge, in spite
> of our need for love, our undeniable lust, and in spite of our

capacity for caring, our inclination to not give a good
goddamn.

We are reluctant to make these acknowledgments because they clash with our image of ourselves as good
people. A good person, we rightly believe, is characterized
by unselfishness, concern for others, and a real ability to
love. Humor, however, is not allied to goodness; it is allied
to nature and to wholeness. To allow our sense of humor
its full development, we must be willing to shift our primary aim from the attempt to be good to the attempt to be
natural.

As I constantly explain to audiences and to interested cor-
respondents, part of the so-called human condition is a natural,
inborn tendency to want to compete successfully; and also: most
of the aggressiveness we dispel in humorous exchanges is almost completely *unconscious*.

And, it must be remembered: much of our appreciation of
humor which we might label as "whimsy" is based upon *victimless* superiority. It is this point that can become a sore point of
contention and a roadblock to understanding and/or appreciation of the "superiority" or "degradation" theory.

Let me explain with an example. Mindness, mentioned
above, agrees with the assumption that there is a great deal of
degradation which is responsible for laughter. However, he *subsumes* jokes which are funny as a result of degrading someone or
some group under his "liberation" theory which, briefly,

> proposes that the most fundamental, most important func-
> tion of humor is its power to release us from the many in-
> hibitions and restrictions under which we live our daily
> lives.[34]

After giving several examples of degradation humor, Mindness
presents two items of "nonsense humor" which, he claims, cannot be explained in degradation terms:

> Q: What is purple, weighs ten tons, and is found in the
> sea?
> A: Moby Plum.

> Q: How can you tell if there's an elephant in your
> refrigerator?
> A: You'll find his footprints in the cheesecake.

Mindness would claim that these bits of foolishness are funny because they give us "Freedom from Reality," (his fifth "chapter") and allow us to delight in childish, lighthearted nonsense. But I think each is eminently explainable by the theory I have outlined. First, let us consider our ten-ton purple sea dweller. Who is he? Moby Plum.

First, let me ask: Suppose you had never heard of Herman Melville's gigantic symbol of evil incarnate? Suppose that, faced with the task of identifying *Moby Dick* in a newspaper quiz you had to guess that this was slang for a certain *rank* of *policeman*? If you were this ignorant, would you laugh, even smile at "Moby Plum"? Of course not. You would more likely shake your head in bewilderment. But: you *have* read Melville's classic; or you have read it in *Classic Comic* form; or you have seen the movie, starring Gregory Peck as Captain Ahab. And when you hear that Moby Plum is something purple, weighing ten tons, and lives in the sea, you see the "natural" connection, the logic of it all, crazy though it is in reality. You *succeed* at the cognitive task thrust at you; and you applaud yourself with the chuckle or smile of self-satisfaction!

And how do elephant footprints in the cheesecake fit our theory? The same mechanism applies. Certainly, if *any* animal is hiding in the refrigerator one would probably find his tracks in the cheesecake! Sheer "logic." And an elephant could hardly *avoid* stepping in the stuff! The reasoning is crystal clear to the quick-witted. Of course, one might argue another way: anyone who would offer such as a clue to an elephant's presence in a refrigerator must be a little loose in the flue. No trouble feeling superior to *him*.

I might say in passing, that Mindness argues that his "liberation" theory subsumes and encompasses "degradation" theories; I would argue that the theory which I propose is "degradation-plus," meaning it includes the smile or laugh which comes, via *generalization*, to symbolize self-satisfaction through verbal problem-solving. And, although I could argue that my theory subsumes and encompasses Mindness' *liberation theory* within *it*, I really shan't bother. He and I agree far more than we do not. Besides, I think you should read his book, also.

Also, Mindness' theory, to my thinking, fulfills the requirement that a theory must possess explanatory comprehensiveness more than most other, competing theories. There is no doubt that humor today in adult, civilized society provides the individual liberation from "conformity, inferiority, morality, reason, language, naivete, redundancy, seriousness, and egotism." I just happen to think the theory provided here which I support does a better job of explaining how laughter came to *be* such a liberating force.

I hope that psychoanalytic theories were properly enough disposed of in Chapter 2, including Freud's, which proposed a "harmless wit" that was completely victimless but for which Freud himself was unable to supply a single example. Bergler's neo-Freudian explanation of laughter as evidence of pseudo-aggression spawned by our inborn drive to live out our lives as "psychic masochists" has, I hope, been dismissed as utter nonsense. Theories such as Eastman's which propose one set of behaviors and neural mechanisms for one kind of laughter and another set for another kind of laughter must also be rejected as useless for describing and explaining the whole spectrum of human laughter.

Other theorists, on the assumption that *no* one theory can encompass all humor-provoking events, have proposed "minitheories" which profess a logical consistency of their own but do not propose to comprehensively explain all laughter. Such a minitheory is proposed by Jerry Suls.[35] He makes a good case for the perception of incongruity as the touchstone of humor; but the examples he uses to support his case are far more explainable using simple superiority or ridicule. For instance he cites the joke about "Fat Ethel" as illustrating his incongruity principle:

> Fat Ethel sat down at the lunch counter and ordered a whole fruit cake. "Shall I cut it into four or eight pieces?" asked the waitress. "Four," said Ethel. "I'm on a diet."

Certainly it is "incongruous" of Ethel to order a whole fruit cake and then, at the same time, fool herself to believe that by having it cut into only four instead of eight pieces she will somehow save herself some calories. According to the theory which I hold to, the joke is intrinsically funny because Ethel suddenly and simultaneously reveals herself to be both gluttonous and *stupid*. Remove her stupidity and we have no way to feel suddenly superior to Ethel; she is no longer funny. Suppose she had said: "Well, I'm going to eat the whole thing anyway, so it doesn't matter; but cut it in four pieces, and maybe I can rationalize to myself in some way that I really am eating less." We cannot feel superior to her now; she has not revealed stupidity; and it has not been revealed suddenly. Perhaps it is because Suls' explanation is not the *only* explanation of this joke that causes editors Paul McGhee and Jeffrey Goldstein to label Suls' work a theory of *comprehension* and not *appreciation* of humorous stimuli.[36] Certainly, humorous stimuli must be understood to be appreciated; but an explanation of understanding is not an explanation of appreciation.

All of which brings me to the question most asked by my live audiences after a lecture on "what makes humor funny." If superiority is the reason for laughter, Professor, why can we laugh at ourselves? That is, how can one feel superior to one's own self?

My answer is two-fold. First, we can laugh as a result of *successfully* achieving what was a puzzle formerly. For instance, I compare my checkbook bank balance against my monthly statement and find that the Citizens and Southern Bank believes that I have $13.97 more in the account than I had calculated. My consternation rises as I check and recheck, add and readd the columns, subtract and resubtract. Suddenly, just as I am about to conclude that the bank's computer contains a weak transistor, I find that an outstanding check for $13.97 has been left out of the calculations. I chuckle a little, partly out of relief (and laughing *does* provide physiological relief!), but also partly at *how stupid I had been just moments ago!*

Second, one of our separate selves can laugh in superiority over the other. One self laugh at another? How can that be?

Each human being is really a collection of several human beings. I, myself, for instance, am a college professor, a husband, a father, a blood donor, a scoutmaster, a researcher, a friend, etc., and, on occasion, I regress to the "little boy" me that lurks in every mature man. As Shakespeare said, a man plays many roles in his life. And one role can delight in seeing the other taken down a peg or two through friendly ridicule. Being a professor, I nonetheless realize that professors can be dull, absentminded, and removed from reality. But when I hear that "A college professor is a guy who has lost touch with reality by degrees," it is the little boy, the "playful me," that smiles at the professor's comeuppance.

Most mature adults realize the welter of conflicting cognitions and emotions which they must constantly balance off against each other. When one is caught exercising one of the more "base" or least socially acceptable cognitions or emotions, the less base or more socially acceptable cognition or emotion laughs in superiority. For example: I believe strongly in being a true-blue husband and upright model for my children. But, like any man alive, I have an archetype of promiscuity inherited from 'way back, and so when my wife catches me staring, openmouthed, at the coed mincing past in short-short cut-off jeans, my upstanding "moral" self enjoys itself by laughing at the expense of my "lecherous" self. And if a colleague kids me for hunching over a typewriter on a Friday afternoon in July instead of watching the bikinis at the pool, my "lecherous" self smiles in conspirational glee at the "stupidity" of my "work ethic." That part of me that is *lazy* occasionally gets off a laugh at my serious, occasional bursts of work; likewise, my *ambitious* self often gets a chuckle at my *laziness*. My *humble* self occasionally gets to laugh at my *proud* self, and vice versa.

And is it not this ability of one part of ourselves to laugh at another that keeps us sane, that keeps us healthy, that keeps our many and various roles *in balance*? Is not the man with "*no* sense of humor" the man with fewer and more rigid roles or selves in his behavioral repertoire? Is he not a flat, unidimensional man, one who can see nothing funny about himself or his beliefs? In short, is he not "*out* of balance?"

Not only do I feel that the theory presented in the last two chapters is the most comprehensive in its explanatory value, since it purportedly can provide a logical explanation for *any* laughter-provoking incident, but I feel that it is therefore the most verifiable. In the case of the present theory, one would be

compelled to predict that as a part of any humorous event one
would necessarily have to find a *victim*, no matter how obscure
that victim might be, and one must find the element of *suddenness* in the victim's loss or "unmasking." During over twenty
years' research in humor, I have been unable to find a humorous
event that could not be found to contain these two indispens-
able elements.

    In addition to the superiority I feel my theory enjoys in its
explanatory comprehensiveness and its verifiability, I believe it
to be more preferred for its *parsimony*, its *simplicity*. Although it
takes considerable time and energy to explain how the mirth experience came about through phylogeny, it is really a simple
proposition to say: "In any humorous situation find an element
of superiority that has been perceived suddenly." The joy of
superiority is easily recognized as pleasurable, and no one needs
a definition of "suddenness." There is no necessity to link this
humor theory with physiological data recorded by complicated
electronic gear; it must not match a personality theory in which
the ego mediates between the id and reality and, in turn, is dominated by the superego; it requires no acceptance of a septet of
unproven baby fears or assumptions that a mother's smile in-
stinctively means to a baby that she will not devour the infant;
it does not require that we have a rash of conflicting minitheories in order to explain apparently disparate forms of humor and laughter; and it does not necessitate a separate neural
subsystem for operating the laugh of scorn and another for the
laugh of play.

    The very simplicity of this theory makes it superior to
others in preventing "the observer from being dazzled by the
full-blown complexity of natural or concrete events," the fourth
criterion of a good theory. And it is this simplicity which makes it
ideal for demonstrating an understanding of the differences and
likenesses between "wit" and "humor," a task taken up in the
next chapter.

5

Humor and Wit

The early pages of Chapter 1 point out the great overlapping of various terms suggested to designate categories of humor. Even the encyclopedic attempt of Evan Esar to classify the various types of humor was found to be wanting. Much of the difficulty in classifying anything so diverse and rich in meaning as what it is that makes people laugh lies in the fact that language and its use among men are not as scientifically specific or universally concise as, say the formula $E = MC^2$. For words do not "possess" meaning, but are only useful as they "stir up" meaning in the nervous systems of people who use them. Lewis Carroll, in Chapter 6 of his *Through the Looking-Glass*, exemplified and, for his comic purposes, exaggerated this truism:

> Humpty-Dumpty said: "There's glory for you." "I don't know what you mean by 'glory,' " Alice said. Humpty-Dumpty smiled contemptuously. "Of course you don't—till I tell you. I meant, There's a nice knock-down argument for you.' " "But 'glory' doesn't mean 'a nice knock-down argument,' " Alice objected. "When I use a word," Humpty-Dumpty said in a rather scornful tone, "it means just what I choose it to mean, neither more nor less."

In this chapter we shall be concerned with developing a

clearer understanding of two terms that have often been carelessly used and sloppily defined—two terms that refer to two
different yet related concepts: "wit" and "humor." Albert Rapp
has clearly spotlighted the problem:

What is the difference between wit and humor?

Nearly every writer on wit and humor in the last one
hundred years has thrown a friendly tackle at this elusive
broken field runner. Some few of these, for a brief instant,
have laid eager fingers on some palpable area. But it always
finally escaped them; and today it is commonly agreed that
the question has not been answered.[1]

Rapp goes on to point out that "humor" is used about half
the time to mean "wit *and* humor," and often is used to mean
simply "wit," as when referring to joke books. For instance,
Nancy Levi Arnez and Clara B. Anthony entitled an article,
"Contemporary Negro Humor as Social Satire."[2] Since "satire"
is generally considered a *type* of "wit," they seem to carelessly
classify *humor* as a type of *wit*.

The same problem of ambiguity plagues our use of the
term, "sense of humor."

Well, if you enjoy [funny] stories . . . , if you enjoy wit
generally, if you are quick at catching the point, if you can
occasionally do a little active verbal sabering of your own,
you may be fairly said to have a good sense of wit. Or, as
people will more likely put it: "sense of humor".

For the term "sense of humor" is used today, collo-
quially, to cover two *substantially different* things: a sense of
wit, and a sense of humor (more strictly). These often
appear together, as do ham and eggs.[3]

The problem is one of lack of suitable and applicable definitions:

One of the most persistent and exasperating phenomena in
the whole field of wit and humor is precisely this: when
you have worked out a fairly adequate explanation for wit,
it makes no sense in connection with ridicule; if it makes
sense in ridicule, it doesn't seem to apply to genial humor;
and the things you might be tempted to say about genial
humor do not seem to bear any relation whatsoever to
riddle laughter. And yet they must all be related, for
laughter is one.[4]

Vivian Mercier suggests that, as judges and lawyers can agree on the "relevance" of a particular item of evidence although they might fail to agree on a *definition* of "relevance," and, although our major networks can differentiate between specific programs as either "information" or "editorial," without agreement upon definitions for each concept, the same operation holds true for "wit" and "humor":

> Like most people who have enough education to make the distinction, I just assume that I can tell at a glance whether a remark is witty or humorous. Probably nine out of ten of my off-the-cuff judgments would be accepted by the average reader of this article. But if he and I tried to produce mutually acceptable definitions of "wit" and "humor", we'd soon become imbedded in a semantic morass.[5]

The "semantic morass" might very well dissipate somewhat if more people had, as does Mercier, a knowledge of how these two words, "wit" and "humor" developed historically in the English language. As he points out, "'wit' was once synonymous with 'intellect,' while 'humor' can to this day mean 'temperament' or 'mood.' "[6] In fact, a brief look at the history of these two words can be quite edifying.

The most comprehensive and scholarly work of lexicography executed upon the English language is the *Oxford English Dictionary*. It specifies not only original sources of a particular word, but where the words were first printed as denoting particular intended meanings. "Wit," which claims parentage from several primitive languages, including Old English, Old Frisian, Old High German, and Old Norse, originally meant: "1. The seat of consciousness or thought, the mind; sometimes connoting one of its functions, as memory or attention." The word with this now obsolete meaning has been traced to about the year 1000. An even earlier use of the word to mean, "The faculty of thinking and reasoning in general; mental capacity, understanding, intellect, reason," appeared in *Beowulf* about the year 589 A.D. By 1325 the word "wit" could be used to mean, "Practical talent or cleverness; constructive or mechanical ability; ingenuity, skill." By 1579 the word "wit" was being used to mean, "Quickness of intellect or liveliness of fancy, with capacity of apt expression; talent for saying brilliant or sparkling things, especially in an amusing way." By 1642 it was used to mean, "That quality of speech or writing which consists in the apt association of thought and expression, calculated to surprise and delight by its unexpectedness . . . later always with reference to the utterance of brilliant or sparkling things in an amusing way". By 1692 the word was used as a noun to refer to "A person of lively fancy, who has the faculty of saying smart or brilliant things, *not always so as to amuse* [italics mine]; a witty person."

On the other hand, we find that "humor" has its ancestry in the Anglo-French *(h)umour,* and is found to have been used earliest in 1475 as meaning "mental disposition" or "temperament." By 1525 it is used to denote, "Temporary state of mind or feeling; mood, temper." It is not until 1682 that the word is found to be used in the sense of, "That quality of action, speech, or writing, which excites amusement; oddity, jocularity, facetiousness, comicality, fun," and, "The faculty of perceiving what is ludicrous or amusing, or of expressing it in speech, writing, or other composition; jocose imagination or treatment of a subject." An Oxford note appended to these definitions reads: "Distinguished from *wit* as being les͜s purely intellectual, and as having a sympathetic quality in virtue of which it often becomes allied to pathos."

So it can be seen that "wit" is historically associated with "intellect" while "humor" is linked with the concept of the more "emotional" activity of *feeling.* This distinction is the one "theory" of the difference between wit and humor that is most often stated by writers in the field. However, this distinction tends to break down if one considers the act of *laughing* to be primarily emotional rather than intellectual. For if a "witty" remark elicits the *emotional* response of laughter, how can it be "purely" intellectual?

Another theory of the difference between wit and humor stems from the thought in the *Oxford English Dictionary* appended to the last definition of "wit," above. As Mercier points out,

> "humor" . . . "connotes kindliness, geniality, sometimes even pathos" in its expression "and a reaction of sympathetic amusement from the audience," whereas "wit" is

associated with "quick, sharp, spontaneous, often sarcastic remarks."[7]

But this distinction is not strictly logical, either. Says Mercier,

> [it] sounds plausible enough until the next time one has occasion to use the phrase "macabre humor;" where are "kindliness, geniality . . . pathos" to be found in *that?* There is such a thing as macabre wit, of course, but I shouldn't call the typical Charles Addams joke witty. And most of the new "sick" jokes I would classify as humor, either macabre or grotesque. The dictionary's theory may be of some use in discussing British humor, but it seems quite inadequate to deal with a quantity of Irish, Jewish, or just plain American comic material which is definitely not witty and just as emphatically not genial.[8]

One difficulty inherent in producing a completely logical distinction between wit and humor is the usual lack of *pureness* in most examples of either. Seldom is one dealing with *pure* humor or *pure* wit. Some element of wit or wordplay is the occasion for much playful and friendly humor. And much wit relies for its effect upon *ridicule,* friendly or not, which, my thesis argues, is the foundation and immediate ancestor of "playful" humor.

The rest of this discussion, therefore, is based upon the theoretical idea that relatively pure wit and relatively pure humor is its proper subject.

Being dissatisfied with both the "intellectual/emotional" and the "sarcastic/kindly" dichotomies used to explain the difference between wit and humor, and demonstrating a thoroughness and depth of scholarship into humor,[9] Mercier has developed his own theory of how wit differs from humor. By permission of the *Nation* magazine I quote extensively from his article in order to demonstrate not only his three-faceted theory, but his argument in favor of its acceptance.

> Oversimplified, Mercier's Hypothesis would run like this: "Wit is always absurd and true, humor absurd and untrue." (Irony, similarly defined, is plausible and untrue.)
>
> In other words, paradox is basic to wit. When an Oscar Wilde character says, "A cynic is a man who knows the price of everything and the value of nothing," the remark momentarily sounds contradictory and therefore nonsensical; then we discriminate between the synonyms "price" and "value" and see the point. This kind of discrimination

requires an intellectual effort unnecessary to the appreciation of humor and also produces the element of surprise
which Addison thought essential to wit. Irony, in the basic
sense of saying one thing and meaning another, demands
an even more complex intellectual response than wit does:
wit confronts us with a patent absurdity and asks that we
make sense of it, whereas really subtle irony can easily be
mistaken for the literal truth.

Humor, on the other hand, remains absurd from start to
finish. My dictionary defines "absurd" as "clearly untrue or
unreasonable, and therefore laughable, ridiculous," etc. In
actual fact, alas, the unreasonable is often far from being
untrue, but for humorous purposes the two become identical. Sometimes we would prefer to describe a humorous
remark as exaggerated rather than untrue, but, as any
fisherman will admit, exaggeration is the commonest form
of lying. The typical response of someone with a poor sense
of humor to a joking remark is, "Surely that can't be true?"
Take the story of the three hermits, the Gaelic of which
suggests that it was current before 1200 A.D. (for all I
know, it may occur in Latin or Sanskrit, too): after they had
been living in the wilderness for a year, one of them said,
"It's a good life we have here;" after another year, the
second replied, "Good, indeed;" after a further year, the
third said, "If you fellows don't shut up, I'm going back to
civilization." On the face of it, this story is untrue; the third
hermit's remark is patently unreasonable, too; still, one
could argue that the story is true to the spirit of the ascetic
life, which it merely exaggerates to an incredible degree;
viewed from any of these three standpoints, the humor of
the story still raises the issue of truth and falsehood, or at
any rate of credibility.

I must admit that denying the truth of humor implies a
challenge to some powerful adversaries. According to the
genealogy supplied by Addison, Truth was the great-
grandfather and Good Sense the grandfather of Humor;
this makes a bastard of Irish Humor, which has nothing of
Good Sense in its composition. According to Max Eastman,
both Aristophanes and Charlie Chaplin have insisted on
their own truthfulness. In an interview with Eastman,
Chaplin said of his audiences, "I make them *conscious of life.*
'You think this is it, don't you?' I say, 'well, it isn't, but *this*
is, see?' And then they laugh."

There is a grain of truth in the Chaplin view: the
humorist does work with materials from life, but he
usually heightens and exaggerates them to the point where
they are just barely recognizable. Life is ugly and terrifying

at times, as we all know, but the whole point of macabre
and grotesque humor is to present life as even more ugly
and terrifying than in fact it is. Our laughter at such humor
is in part motivated by a feeling of relief that things aren't,
thank goodness, quite *that* bad. Maybe I'm a Pollyanna, but I
think this response accounts for the popularity of sick jokes
more often than the release they give to feelings of
repressed hostility. The humor typical of armies and board-
ing schools the world over depends on wild exaggeration of
real hardships. . . .

There is another fairly important distinction between
wit and humor that the standard writers on the subject
don't pay enough attention to: wit is more purely verbal
(and thus again more intellectual) than humor. I can't think
of an uncaptioned cartoon or a sequence in a silent movie
that one could fairly describe as witty. Furthermore, to
deny that puns are witty or to describe them as the lowest
form of wit seems to me completely wrongheaded. I doubt
whether wit can exist without some kind of play on words.
This is where I quarrel with Addison, who takes the usual
dim view of the pun. To see if he lives up to his own
program, let's look at his example of a witty simile: ". . .
when a Poet tells us that the Bosom of his Mistress is as
white as Snow, there is no Wit in the Comparison; but
when he adds, with a sigh, that it is as cold too, it then
grows into Wit." To say that a bosom is as white as snow
isn't witty, of course, because it lacks absurdity; the statement is at once recognized as objectively verifiable. On the
other hand, anyone who owns a clinical thermometer can
prove, if the poet and/or the mistress consents to the
experiment, that her bosom is no colder than that of any
other human being. Only when the metaphorical meanings
of "bosom" ("seat of the affections") and "cold" ("unemo-
tional") are considered does the poet's absurd statement
become "true". Thus "bosom" and "cold" are puns; the play
on these two words makes an objectively absurd remark
metaphorically true. Not all puns are witty, but perhaps all
witty remarks are in this sense puns. . . .

One final point: unconscious humor turns up every day
in the behavior of people who take themselves very
seriously, but can we also speak of unconscious wit? Freud,
if I understand him correctly, would say yes; from his point
of view even our dreams can be witty. Having laid so much
stress on the intellectual nature of wit, I'm not sure that I
ought to agree with him. Still, it cannot be denied that
unthinking comments may show the same formal characteristics as deliberate witicisms. The so-called "Irish bull" at

its best can be astonishingly witty. Sir Boyle Roche, a
member of the Irish Parliament just before the Union with
Great Britain in 1801, gave utterance to several bulls that
would have won any other man vast reputation as a wit.
According to Sir Jonah Barrington, it was Sir Boyle who
made this brilliant remark, in a debate on taxation: "I would
ask the honorable gentleman . . . why we should put
ourselves out of our way to do anything for posterity, for
what has *posterity* done for *us*?" Barrington tells us that
Roche was puzzled by the laugh which followed this
remark and tried to clarify matters, saying that "by posterity he did not at all mean our ancestors, but those who
were to come immediately after them." Obviously the
second remark was so nonsensical a blunder as to be barely
humorous, even, but the first contained a truth that has
great appeal for politicians of all eras.[10]

I consider Mercier's postulations a contribution of real
merit to furthering our understanding in this area. However,
some niggling comments must be made before passing on to
other considerations of the same topic.

First of all, when Mercier states that "Wit is always absurd
and true, humor absurd and untrue," he is engaging in semantic
paradox. The usual meaning of "absurd" is that specified by my
dictionary: "Contrary to reason; not agreeing with truth or
common sense; ridiculous. . . ." So, how can it be both "true"
and "not agreeing with truth?" And, is not the statement that
what is "untrue" is also "absurd" a redundancy? Of course,
Mercier goes on to explain his position in enough detail to rebut
the semantic argument: we know what he means, I think.
However, he labels as an "untruth" simple *exaggeration*. And it
seems to me that a great deal of exaggeration can appear in a
witticism without allowing that witticism to be considered
"humor" instead of wit. There is, for instance, the famous
retort to a politician who predicted that his opponent would die
either on the gallows or of a venereal disease: "That depends
upon whether I embrace your principles or your mistress." Is
this not untrue, or at least exaggeration? Is one to really believe
that the angry recipient of this retort has principles that will
inevitably lead to his hanging? Are we actually to believe that he
has a mistress? And that she undubitably must have the disease
in question?

I think that what Mercier really intends here is that "wit"

has a stronger grounding, on the average, in reality, than does what we would label "humor." It is a matter of degree, not one of kind. Macabre and "sick" humor certainly must be taken as "untrue," that is, *not literally*, if it is to be received as humor. This is the point I was making in Chapter 1 regarding the conversation between two brothers, one of whom had just pushed his mom off a cliff. It must be "taken as a joke," and not seriously, or it is not the least bit funny. It appears to be a major point, also, in William F. Fry, Jr.'s book, *Sweet Madness*.[11] We must have a "play frame" around our jokes in order to recognize the "untrue" nature of their content.

Not only must Mercier's "true/untrue" difference between wit and humor be considered one of only degree and not of kind, so must, according to my thinking, be his "verbal/less verbal". Certainly the vast majority of witty events are verbal; of this there can be hardly any doubt. And certainly a great deal of humor can be entirely visual, without the slightest trace of plays upon words. Visual humor is much more akin to childish (emotional) play, while language is almost universally required for the more intellectual games of wit-work. But, contrary to Mercier's assertion that he cannot "think of an uncaptioned cartoon . . . that one could fairly describe as witty," I think I can assert that I can. Quite often I have remarked to myself how a witty caricature in an uncaptioned political cartoon has visually carried the field in performing its satiric work. And I can remember one devastatingly *witty* uncaptioned piece in *Playboy*.

Playboy had been running a series (one per month) of well-known classical works of art, rendered extremely faithful to the original—but with one tiny, hard-to-detect detail altered. The one I remember most vividly was Grant Wood's *American Gothic*. The dour-faced farmer and his wife stared out realistically from either side of his pitchfork; the rendition of the barn in the background was painstakingly accurate to the original, as was each nuance of expression on the two faces. I searched and searched the picture, thinking at first that perhaps the printer had mistakenly left out the one "defect." Finally a tiny red spot became evident on the bosom of the lady's dress. Close scrutiny revealed that it was a tiny red button reading simply, "Goldwater."

Again, such visual wit is far less evident than is verbal wit;

the purely visual stimuli for laughter can almost unanimously be called "humor" rather than *wit*. But there are exceptions.

I agree wholeheartedly with Mercier that there can be such a thing as "unconscious humor" but that "unconscious wit" is impossible. However, I regret his theory's incompleteness in that it leaves out consideration of what Albert Rapp and I consider an important dimension: that of aggression/kindliness.

As mentioned before, Freud postulated that there is "tendency wit" (aggressive) and "harmless wit." "Harmless wit" depended upon form, not upon a "victim." Even though, as pointed out in Chapter 1, Freud could not supply a single example of completely harmless (victimless) wit (or, humor), there are laughter-evoking stimuli that can vary widely in the specificity of who or what is being attacked, and how strongly. Contrast Nietzsche's mentioning "two great European narcotics, alcohol and Christianity," with the milder

> I was flying in a plane from New York to California and suddenly the plane was hit by lightning. A little old man sitting opposite me screamed: "Do something religious!" So I took up a collection.

Rapp is another modern writer who has grappled meaningfully with the difference between "wit" and "humor," or what he often calls "humorous laughter." His stand, based as it is on the phylogenetic development of laughter in man, is generally quite agreeable to me.[12] He makes five points in differentiating the two concepts.

First, he insists that humorous laughter *must* be accompanied by a "predominate measure of affection or love," for that is its nature. Descended as it has from what he calls "thrashing laughter" (what I call "roar of triumph") to "ridicule" to "affectionate ridicule," it contains more of the civilizing balm of human kindness. Wit, of course, may be openly hostile, although it need not be; "humor" may not be at all.

I can agree with most of this first point, although I agree with Grotjahn that there can never be anything *like* a completely victimless laughter-provoking stimulus. Again, it must be a matter of degree. Certainly, there are jokes so mild that the victim seems so obscure as to be unrecognizable; sometimes one must search diligently to find him. But as I hope I demonstrated in the last chapter with the examples given by Mindness and Suls (pp. 85–88), one might suppose that sheer foolishness or simple incongruity alone could produce laughter, but that the humor can disappear like steam in the arctic without someone or something being demeaned at least somewhat.

To illustrate how the love/aggression difference can operate, let us consider comedian Dick Gregory. During a nightclub performance he is likely to be heckled by drunk bigots in the audience. To these he can respond with any one or more of several hecklerisms I would personally classify as "wit," and of the "aggressive" kind, such as

> Man, trying to get you to shut up is like trying to explain integration to a lynch mob!

> Don't just sit there and heckle me. Pay your check, burn your cross and leave!

He can be gentler, more kindly in what I would call "humorous" comments, too. At one public appearance he was questioned as to how he can demand respect and love of the white community when he talks about such deadly things as burning down our houses. He responds that he would "just make sure you weren't home at the time." Even milder still, he will comment:

> People keep telling me some of their best friends are colored. Let's face it, there just aren't that many of us to go around. . . . Personally, I like Negroes. I like them so much, I even had them for parents. . . .

Joshing, self-ridicule, yes. But there is still the tinge of criticism of Whitey under the surface.

Rapp's second point is that wit is intellectual, a duel of wits, whereas humor is not. Humor need not even be verbal, but may exist as visual, slapstickish. In this respect Rapp agrees with both Mercier and me.

Rapp's third difference: "In humor it is nearly always clear who it is you are laughing at (and with). In wit it is occasionally clear, but usually not. That is why, in wit, people often think they are laughing at a word or phrase or play on words [Freud's supposed 'harmless wit']. . . ." My own position is that this distinction can be applied only partially. Certainly, many victims of puns *do* think they are laughing at "plays on words," but

again: it depends upon the *target* of the pun. Generally, I should
guess that when the target of the pun is oneself, one may have
difficulty in consciously assessing himself as the direct antagonist. However, if the pun is a witty attack on someone else, the
audience to the pun might easily detect the target of the aggression. For instance, if someone cracks to you, "Where do you find
mangoes? Why, where woman goes!", you might (if you even
thought of it) chalk up the "laugh" or groan to the "play on
words"; but when critic Irving Hoffman said about Ilka Chase's
performance in a play: "She makes me Ilka," the audience can
have little doubt as to who is the victim of the pun.

Point number four, according to Rapp, is that wit is artificial and deliberate, whereas humor is more "natural" and spontaneous. The creator of wit, the person who tells a gag, or
makes a witty comment, is *deliberately* creating, and showing his
skill. Again, Rapp could get little argument on this point from
Mercier or me.

Rapp's last point is one which the results of experimental
psychological studies have validated.

> The witty person, therefore, tends to be characterized by
> vanity, narcissism, extroversion, intellectual skill, verbal
> skill, sadism, aggressiveness. The person given to humor-
> ous laughter tends to be characterized by an affectionate
> attitude toward his fellows, by tolerance of sin and weak-
> ness, by sympathy with sufferers, by an objectivity of
> attitude, by patience, by masochism, by maturity.

Since this chapter takes issue, however mildly, with the position
which Rapp has taken, it is only fair to point out that he himself
has pointed out that his stated differences between wit and
humor are generalizations, "which is to say that they are not
always necessarily true." He is also fond of pointing out that
humor and wit often are found in the same story, as in the
example he provides:

> "I meant to have told you of that hole," said an Irishman,
> to a friend who had fallen into a pit in the Irishman's
> garden.
>
> "No matter," said his friend. "I've found it."

To repeat again, wit and humor, to my mind, differ only in

degree and not in kind. Humor generally carries more affection and love, whereas wit *more often* is hostile. Wit is more intellectual than is humor, in general; in humor it is more often that one can tell who is being laughed at, and/or with, than in wit—with some glaring exceptions. Wit tends to be more artificial and deliberate than does humor, although "humorists" *deliberately* invent and stage the display of their work. And "wits" tend to be more aggressive than the more gentle "humorists."

An understanding of the differences between wit and humor can be further understood by means of an extended analogy. The analogy is a comparison of the relationship between wit and humor as compared to that between *rhetoric* and *poetic*. It is probably quite true that very few ordinary citizens have bothered their heads over the differences between *rhetoric* (defined by Aristotle as "the faculty of observing, in any given case, the available means of persuasion,") and *poetic*, meaning usually "literary discourse." But the problem has been stimulating enough to foster a small but energetic scholarly literature.[13]

It is not the purpose of this section to develop interest in the scholarly pursuit of the ways in which rhetoric differs from poetic, but merely to use those differences to develop further insight into the subject of wit and humor. For the better we understand humor, the better we can understand the tactics, rationale, and problems of much of the research explained in the next two chapters.

In general, it will be argued that the differences between wit and humor are very much like the differences between rhetoric and poetic, that wit tends to be more like rhetoric, and humor tends to be more like poetic. The comparison will be specifically drawn between the wit/humor and rhetoric/poetic differences of (1) Purpose, (2) Medium, (3) Method, (4) Audience and Occasion, (5) and Subject Matter. Left unargued will be the question of which forms of the compared discourse types require the most "gift" or "genius."

For its definitive explication of the differences between rhetoric and poetic, this chapter selects that as presented by Gordon E. Bigelow in an article, "Distinguishing Rhetoric from Poetic Discourse."[14] His analysis is generally supported by two

other important scholarly articles.[15] Various sources will be
cited to support the corresponding differences between wit and
humor.[16]

Purpose

For analytical clarity, *purpose* here is considered in two parts,
function and *motive*. "Function" refers to what the particular mode
of discourse is expected to accomplish; "motive," of course,
refers to the intent, the *raison d'être* of the producer of the
discourse. It is these two elements making up the purpose of
a particular discourse that most clearly distinguish wit from
humor and rhetoric from poetic. Let us first consider function.

Function. As one might conclude from the simple definitions
above, the proposed function of rhetoric is quite a practical one,
whereas the function of poetic is aesthetic. As Bigelow puts it:

> In very brief terms, the distinctive Function of poetry is to
> give aesthetic pleasure rather than to persuade, to express
> or exhibit rather than to communicate. . . . Rhetoric may
> propose both to please and to persuade, but the emphasis is
> on persuasion; poetry may also propose both to please and
> persuade, but the emphasis is on pleasure.[17]

To illustrate: in his Inauguration Address (rhetoric) a U.S.
President will generally attempt serious and important persuasive functions, such as a uniting of the people divided by the
election, or to secure acceptance of his broad legislative program. But it would be an immensely modest speaker on this
occasion who did not also attempt some flashes of vivid style
that would please aesthetically enough to make his speech
memorable. It is the style of rhetorical pieces and not simply the
unadorned thought which has captured and retained the imagination of millions. Roosevelt's "We have nothing to fear but
fear itself," and John Kennedy's "Ask not what your country
can do for you, but what you can do for your country!" state
simple ideas, but in language artful and graceful enough to
conceal that art. By the same token, a poem, such as Housman's
"To An Athlete Dying Young," appeals primarily to the emotions through vivid word pictures and its airy, "sweet" style; it
only secondarily makes a wry rhetorical point.

And what of the function of wit vs. the function of humor? Edgar Johnson, in a definitive work on satire [a species of the genus *wit*], discriminates between burlesque as satire and burlesque as humor: "When burlesque inflates things to grotesqueness *just for fun* [italics mine], it is one of the forms of humor; when it inflates them in order to deflate them it is satire."[18] Johnson further denies the label "satire" to any laughter-provoking stimulus which attempts to achieve no *serious* function:

> No description of satire can hold water unless it takes *all* aspects of satire into account. . . . The one ingredient common to all . . . from satire in cap-and-bells to satire with a flaming sword, is *criticism.*[19]

Gilbert Highet generally upholds this distinction advanced by Johnson:

> The purpose of comedy and farce is to cause painless undestructive laughter at human weakness and incongruities. The purpose of satire is, through laughter and invective to cure folly and to punish evil.[20]

Marie Collins Swabey agrees that irony (another form of *wit*), as well as satire, proposes to persuade through criticism:

> Closely related to irony is another variety of the comic involving adverse criticism known as satire. To ridicule the vices and follies of mankind is the business of satire . . . satire by its imaginative eloquence excites anger at human misdeeds and cruelties.[21]

Persuasion is also the usual proposed function of most "serious" (that is, political and/or otherwise satirical) *cartoons.* As the late Edmund Duffy, whose cartoons have been described as "more effective than a well-aimed brick," put it once, "The best cartoons are against something."[22] There can be little doubt, for instance, that the heavy-browed, unshaven likenesses of Richard Nixon drawn by editorial cartoonist Herblock were designed to lower our estimate of Nixon. As the creator of Pogo, Walt Kelly, has emphasized: "Cartoonists are subversive. . . . They are against things."[23]

Occasionally the ability to employ witticisms is perceived as

a weapon in the hands of one's adversary. Stephen A. Douglas
was supposed to have feared Abraham Lincoln's wit. When he
heard that the Illinois Railsplitter was to be his political opponent, Douglas is reported to have said of Abe: "I shall have my
hands full. He is the strong man of the party—full of wit, facts,
dates, and the best stump speaker with his droll ways and dry
jokes."[24] And wit is occasionally given credit for accomplishing
the function for which it was designed. Thomas Dewey's failure
to achieve the Presidency has been partially attributed to a
comment by Alice Longworth, who described Dewey as re-
sembling "the bridegroom on the wedding cake."[25] Richard
Nixon's 1960 bid for the Presidency, it has been widely felt, was
thwarted at least in part by a witty comparison: "Would you buy
a used car from this man?" The French satirist Voltaire "probably had more influence on society than any other Western
satirist," probably because "he was so persistent, so prolific, and
so long-lived."[26] However, as we shall see in the next chapter,
the overall persuasive function of satire has probably been
grossly overestimated.

Of course, it cannot be said that the only, or even the most,
important function of wit is persuasion or aggression. Like
humor, whose primary goal is entertainment, the various forms
of wit are also designed to elicit pleasure. As Leonard Feinberg
says of satire:

> The chief effect of satire is pleasure. That pleasure may
> consist of relief from dullness, as in Charlie Chaplin's
> definition. "Slapstick is a break in the monotony of normal
> conduct." It may be relief from "the tyranny of reason," as
> Schopenhauer suggested. Or, in Freud's view, it may be
> relief from authority. Satire offers the consolation of
> superiority, which is useful even if it is ephemeral; for
> many people even a momentary feeling of superiority is
> rare. Satire may also provide a fresh perspective, detach-
> ment, or balance. But essentially it offers aesthetic plea-
> sure.[27]

In summary, then, it can be said that rhetoric's primary function
is to persuade, but may also please aesthetically; poetic's primary function is to please aesthetically, but may also serve to
persuade. And wit may function to both persuade or chastise
and please; humor is more strictly aimed at pleasure.

Motive. Rhetoric and poetic generally differ in how consistent the motive behind each remains to its function. The rhetorician's motive is usually highly consistent with the function of his discourse, whereas the user of poetic discourse may have a motive not at all in keeping with his work's primary function. As Bigelow explains,

> In poetic discourse, moreover, motive may be relatively independent of the function. One strong component of the poet's motive is simply that the discourse shall *be*, without much reference to what it shall do.[28]

The motive of the political candidate on the campaign trail is to secure votes, the intended function of his rhetoric; the poet might produce a dazzling array of images which function to thrill the aesthetic sensibilities of his readers, but his motive may have been simply to produce an enduring work of art.

One's motive for telling "a good one" at the shop or office is usually quite consistent with the function of the joke itself—to entertain. But the jokester may also have other, less consistent motives in sharing his jokes. He may find this a productive way to "kill time" that would otherwise hang heavy over his head; he might seek to increase his popularity with his fellow workers; if there are females present, and the jokes he tells tend toward the scatalogical or the obscene, his motive may be aggression, even seduction, toward the females.[29]

On the professional level, the motive of the comedian can be quite disparate from his function of entertaining. He performs his act to make people laugh, certainly; but he seeks to make his living at it, also. A quest for fame would not be inconceivable.

In rhetoric, of course, the rhetorician's motive would usually be quite consistent with the persuasive function of his discourse.

Not only does the consistency of function and motive differ between wit and humor, but the actual motivation behind the two forms usually differs. Whatever his other motives, the purveyor of humor hopes to entertain; but the motive for wit is usually more "serious." The story is told that William Jennings Bryan, finding no platform to speak from at a country meeting, climbed onto a manure spreader and proclaimed: "Ladies and gentlemen! This is the first time I have addressed an audience from a Republican platform." Quite obviously, the Great Commoner had a political point to make in addition to his hopes of getting a guffaw from his audience. Much the same kind of double motivation was probably behind Emory Storrs' statement that "the Democratic party is like a mule—without pride of ancestry or hope of posterity." Producers of the wit-form known as satire have "serious" motives, also. As Highet puts it:

> the motives of the satirist? . . . First, he is always moved by personal hatred, scorn, or condescending amusement. . . . The second impulse is openly avowed by many satirists. They wish to stigmatize crime or ridicule folly, and thus aid in diminishing or removing it.[30]

"The laughter of comedy is relatively purposeless," David Worcester chimes in. "The laughter of satire is directed toward an end."[31]

Therefore, as rhetoric differs from poetic in seriousness and practicality of function and motive, so does wit differ from humor in overall purpose.

Medium

Rhetoric deals with reality, with real events, proposing solutions to real problems and praising or blaming real people and institutions; poetic is more apt to deal in fancy. The language of rhetoric focuses the attention of its audience upon the world as it is, but the more figurative language of poetic is more apt to fly into the imaginative. On this contrast Bigelow quotes Longinus' "On the Sublime:"

> It is no doubt true that those [images] found in the poets contain, as I said, a tendency to exaggeration in the way of the fabulous and that they transcend in every way the credible, but in oratorical imagery the best feature is always its reality and truth.[32]

The same distinction can be said to exist between wit and other comic forms. We have already seen, above, Mercier's insistence that it is the relative truth or falsity between wit and humor that distinguishes them ("Wit is always absurd and true, humor absurd and untrue "). Other experts agree, such as

Feinberg who wrote: "Significant satire is concerned with the nature of reality."[33] Two comments from Johnson:

> For satiric purposes . . . abuse has to be damaging, and to be damaging it must strike us as really true. *The sudden revelation of a damaging truth is what makes comedy wit* [italics mine]. . . . Even comic satire derives its significance from the truth.[34]

> But wit has its eye glued on reality. . . . Its theme is always reality; its standards are truth and sanity . . . it is a true instrument of satire . . . wit is not necessarily amusing. Serious wit may be only a powerful searchlight thrown on reality.[35]

Further insistence that the wittiest of humor represents "truth or sense" comes from Cecil Northcott. He even goes so far as to entitle his brief article, "I Just Tell the Truth," from the assertion by Mort Sahl.[36] Sahl, one of the more outspoken and satiric of the so-called "New wave" comedians, thus describes what he does. He does not "tell jokes," but rather, capsulizes and condenses *truth* in a "kind of shorthand." Consistent with his claim is the fact that a typical prop in his nightclub monologue is a rolled-up newspaper. And regarding satire, playwright Gore Vidal concurs: " . . . for is not satire, simply, truth grinning in a solemn canting world?"[37]

Method

The difference between the method of rhetoric and poetic is one already mentioned as existing between wit and humor: the method of rhetoric is more reasonable, appealing more often and more directly to the intellect; the method of poetic is imaginative, emotional. As Bigelow explains:

> [R]hetoric . . . is characteristically logical, a progression of ideas determined by reason and appealing chiefly to reason in the hearer . . . the method of poetry [is] alogical, dependent upon emotions rather than on reason . . . poetic discourse is essentially alogical . . . appealing to imagination or emotion.[38]

Johnson asserts pretty much the same difference between wit and humor:

Humor remains closer to the childhood mood of hilarity
than wit does. Humor may be sheer playful nonsense. It is
indifferent to whether its fun is anchored in reality or
adrift in fantasy. It is high-hearted and cockeyed; if it has
any meaning at all the truth or the importance of that
meaning is the last reason humor would have for its
happiness.[39]

The Audience and Occasion

The rhetoric/poetic and wit/humor difference in audience
and occasions prompting them is probably second in importance
only to that of *purpose* at distinguishing the discourse types. The
audience and occasion of poetic is generally a great deal more
universal and certainly less confining than that of rhetoric.

[T]he orator's discourse is determined to an important
degree by a specific occasion . . . . The poet is aware of
some audience and some occasion. But these are both
characteristically much broader than in rhetoric . . . The
poet might speak to anybody, to everybody . . . or to
nobody. He often appears to be speaking to all mankind and
for all time. But the most important consideration here is
that neither audience nor occasion has a direct or shaping
influence on the nature of his discourse except in a comparatively broad sense.[40]

It is, rather, the subject that holds the poet's mind:

The poet, as Wordsworth reminds us, keeps his eye not on
the audience or occasion, but on his subject: his subject fills
his mind and engrosses his imagination, so that he is
compelled, by excess of admiration or other emotion, to tell
of it; compelled, though no one hear or read his utterance.[41]

Not so with the rhetorician:

The rhetorician stands at the opposite pole. He composes
his discourse with his eye upon his audience and occasion.
The occasion may dictate his very subject; and it may well
be a subject quite other than that he would have chosen if
left to himself.[42]

The distinction generally holds true for wit and humor. Of
course, some wit does seem to speak to broad segments of the
human race without much dependence upon time and place of

occasion. Such witticism as G.B. Shaw's remark, "Englishmen will never be slaves; they are free to do whatever the government and public opinion allow them to do," or Bierce's definition: "Immoral: inexpedient," seem to be recognizable examples. But much wit was created for a particular occasion and audience, and, as such, quickly becomes "dated." Dorothy Parker once admitted of her satiric poetry: "Let's face it, honey, my verse is terribly dated." Much wit, indeed, is directed against particular people, knowledge of whom would be necessary in order to "catch on" to the witticism. H.L. Mencken, for instance, thrust out at a particular politician in his definition: "Democracy is that system of government under which the people, having 37,000,000 native-born adult whites to choose from, including thousands who are handsome and many who are wise, pick out a Coolidge to be head of state."

Little that can be classified as more humorous than witty depends for much of its impact upon specific audience or occasion. These factors no more restrict the mimic comedy of Red Skelton or Charlie Chaplin than they have the pratfalls and mummery of jesters of any age. Jack Benny, kidding himself endlessly over his vanity and his stinginess attracted something akin to a universal audience. The circus clown plays equally well to the child, the adult, or the aged.

But it is the young, the "cool" and "in" crowd that attends to a Mort Sahl or a Lenny Bruce. The acerbic and biting savagery of Bruce's witty monologues brought down upon him much "establishment" ire and harassment, which must have combined with his many personal problems to bring him to an early grave. Sahl cannot secure or maintain a regular sponsor. Show folk know well the maxim: "Satire closes on Saturday night."

As with the other areas of difference between wit and humor, there are exceptions to the "rule." Some humor is audience/occasion-bound, and some wit is a statement of universal truth. But on a continuum from "humor" to "wit," the work of such comedians as Skelton, and Benny, and George Gobel would stand toward the humor end, and that of Bruce and Sahl toward the wit end, in terms of dependence upon audience and occasion. The reader of Swift's "A Modest Proposal" might think it either foolish or satanic unless he were familiar with the eighteenth century barbarity which Swift was satirizing.

Subject Matter

If a form of discourse differs from another in specificity of audience and occasion, this fact would necessitate a similar difference in subject matter. In the case of rhetoric vs. poetic discourse, the usual subject matter difference is in breadth and timeliness of theme. Writes Bigelow:

> [R]hetorical themes tend to be more limited in application than the themes of poetic discourse; and conversely, in keeping with the aesthetic purpose and the more general audience and occasion of poetic discourse, poetic themes tend to be more timeless and universal than rhetorical themes.[43]

Of course, some rhetorical masterpieces find themselves enshrined in a nation's or the world's literature because their originators spoke beyond their immediate audiences and occasions and touched upon universal and timeless values. Examples that come to mind are Lincoln's Gettysburg Address and R.G. Ingersoll's funeral oration at his brother's grave. But such examples are as apt to be called "poetical" or even "flights of poetical fancy" as rhetoric. And, certainly, some poetry is written for a particular audience or occasion, and thus emphasizes temporal, immediacy-ridden themes. The world of letters is strewn with the poetry written almost on demand by persons in high office, and with poetry written to commemorate particular events and to enlist people in specific causes. An example of "poetry on demand" is the well-known poem of Oliver Wendell Holmes, "Old Ironsides," written to further the cause of preserving the historic warship U.S.S. Constitution. But, by and large, most poetry addresses itself to broader, more universal themes; rhetoric speaks to the particular issue.

The subject matter of humor, as hinted above in the section on audience and occasion, has a kind of universal and timeless appeal; primarily this is because to engage in the business of humor is to enter a "play" world, however temporarily. When we open our newspaper to "Peanuts" or "Beetle Bailey," when we seat ourself in the nightclub or before the television set to attend to the stand-up comic, when we tell or listen to jokes at parties or at the office, we renounce the serious, "real" world around us and ready ourselves to hear or read nonsense, exaggeration, even idiocy or silliness. Max Eastman has insisted that the world of humor is a place to which we temporarily and symbolically return to the playful and happy mood of child-hood,[44] a view which he shares with Freud. The successful comedian, then, is one who develops a routine of stock material with wide audience appeal, drawing laughs (many at himself) because of human shortcomings widely and easily perceived. And this routine or stock material must be fanciful and exagger-ated enough to create the "play frame" or attitude so that the audience can childishly dispense with reality-testing while enjoying the laughter. Thus we can laugh at Jack Benny's miserliness and vanity knowing full well that no one could be that cheap and vain. We roar at Red Skelton's Willie Lump-Lump without the necessity of wondering how Willie ever makes it through a routine day. We can enjoy the outrageous stories Alan King tells of his troubles with his wife and family, without really worrying about his home life. We can chuckle at Rodney Dangerfield's self-deprecation knowing that, in the real world, no doorman would really ask Dangerfield to call *him* a cab.

But the subject matter of the professional wit is usually of the here and now, the immediate, the real. The point has already been made that wit deals mostly with truth while humor deals more with the absurd, thus false. Many witticisms are made on the spur of the moment, and become unrecogniza-ble as wit outside of the particular event prompting it. Thus Tallulah Bankhead said after seeing a particular play, "There is less here than meets the eye." Irwin S. Cobb, upon being informed that his mean boss was ailing, is reported to have quipped: "By God, I hope it is nothing trivial." And to enjoy much of what we could call "wit," we must usually be in possession of certain, particular knowledge. When Art Buch-wald symbolically laments with other political humorists that there is nothing funny they can say or draw regarding George

"WITTY
HUMOR"

M   M
O   O
R   R
E   E

M ||| M
O ||| O
R ||| R
E ||| E

W ||| H
I ||| U
T ||| M
  ||| O
T ||| R
H |||
A ||| T
N ||| H
  ||| A
  ||| N
H |||
U |||
M ||| W
O ||| I
R ||| T

"HUMOROUS
WIT"

Rhetoric/Wit tends to be:

in *Purpose:* practical in function, in motive, consistent with function

in *Medium:* truthful, real

in *Method:* logical

by *Audience, Occasion:* more influenced

in *Subject Matter:* on more specific, limited issues

Poetic/Wit tends to be:

in *Purpose:* aesthetic in function in motive, not necessarily consistent with function

in *Medium:* fancy, exaggerated

in *Method:* alogical

by *Audience, Occasion:* less influenced

in *Subject Matter:* on broader, more universal themes

Figure 5-1. Graphic Representation of the Differences Between Wit and Humor

114

McGovern because he "looks like everyone's high school chem-
istry teacher," we must know McGovern's demeanor and
something of his history to enjoy it. A reader knowing nothing
of Richard Nixon's political career would find little to laugh at in
one of Buchwald's columns depicting a debate between the
"New Nixon" and the "Old Nixon" who has just come out of the
closet where he has been kept in mothballs. To enjoy a Mort
Sahl routine one must be up on current events and have read
today's newspaper.

It cannot be denied that some statements one could define
as "witty" address themselves to universal human themes. The
English language abounds in witty comments on the world that
strike one as universal truisms.

> Conservative: A Statesman who is enamored of existing
> evils, as distinguished from the Liberal, who wishes to
> replace them with others. (Ambrose Bierce)
>
> Two-party system: Political system composed of two par-
> ties, the Ins and the Outs. (Richard Armour)
>
> A pessimist is a person who has had to listen to too many
> optimists. (Don Marquis)
>
> Man is the only animal that blushes. Or needs to. If you
> pick up a starving dog and make him prosperous, he will
> not bite you. That is the principal difference between a dog
> and a man. (Mark Twain)
>
> Everyone can master a grief but he that has it. (Shake-
> speare)
>
> The only thing to do with good advice is pass it on. (Oscar
> Wilde)[45]

The point to be made here is that what we can call "humor"
almost invariably is based upon broad and timeless themes; wit
may be so based, but is also often much more specific and rooted
to a particular moment and location.

The chart in Figure 5-1 summarizes what this chapter
argues are the relative differences between wit and humor.
Again, let it be perfectly clear that it is a matter of relativity, of
degree, which separates a primarily witty stimulus of laughter
from a primarily *humorous* one. One might be hard put to find a
dozen examples of "pure" wit containing no humor or "pure"

humor without any wit. But it seems to me that it makes sense to say that wit is relatively more practical and persuasive in purpose than humor, deals more often with real events while humor more usually deals with fantasy; that wit appeals more to the intellect while humor has a more emotional element; that wit is generally addressed to a more specific audience on a more specific occasion than is humor; and that wit appeals more to the events of the here and now while humor is broadly based on universal human themes.

II

PRACTICAL CONSIDERATIONS:
Laughter-Provoking Stimuli as Communication

6

Humor,
Satire,
Schmatire:
Persuasive?

In Theory

Every so often some journalist or another will decry the present lack of humor in politics, especially in Presidential campaigns. Implying that the candidate who shows the best sense of humor would make the best president, such journalistic complaints sometimes suggest that the candidate who shows the best sense of humor in his public statements also might persuade the most people to vote for him.

One such lament on the lack of Presidential humor appeared in the *Wall Street Journal*.[1] In his article, Elliot Carlson pointed out that Lincoln knew how to disarm his critics—with humor—but that President Nixon rarely relies upon funny stories for any purpose, much less "as a political weapon."

Carlson states that "From Andrew Jackson onward, Presidents and presidential aspirants were expected to entertain and, frequently were judged as much on their wit as their policies." He points out that several Presidential candidates used humor to "demolish critics." For instance Franklin D. Roosevelt "countered critics' thrusts with a light, tongue-in-cheek talk, the famous 'Fala Speech,'" thus robbing his opponents of the argument of his frivolous spending of taxpayer money to transport his dog.

Carlson gives several other examples where politicians have used humor and/or wit, supposedly with telling effect. FDR once chided the Daughters of the American Revolution by addressing them, "Fellow Immigrants," his way of saying that we are all immigrants and should brook no antiimmigrant feeling. FDR is also supposed to have "humanized" Stalin at the Teheran Conference by continually kidding Winston Churchill for his "Britishness," his derby hat, his cigar, and so forth. Stalin finally broke his reserve, laughed, told some jokes of his own, and began discussing the issues like a brother. Adlai Stevenson, twice defeated by Eisenhower, was delayed in traffic by a soldier's funeral procession. He cracked that "Military heroes always seem to be getting in my way."

In the Lincoln-Douglas debates, Douglas accused Lincoln of being two-faced. Said Lincoln to his audience: "Ladies and gentlemen of the audience, I leave it to you: if I had two faces would I be wearing this one?" Someone threw a cabbage onto the platform where stood William Howard Taft, who quipped: "I see that one of my adversaries has lost his head." Harry Truman would introduce himself during his reelection drive: "My name is Harry S. Truman. I work for the government and I'm trying to keep my job." Even Jack Kennedy attempted to disarm with humor his critics' complaints about appointing his brother, Robert, Attorney General of the United States. His reply was, "I see nothing wrong with giving Robert some legal experience before he goes out to practice law."

Carlson does record *one* humorous remark by Nixon; asked a so-called "in house" question at a press conference, he replied, off the cuff: "You wouldn't ask an out-house question, would you?" He also does point out that McGovern, after winning the California primary, mimicked the famous Alka-Seltzer commercial: "I can't believe we won the whole thing." However, his general conclusion is highlighted in the title of his by-lined article: "Wanted: a Bit of Campaign Humor." Carlson was definitely not satisified with the politics of dourness.

Regardless of the wishes of journalists, would it really help candidates or other persuaders to use humor in their public discourse? When one turns to the leading theorists for an answer, he finds a wide variety of answers. For instance, in summarizing the advice of the leading ancient-through-nineteenth-century rhetoricians, Wilma Grimes points out:

> Regarding the worth of laughter and its function, almost all the rhetoricians had their say. In the writings of Aristotle, Cicero, and Quintilian, propriety and the rhetorical efficacy of laughter were prominent. Throughout the Renaissance, writers justified laughter and the artistic forms arousing it in terms of its power to shock human beings out of their own faults. In the main, eighteenth century writers expressed greater curiosity about causes and emotions in mirth than about its practical use, but in the nineteenth century rhetoricians again focussed attention upon the propriety and function of mirth. Whately in particular questioned the utility of humor in argument.[2]

At the end of her own dissertation study, Grimes seemed skeptical that humor has much of a place in persuasion. She points out that, in a serious, persuasive speech, the use of humor actually causes an "interruption" of the train of thought, and may thus be dysfunctional to the speaker's purpose.[3] She admits that humor in a speech produces "relief," but questions whether this is an appropriate response for a persuasive speaker to seek. She argues that introducing a speech with humor will not *produce* audience friendliness, but may merely determine if it exists.

> Actually, an introductory anecdote or joke might signify that all is well, that the speaker and audience are in a state of well-being and no danger exists, that we are all superior to whatever may occur. In this sense, humor can be useful in dispelling strain, and helping the audience to relax and receive whatever the speaker has to say. For instance, political lampooning *satisfies the lampooner and the members of his party that they are free of the dangers which their opponents have embraced, e.g., graft* [italics mine].[4]

The italicized lines, above, incidentally, seem to indicate that political lampooning may be self-satisfying, but hardly damaging to the opposition.

Grimes does seem to agree with a couple of ancient rhetoricians that humor might be useful for persuasion toward *in-action*: "As Aristotle and Cicero declared, however, when one is opposing a measure, humor is a great aid in clouding issues and delaying judgments, since it forces an interruption, whether welcome or not."[5] But the final paragraph of her dissertation furnishes little hope for humor's efficacy in persuasive speaking:

> Thus it appears that many claims for the value of humor in public speaking are open to question. If one wishes to use it, he must risk, as does the poet, the misunderstandings to which connotative language is liable. Since we call *humorous* only those situations arousing mirth, and since mirth is an emotion, humorous situations are emotional situations, stimulated by emotion-arousing language. As emotional situations, they demand the exercise of great wisdom and judgment. An organism can participate in only one event at a time, can feel only one emotion at a time. When the emotion of humor dominates the organism, all action except laughter is excluded. The speaker must decide whether the relief of laughter is so essential to his purpose that he can risk shocking his audience out of its preoccupation with an avowed goal.[6]

William S. White has quoted a "British politician" friend of his on the use of political humor. The Britisher is alleged to have said that political humor must

> make people laugh, but far preferably at issues and situations, and perhaps then at the other candidate. It is tolerable for this laughter to be *with* the speaker himself. But there is great danger that laughing *with* him may merge, imperceptibly and at any moment, into laughter *at* him. And this is fatal.[7]

Senator Tom Corwin of Ohio, who attempted humor in much of his public speaking, finally decided that humor was out of place in political persuasion, and formulated the "Corwin Law of Solemnity:" "Use humor, if at all, only in the speech introduction."[8]

White apparently believes that humor can be an effective weapon, depending upon who uses it and where and how. He said of Lyndon Johnson, just before the campaign of 1960: "A Johnson anecdote most often is told to destroy an opponent's argument, or simply to put an opponent off-balance. . . . No man in public life can use irony more effectively in personal relations."[9] And Steve Allen claims that some humor can have an "educational" value, although it may tend to irritate some.[10]

So far, the discussion has been concerned more with what the last chapter defined as "humor" rather than with what it defined as "wit." Surely some of the political jibes of Presidential aspirants detailed in the *Wall Street Journal* article of Carlson can be called "witty" and not merely humorous; but many were relatively "harmless" humor, too. What about "wit"? And, what about the special kind of "wit" called *satire*? Regarding this literary genre, there is also a wide variety of opinion as to its persuasive usefulness.

The proponents of satire's persuasive effectiveness often argue for it adamantly. Gilbert Cannan has said,

> No tyrant, no tyrannous idea ever came crashing to earth but it was first wounded with the shafts of satire: no free man, no free idea ever rose to the heights but it endured them.[11]

Edgar Johnson writes that, "For satiric purposes . . . abuse has to be more than funny, it has to be damaging." He further insists that all satire must contain one critical element: "No description of satire can hold water unless it takes all the aspects of satire into account . . . the one ingredient common to all . . . from satire in cap-and-bells to satire with a flaming sword, is *criticism*." He further insists that satire must criticize, must attack: "evil arrogant and triumphant," "conventional respectabilities which are really hidden absurdities," "foolishness foolishly convinced that it makes sense."[12]

Marie Collins Swabey asserts that satire "excites anger at human misdeeds and cruelties,"[13] and Gilbert Highet writes that the very purpose of satire is "to cure folly and to punish evil . . . to expose evil to bitter contempt."[14]

The work of Edmund Duffy, the late editorial cartoonist, who insisted that "the best cartoons are *against* something," has been described as "more effective than well-aimed brickbats."[15]

Apparently the Central Committee of the USSR at least hopes for some persuasive results from their own use of "humorous criticism." The *New York Times Magazine* has published cartoons from a Russian magazine, *Krokodil*, with the following comment:

> Cloaked as humor but bearing sharp lessons, the cartoons that appear in the Soviet magazine *Krokodil* are one of the best-known mediums of Soviet self-criticism—a means of pointing up faults the Soviet leaders want to see corrected. The cartoons cover a wide range of targets, though some things are off-limits. Top Soviet personalities, delicate matters like relations with China, resentment over consumer prices—these are among the topics not lampooned in *Krokodil*. But there are other things to jibe at.[16]

The "other things" that *are* jibed at are illustrated: "organization mania," "special privileges," "bad management," "graft," "shortages," "black marketing," "poor planning," and "scarcity of help."

Benjamin S. Rosenthal, Congressman from New York, has implied that satire is an effective weapon against individuals in his praise for the satire magazine, *Mad*:

> Mr. Speaker,
> this month marks the 10th anniversary of a publishing phenomenon that exemplifies one of the strengths of our free society. I refer to *Mad* magazine, which for the past ten years has humorously pointed out the laughable foibles of business, labor, advertising, television, sports, and entertainment, to say nothing of politics.
> *Mad* magazine has let people laugh at those in high places without damage to those high places themselves. It has poked fun at many aspects of the American scene, and the country is the better for its raillery.[17]

In direct opposition to the above claims for satire's effectiveness as an agent of persuasion (and, therefore, of change), is Leonard Feinberg, professor of English at Iowa State University. Feinberg, author of two books on satire, demurs.

> In spite of these claims, the notion that satire has played an important part in reforming society is probably a delusion. Satirists themselves know better. Swift said that mankind accepts satire because every man sees in it his fellow's failings, never his own; a few months after the publication of *Gulliver's Travels* Swift wrote a letter pretending to be amazed that society had not already reformed itself.[18]

Feinberg allows that, "Aesthetic effect satire has had, as every literary form should have." But, he adds: "The chief effect of satire is [personal] pleasure."[19]

Feinberg offers an analytic explanation of why satire is both ineffective as persuasion and, in the bargain, not a particularly popular or well-loved form of literature. He points out what are the "limitations" of satire.[20] I paraphrase his list of such limitations:

1. Good satire appeals more to the intellect than to the emotions.
2. Satire is often puzzling.
3. Pure satire is rarely able to hold a reader's interest for a prolonged period of time.
4. Some truths are simply too uncomfortable to admit.
5. Satire is, or is generally regarded as being, cruel.
6. Satire is accused of being negative.
7. Satire dispels illusions (and man needs his illusions).
8. Satire has a short life.
9. Satire provides neither the catharsis of tragedy nor the escapism of romantic literature (The effect of satire is ambivalent and ambiguous).

So there we have a generally representative cross-section of the arm-chair opinionizing, the more or less thoughtful theorizing about the persuasive effect (or its lack) one can claim for humor and/or wit. This theorizing has undergone several more or less rigorous tests via laboratory experimental studies. Through a review of these studies and their more or less quantitative results, I hope that a more thorough understanding of the value of humor and/or wit as persuasion is developed.

Empirical Studies

The earliest known study to test the value of including humor in persuasive speeches was conducted by P.E. Lull in 1939.[21] For his experiment he wrote four speeches, two of them for and two of them against the idea of a system of state medicine. One speech *for* state medicine and one *against* state medicine were "humorous," that is, contained cracks, anecdotes, and puns, and one speech for and one speech against state medicine were completely humorless.

Experienced college speakers delivered these speeches live to groups of college students at Purdue and at the University of Wisconsin. Two weeks before these student subjects heard the speeches they responded to a Thurstone-type attitude scale measuring their attitudes toward the idea of "state medicine." Immediately after hearing one of the four speeches, each student in the experiment responded to an alternate form of the attitude scale. In addition, he rated the speaker from 0 percent to 100 percent on attributes, "interestingness," "humor," and "convincingness."

The "humorous" version of the speech favoring state medicine began with a lengthy introduction with several quips and "cracks" in it. It is provided here in full:

> The illness of a good friend of mine a few months ago first aroused my interest in our present system of medical practice. Adolph lives with his wife Gretchen, and their small son, Adolph, Jr., in a nearby city. He supports his little family by selling corsets, but lately his business has been falling off, so that his income is barely $2,000 a year. One day after an unusually heavy breakfast of sauerkraut and pig hocks, Adolph developed a pain in his side. A doctor was summoned. Much to Adolph's surprise, the case was diagnosed as acute appendicitis. They rushed him off to a hospital. His wife Gretchen was greatly excited and urged the doctor not to spare any expense. The urging was really unnecessary. The doctor didn't—neither did anyone else. A few minutes later the routine operation was quickly performed. The kindly old surgeon said to the anxious wife: "Gretchen, your worries are all over." And they were until the next morning when a bill for $35.00 arrived from the doctor who had given the anaesthetic. A few days later the hospital presented the weekly bill to the still groggy patient—seven days at $6.00 a day, with additional charges for the operating room, special nurse, medicines, and apparently about everything else they could think of, including a new tie for the janitor. Then the doctor, who was skilled in the important matter of the correct diagnosis of the maximum fee, came in and he and Adolph had a little heart-to-heart chat about finances. The doctor said: "My usual charge is $200.00 *but* . . ." He was awfully decent about it. He had been collecting fees from the unfortunate Adolph for twenty years, so he said: "The charge won't be over $175.00." After the doctor had gone, Adolph and Gretchen added up the bills. The whole thing amounted to only $300.00—not much more than the cost of a Prom week-end. But they didn't have $300.00—as a matter of fact, when he went to the hospital Adolph had only $26.18 in cash, which included the contents of the baby's bank. He and Gretchen had been budgeting as closely as possible, but

were just able to get along. They had no house to mort-
gage. They still owed a few installments on Adolph, Jr. But
the doctor had to be paid.

A long paragraph later the speech tells of a "reliable report"
showing shocking numbers of physical defects among Americans, which "is not padded or exaggerated in any way by the inclusion of such piffling products of the advertisers' imagination
as 'halitosis,' 'ash-tray breath,' 'dish-pan hands,' 'office hips,' and
the like."

Almost a typewritten page later is the anecdote:

> There [is] more truth than humor in a typographical error
> which appeared in a large newspaper not long ago. The
> sentence read: "The doctor felt of the patient's *purse* and
> admitted that there was nothing he could do."

Almost another typewritten page later appears this gem:

> Recently, an established physician was talking to a group of
> medical students about the matter of fees. "Now, I charge
> $25 for a call at a residence," he said, "ten dollars for an
> office consultation, and five dollars for a telephone con-
> sultation." At this point one of the students called out:
> "Say, doc, how much do you charge for passing a man on
> the street?"

This was followed immediately with: "Another doctor suffered a
heart attack not long ago when he charged a patient only $75 and
then discovered that the man had $200." Another story appears a
bit later:

> The story is told of the man who was filling out an appli-
> cation for life insurance. He was asked whether he had ever
> had appendicitis. "Well," he answered, "I was operated on
> but I have never felt quite sure whether it was appendicitis
> or professional curiosity." It is reported that in this same
> case, after the operation, the doctor pinned a label on the
> patient which read: "Opened by mistake."

After another page and one-half appears this now untimely
crack: "Today even the bachelors, grass widows, and old maids
help to pay for our educational system, so that even children of
Republicans and Prohibitionists are not denied the advantages
of a free public education."

Two pages later appears a humorous quotation to reinforce the idea that British doctors love their own form of

national health care: ". . . only last month Dr. D.W. Orr asserted: 'Nine out of ten British doctors would give up health insurance only over their dead bodies.'" Two pages later the argument that doctors get paid only when people get sick is backed up with: "Some of them [doctors] may be high-minded enough to really try to prevent disease, but if no one got sick under the present system—all the doctors would starve to death—or the poor-houses would be jammed to the window-sills with poverty stricken physicians."

Lull reports that, when the speech containing the above humorous items was presented to his groups of student sub-jects, it evoked from four to nineteen laughs per group. The speech *for* state medicine but containing *no* humor produced no instances of laughter. Lull offers this evidence, plus the ratings to be mentioned later, as proof that the "humorous" version was, indeed, *perceived as* humorous.

The humorous speech *against* state medicine also began with a lengthy introduction with several possibly humorous cracks in it. It is presented here in full.

> One of the most interesting books that hasn't been written yet, will be published someday under the title: "How to Skin Friends and Influential People." It will deal with the countless schemes that have forced the govern-ment into almost every known activity. It has been sug-gested that the government take over the railroads, mines, electric utilities, and—Mae West. Even the medical pro-fession has not escaped the attention of those who insist on putting their political fingers into every bowl of soup. As a group, the plans to have the government take over medical practice can be classed as various types of State Medicine. Briefly, State Medicine involves setting up a system of complete medical service, organized, controlled, and regu-lated by the state, available to all citizens, and which would be paid for out of government funds—if the government happened to have any funds at the time. Because of the vital importance of the situation to which these proposals relate, it seems essential that we should analyze State Medicine thoroughly and determine its probable conse-quences instead of giving it a blind endorsement.
>
> Advocates of state medicine describe a health situation in this country that would draw iron tears down Pluto's

cheeks. But what are the facts? Perhaps some of you have the same attitude as the man who was seated in the reading room of a library. Next to him sat a man who was poring over birth and death statistics. After while the second man turned to the first and said: "Do you know that every time I breathe a man dies?" The first man replied: "That's very interesting, but why don't you chew cloves?" Yes, statistics are boring, but the fact is that our medical facilities have been and are being constantly improved. There has been a steady increase in the number of physicians, nurses, hospitals; even X-ray machines, iron lungs and hot-water bottles. We have 150,000 active doctors—why, that's one doctor for every person in Kankakee, Keokuk, and Kalamazoo—including those imbedded in the cemetery. Altogether, more than one million people are now devoting themselves to health work. Further investigation reveals that the quality of service that these people are rendering is being constantly improved. Longer training requirements have been established for doctors; more rigid requirements for licensure have relegated quacks and incompetents to the limbo of the Indian Medicine Men and Snake Oil salesmen.

Half a paragraph later U.S. medicine's contribution to human longevity is lauded: " . . . the span of life has been increased 15 years—just think how many extra games of pinochle that means for the old folks; and, in spite of increasing deaths due to auto accidents caused by one-armed drivers and others, the death rate has been lowered. . . ." Two paragraphs later the idea of scrapping private medicine for its "few faults" is ridiculed: " . . . the faulty reasoning back of these unwarranted charges is similar to that employed by one of Mark Twain's characters who advocated abolishing beds because 'So many people died in them.'"

The inability of people to be able to pay for private medicine as a reason for turning to state medicine is ridiculed a paragraph later:

> many people don't earn enough to buy fresh artichokes in January, or orchids for every date they take to a Union dance, or Pierce-Arrow motor cars. Yet since some people cannot buy everything, it is hardly a good argument for

turning all the grocery stores, florist shops, and automobile companies over to the government.

A full page later the "poor distribution of health services under
the present system" argument is attacked humorously:

> And the mere fact that there are more doctors in Califor-
> nia than there are in North Carolina may be caused by the
> fact that there are more wealthy widows and tempera-
> mental movie stars in California who are quite susceptible
> to imaginary illnesses. Strangely enough, no one, not even
> the Los Angeles Chamber of Commerce, has ever attempt-
> ed to prove that the people of California are healthier than
> those of North Carolina.

The next paragraph attacks the argument that private medicine
does little for preventive medicine, and contains the following
jibes:

> In spite of all the preventive efforts of the doctors, ill-
> nesses will probably continue to develop—small boys will
> disregard the best advice, eat green apples, and come down
> with the stomach-ache; bigger boys will race around in
> ancient jalopies, smash up and find themselves in hospi-
> tals; and older boys will gorge on porterhouse steaks,
> develop distended waist-lines, and high blood-pressure.

Almost a page later the "mechanization" of medicine resulting
from state control is argued. The argument contains this crack:
"When you become ill you will have to take whatever politically
appointed pill-peddler is assigned to you, and furthermore, you
will be rushed through a routine treatment faster than a Ford
chassis through an assembly line." A few lines later in that paragraph appears this story:

> An interesting story is told of an experience one man had in
> the offices of a clinic where patients were shoved through
> in a steady stream. This young man came into the reception
> room one morning and asked to see one of the doctors
> privately. The nurse asked if he had an appointment. He
> replied that he hadn't. "Then," said the nurse, "go into that
> dressing room there, remove all your clothing, even to
> your shoes and socks. When the bell rings, enter Dr.
> Martin's office through the door in the dressing room
> marked 'office.'" The young fellow started to protest—but
> the nurse, informing him that the rules were never modi-
> fied for *anyone*, pushed him into the dressing room. Finally

he disrobed. When the bell rang, he tripped into the doctor's office, wearing only a few beads of perspiration. "Well," barked the doctor, "what's the matter with you?" "They ain't nothing the matter with me, doc," answered the new arrival. "Well, what in blazes are you doing in here then?" thundered the doctor. "I came," said the boy, "to see if you'd care to renew your subscription to the *Saturday Evening Post.*"

Half a page later, in discussing the lower quality of physicians which state medicine produces, a story of Russian state medicine appears:

> One of the medical students in Russia, in an examination, gave the composition of air as 10% oxygen, 5% hydrogen, 65% nitrogen and his temperature. How would you like to have to entrust your life to a doctor like that one?

Two lines later, in a discussion of books lauding socialized medicine overseas, appears:

> The glowing reports of socialized medicine in Russia in American books and magazines have been a source of amusement. . . . Always we have wished their authors only one punishment—a week or so as patients in the second-best hospital in Russia.

Seven lines later appears another joke ridiculing *British* socialized medicine:

> In one of the state operated hospitals the practice is followed of indicating the patients' illnesses in the hospital records by certain letters, such as "TB" for tuberculosis. One day one of the younger doctors—a newcomer—was going through the records when his curiosity was aroused by the large number of cases on which the letters "G.O.K." had been written. He went to the head physician and said, "There seems to be a severe epidemic of G.O.K. in this city. What is it, anyhow?" And the older doctor replied, "Oh, that means 'God Only Knows!'"

A full page later, after details of some problems German state medicine is having with "malingering," a crack against the social-political situation in 1939 Nazi Germany appears: "Now, it may be, what with conditions the way they are in Germany today, all those people [going to the hospital] figured that they were a lot safer in a hospital than anywhere else." The next

paragraph continues the "state-medicine-produces-malin-
gerers" argument, including: "'Bottle addicts,' became so numerous that the late Sir Frederick Treves, a famous English
surgeon said that 'The craving for bottles of medicine in England is second only to the craving for bottles of drink.'" A page
later the "malingerer" argument is still being pursued:

> Don't forget that if State Medicine is adopted, you'll pay for
> other people's pleasure. You'll give those who like to talk
> about their operations even more to talk about—you'll
> have to pay for not only the real—but also all the imagined
> illnesses of everybody else—from week-old babies to weak
> old men.

The last humorous item appears in the "state-medicine-pro-
duces-expensive-bureaucracy" argument: "Before we let the
State control medicine, we'd have to put every politician on the
operating table and cut out *his* acquisitive instincts."

Lull reports that, when presented to his groups of student
subjects, the speech containing the above humor elicited from
six to twenty-three instances of laughter. No laughter occurred
during the presentation of the *serious* antistate medicine speech.

The number of laughs which the humorous speeches
received, in contrast to the absence of laughter for the serious
versions, seems adequate proof that the humorous versions
were, indeed, perceived as funny by the student audiences.
However, that was not all the proof of humorousness which
Lull collected. Analysis of the *ratings* of the "humorousness" of
the speeches overwhelmingly supported his contention that
there was a difference in humorousness between the two sets
of speeches. However, the humorous speeches were not found
to differ in average ratings on "interestingness" and "convincingness."

Analysis of the pre- and post-speech attitudes of the subjects revealed that each of the four speeches seems to have been
effective in changing attitude, on the average. However, there
appeared to be no difference in the average amount of attitude
shift produced by the humorous speeches as compared with the
serious speeches, and vice versa.

As a follow-up to the immediate attitude change produced
by hearing the speeches, Lull measured his subjects' attitudes

again three weeks after they had heard these experimental speeches. He found that, during the three week period, the students' attitudes had regressed somewhat toward their original (pre-speech) attitude level (a common finding in studies of this kind), but that each group still showed the persuasive influence of the speech it heard. Also, he found that there was still no difference in attitude between those who had heard the humorous speeches and those who had heard the nonhumorous ones.

Lull's conclusion as a result of his experiment was that it seems to make no difference whether one does or does not use humor in persuasive speaking. The implication for speech teachers, he further implied, is that no blanket rule on whether to use or not use humor in persuasive speaking should be laid down.

Lull's findings were so overwhelmingly "negative" for communication scholars interested in humor, and, in addition, his experiment was so carefully and thoroughly conceived and carried out (it was his doctoral dissertation at the University of Wisconsin), that it apparently discouraged further study of the phenomenon of humor in persuasive discourse for over twenty years.

Donald Kilpela finally performed a similar study for his master's thesis at Wayne State University.[22] Like Lull, Kilpela used speeches on "state medicine." The specific thesis argued in each of his two speeches, one containing humor, the other not, was that "The Federal Government Should Adopt a Program of Socialized Medicine."

The humor used in his funny speech was a series of what I would call "wisecracks," mostly, and a few outrageous puns. Unlike Lull, he used only one example of what I would call a "joke," a narrative with a surprise, funny ending. It occurred almost in the middle of the speech:

> When I was a youngster, a city boy, I used to spend two weeks each summer on the farm. The farm boys always told me that black horses eat more hay than white horses. And, incidentally, this is absolutely true. The reason? More black horses.

The anecdote is offered as an introduction to an attack on AMA statistical reasoning which argues that present U.S. medicine is just fine. I hereby simply list the other instances of humor used by Kilpela, the wisecracks and the puns, in the order in which they appeared in the speech:

> Sounds like the fourth Kennedy-Nixon debate–if you still remember who Nixon is.

> Who knows what may come next? Just last week, Doctor Abe Snake perfected a medicine that will make your hair heavier. Only one hair, of course, but it weighs 28 pounds.

> As your friendly family physician carefully operates on you and your wallet he will undoubtedly tell you that most Americans are perfectly satisfied with the traditional system of medical care. If you object, you are either part of the lunatic fringe or un-American or your name is Khrushchev.

> You cannot tell, furthermore, whether your next sickness will be a five dollar tune-up or a $500 dollar overhaul. You can't tell *when* or how *much*. That is why you attempt to protect yourself with voluntary health insurance of some kind. That is why you delay going to a doctor until they begin looking for the will. That is why you tend to worry about the family plot. That is why you tend to worship the old rugged Blue Cross. This doesn't concern only the poor; it concerns everyone except your friendly family undertaker.

> Even Hollywood has gotten into the act with a new movie—"The Surgeon's Knife" starring Lana Turner's daughter and Johnnie Stompanato.

> Other programs offered by business, labor, and government leaders call the same program by other names such as Compulsory Health Insurance—after the British system of Socialized Medicine—State Medicine—after the Swedish system of Socialized Medicine, medical care for the aged—after the politicians finished compromising, and a variety of euphemisms that essentially mean the same thing—get the AMA!!

> For reasons of necessity, the state has taken over the obligation for the education of our youth. True, you won't find "progressive" education where the students run around in the nude playing fish, but you will find classes where students get hooked into learning how to do the Virginia Reel; Fishical Education 101, a class with a porpoise, and I think it's a whale of an idea.

If medical bills can best produce ulcers, then we turn to Household Finance.

At this rate we ought to save ourselves into bankruptcy. I don't want to say that my doctor is expensive, but he sends me a thank-you note before he sends me the bill.

And notice, complete sentences [of Eisenhower quote].

Of course we cannot overlook the AMA discovery of the three major causes of headache; tension, overwork, and John F. Kennedy.

This plan, a combination of five ingredients, is like a doctor's prescription. Taken immediately it will fight depression fast, relieve medical bills fast, and end paycheck paralysis fast.

Even my doctor wants to go there—for a vacation. He went too. The trip only cost him the price of my tonsillectomy. No, really he went over on Khrushchev's private steamer, as his private physician. Seems that Nikki caught a cold in one foot. The trip didn't cost him a cent—after he sold the story to the C.I.A. He was asked to leave—over the side—when he butted into foreign affairs—Mrs. Khrushchev and the first mate, Fidel Castro. He went along to help Nikki grow a beard—on his head.

The two versions of the speech were tape-recorded, keeping style of "delivery" constant. The results: quite similar to those of Lull—both speeches were found to be persuasive, but the humorous and the nonhumorous were equally persuasive. Again, no superiority for humor-laden persuasive speech was found.

Again, there seems to be a lull in experimentation utilizing humor in persuasive discourse to determine humor's effectiveness in added persuasion. It may be that Lull's negative results, now supported by very similar findings by Kilpela, delayed further similar experimentation. For it was now another ten years later before serious, publishable experimentation on the question of whether humor added to a persuasive speech would add persuasive impact.

Allan J. Kennedy, in his doctoral dissertation,[23] tackled the question of whether humor added to persuasive discourse would add persuasive impact. In his study, he added a few new

"wrinkles" in order to test certain other hypotheses in addition
to his main one about added humor's possibly producing added
persuasiveness.

Kennedy's basic, serious speech was one advocating greater
censorship of movies, on the grounds that they have become
both too violent and too-sex-ridden. To create his "humorous
version" of the speech, Kennedy added a number of wisecracks,
puns, and anecdotes to his "serious" speech. But then he went
one step further: on the assumption that one's potential
response to "humorous stimuli" would depend partly upon the
"set" or "expectancy" he had been led to adopt, Kennedy produced a third version of the speech with a special "laugh-
begging" introduction designed to "tip off" his subjects in
advance that the speech they were about to hear *did* definitely
contain *humor*. That special introduction to the speech he labeled
"Hu2" (for HUmorous speech #2) was worded thusly:

> I hope my presentation this afternoon (evening) is both
> funny and serious. It is supposed to contain a few gags that
> are worth a laugh or two. So, out of respect for my gray
> hairs and my advancing years, if I say anything that sounds
> funny, for Heaven's sake, laugh. Besides from all the
> college lectures I've had to listen to, I've learned one thing.
> If all the people who go to sleep in college classes were laid
> end-to-end—they would be far more comfortable!

The remaining humor, in both the "Hu2" version and the
"regular" humorous version (without the laugh-begging introduction) was scattered throughout. It consisted of a variety of
humorous verbalisms, which are here listed in chronological
order as they appeared in the two humorous speeches:

> The other evening I went to a local movie. About a third
> of the way through the feature a young mother who was
> sitting in front of me with what looked to be her eight-
> year-old daughter, bolted up from her seat and urged her
> daughter to get ready to leave. The film had just revealed a
> scene showing two half undressed women beginning to
> make amorous advances to one another. The mother ex-
> claimed to her little girl, as she rushed her out of the
> theater. "Yes, it's bedtime for everybody! See, those ladies
> are already half undressed!"

You know, the minute someone like me, a college

student majoring in business administration, who has just begun to learn that a college education never hurt anyone willing to learn something—afterwards—begins to talk about why we should again start censoring films, I get all sorts of challenges hurled my way. Especially now that the President's Commission on Obscenity and Pornography has released its report. In fact, it makes me feel a little like Spiro (what's his name)—Agnew.

Movies are really getting strange. The other evening I called the Valentine Theatre for the movie times. The cashier answered the phone with "The movie begins at 7:30. With the orgy scenes at 7:50, 8:10 and 8:30."

Groucho Marx once said, we look upon a censor as a man who knows more than he thinks you ought to.

And, don't forget, France was the country where they originated the phrase, "Movies are bedder than ever."

That reminds me about the story of a college professor who had loaded down his class with enough problems to keep them engaged for several hours. After 15 minutes, a student inquired, "Sir, do you have any more problems?" Somewhat aghast, the instructor queried, "Do you mean you have finished all those I assigned?" "No," answered the student, "I couldn't work any of these, so I thought I might have better luck with some others."

I'm afraid that if couples at the drive-ins ever glanced up at the screen to watch the film they would never again return.

I fully expect that if the trend continues, my children will be viewing films on television like "Son of I a Woman" brought to you by the makers of "I a Woman, Part Fourteen" and "Snow White and the Seven Homosexuals." And after viewing it, I suspect some of them may have some doubts about Snow White, himself.

Why, the other evening, Bob Hope stated that the endings of new Westerns will suggest that when a cowboy rides his horse off into the sunset, it may be the start of a tender new relationship.

What passes for entertainment on a lot of theatre screens today is *a crime.* . . . Now, I realize that no one is going to rush out to kill his mother-in-law just because he saw a violent act performed on the screen. However, movies have gotten so violent, it has been suggested that you should only go with someone you hate.

I suppose I'm just a cynic, but I'm beginning to think movies would be better if they shot less film and more directors.

The only thing that has redeemed some of the violent deaths in our current films, is the fact that more and more actors are dying from pneumonia since they have to make so many films without their clothes on.

Why the other day, I overheard two ten-year-old girls discussing a film they had seen. One girl said, "There was one scene in the picture last Saturday where the girl's father found a contraceptive on their patio." To which the second girl asked, "What's a patio?"

A film reviewer for a local police department recently tried to stop the exhibition of a new flesh flick because the picture contained an extremely graphic orgy scene. The film maker readily defended his film by asking, "What's the matter, haven't you ever seen seven men, four women, and a sheep all madly in love with each other?"

. . . the new sexploitation cinema can claim . . . that it's helping many new actresses become exposed to larger audiences.

Why the films nowadays are so dirty that after reading about them in the "Peach" section of the paper, I almost feel compelled to wash my hands before I eat anything. And after actually seeing a few of them, I usually don't want anything to eat.

Perhaps Art Buchwald is right when he charges that "The major studios are trying to outdo each other making films about revolution, dope, and sex in a desperate effort to attract the two major groups who still go to the movies—young people and dirty old men."

The Commission's Report only proved what I've always known about committees. About the only thing that committees are good for is keeping minutes and wasting hours. One reason why the Ten Commandments are so brief and so concise is the fact that they were issued in a direct manner and were not put through the process of committee action.

. . . these sexploitation theaters only prove that dollars and sense do not necessarily travel together.

As Bob Hope pointed out at last year's Academy Awards, "It's getting so bad that the only time you'll ever see all of the stars in some films fully clothed is at the Academy Awards presentation."

Kennedy used two types of students in his experiment. One was a fairly large class of day students at the University of Toledo, the other a group of older, more mature adult night students at the same institution. He kept the results from these two types of students separate for data analysis.

The subjects responded to the speech they heard by rating it for funniness, by taking an objective examination over its content, by responding to a scale depicting their attitude toward the censorship of movies (a Thurstone-type scale developed for the study), and scales designed to measure the speaker's *ethos*, or "image."

The results? In terms of attitude change elicited by the various versions of the speech, again the results were the same as for Lull and Kilpela. No difference in attitude change due to humor, or when the humor was introduced as "to be expected." Which speeches were perceived as the funniest? In general, the speech introduced *as* funny ("Hu2") *and* containing the humor was judged funniest; the humorous speech *not* introduced as funny was perceived as next funniest. The "serious" speech was perceived and rated as least funny.

The results on the test of information recall over the content of the speech and the ratings of speaker "image" or "ethos" will be discussed more in context in the following chapter. Our main concern here is that, although the humor added to the speech definitely added humorousness to that persuasive speech, and even though introducing the humorous version *as* humorous added to its humorousness rating, no difference seems to have occurred in terms of attitude change.

One important clue to humorous stimuli and its reception seems to be provided by the Kennedy study. Theorists have long and often pointed out that a "play frame" needs to be placed around a particular joke, riddle, cartoon, etc. for maximum enjoyment of it. Kennedy began his "Hu2" speech with just such a verbal "play frame." He gave the audience of that speech a definite expectation that jokes were coming their way, and that they should laugh when they came. The decidedly higher humor ratings given that speech over the same speech without the "play frame" seems to validate the conclusion that that "play frame" is effective in increasing humorousness and, thus, enjoyment.

At about the same time that Kennedy was working on his project, Paul Brandes was working on a similar one at the University of North Carolina. However, he was going about it a bit differently. He was interested in the persuasiveness of different *types* of humor. His findings first found their way to the light of day through a professional convention program.[24]

Brandes began with a "regular" speech entitled "What Every Yale Freshman Should Know." It was already "slightly" humorous, but such "slight" humor was left in for the sake of "normalcy" for the control speech. It was rewritten to bring it more up-to-date, making it more relevant to high school audiences, and to limit it to ten minutes delivery time.

Then three "humorous" versions were made, each with a different "type" of humor added. To one version was added six jokes; to another, twelve puns and plays-on-words were added; to a third, twelve items of "sarcastic humor" were added. The various forms of humor were validated as belonging to the classes named by pretesting procedures. The four speeches were delivered before persons trained in speech. These speech-trained persons rated the humor on its humorousness, its germaneness to the subject matter in which it was imbedded, and its suitability to high school audiences. Based upon these ratings, some changes were made in the humorous items. The items actually used, then, in the three "humorous" versions of the speech, were as follows:

> Your boss may wish to make a show of knowledge, when he knows nothing at all. Mark Twain was invited to be the guest of a rich box-holder at the Metropolitan Opera House to hear "Aida," the humorist's favorite opera. However, his host and hostess talked so much through the performance about how good or poor the singers were and how this opera compared with other operas by Verdi that Twain could not follow the music. As the last curtain descended, his hostess turned to Twain and said effusively, "My dear Mr. Clemens, I hope you can join us again next Thursday evening. The opera is *Tosca* and I'm certain you'll enjoy it." "I'll be delighted," responded Twain. "I have never heard you and your husband in that one before."

When you do know something, there will always be someone who doesn't believe you. For example, there was the somewhat drunk Texan in a bar who said to the bartender, "You know, bartender, I know just about everybody in the world. Why I know old Lyndon Johnson. I know Dickie Nixon. I know just about everybody. I'm good old Tex Thompson from Houston, Texas. Everybody knows me." At the other end of the bar, a fellow got tired of hearing the Texan talk and said, "Aw, you're just drunk. You don't know Lyndon Johnson." "Ok, friend," said Tex Thompson, "let's go over here to the telephone and I'll call old Lyndon up." They do, and greatly to the surprise of the stranger, once Tex gives his name, he gets right through and he and Lyndon have a long conversation. After he hangs up, the doubter says: "Well, you may know Johnson because you're a Texan, but you don't know Nixon." "Sure I do," said Tex Thompson. So he goes to the telephone, asks for the White House, gets right through to Nixon, and has a good conversation with him. By now the doubter is really mad. "Well, you may know Johnson and you may know Nixon, but you don't know the Pope." "Well," said Tex, "the Pope. Sure, I know the Pope, but you can't just call him on the telephone. Tell you what. We'll fly to Rome and you stand in St. Peter's Square, and, if, when the Pope comes out to bless the crowd, I'm standing beside him and he has his arm on my shoulder, will you believe I know just about everybody, including the Pope?" "Sure, but you can't do that." So they get on the plane, and Tex goes off, and the doubter gets there early to St. Peter's Square. Soon the place gets just packed with Italians. Finally, out comes the Pope, and there is Tex Thompson right beside him and the Pope has his arm on Tex's shoulder. The doubter can't believe what he sees. He hits himself on the forehead, pokes the Italian next to him, and says, "Is that really the Pope up there?" "I dunno about the Pope," says the stranger, "but that's Tex Thompson from Houston, Texas, that the fellow with the robe has his arm on."

I am reminded of the story of four Englishmen who entered the same small compartment in a train bound from London to Edinburgh. You know how conservative Englishmen are, so that the train was halfway to Scotland before the silence was broken. Finally, one dignified Englishman put down his *Times* and said as a dare to the others: "I'm Albert Ashley, brigadier general, retired, married, two sons, both clergymen." After a moment, a second dignified Englishman put down his *Times* and said: "I'm William Wooten, brigadier general, retired, married, two

sons, both barristers." Then the third dignified Englishman put down his *Times* and said: "I'm Richard Ralston,
brigadier general, retired, married, two sons, both physicians." Finally, and somewhat slowly, the fourth Englishman put down his *Times*, and said: "I'm 'erbert 'inton,
sergeant-major, retired, never married, two sons, both
brigadier generals."

They [pleasure-seeking-students] are like the patient in
the hospital who said to the doctor: "Doc, when I get well,
will I be able to play the piano?" "Of course," responded the
doctor. "That's really super. I never played it before."

. . . the first three hundred passengers on the first fully-
automated rocket plane flight from New York to Paris had
just taken off, and at 20,000 feet a voice with infinite assur-
ance announced over a loud-speaker: "Ladies and gentlemen, there is no crew on this aircraft, but there is nothing
to worry about. Automation will fly you to Paris at a speed
of twenty-five thousand miles per hour. Everything has
been tested and retested so exhaustingly for your safety
that there is not the slightest chance anything can go
wrong. . . go wrong. . . go wrong. . . go wrong. . ."

Five undergraduate speech students were trained to deliver
the four speeches with minimum delivery differences. They
went to five different high schools in North Carolina and delivered the speeches. High school student subjects responded to
an attitude scale on the thesis of the speeches. They also rated
the sincerity of the speaker toward his topic; and how much
respect the speaker seemed to have for his subject.

Brandes' findings were, in general, in line with the findings of studies previously reported in this chapter. He found no
difference in attitude change favoring the speeches containing
humor; further, he found no one "type" of humor added more
or less persuasiveness than any other did. In fact, the high
school age subjects seemed to have difficulty in distinguishing
between types of humor at all. An additional finding is en-
lightening: the student subjects did not find the speakers using
various forms of humor to be any more or less "sincere" or
"respectful" regarding their speech topics.

Again, the generalization seems to be: adding humor does
not seem to hurt or help one's potential for persuading.

One somewhat different study utilizing humorous material
imbedded in an otherwise straightforward persuasive speech
should be considered in this section. Charles Gruner and

William Lampton became intrigued by the question of what would occur as a result of the inclusion of humorous material in a persuasive *sermon*.[25] After all, no such study appeared to exist, and "common sense" indicates that, usually the sermon which contains some humor seems to be more appreciated by congregations than is the humorless one.

The experimenters began with a sermon once delivered by the Reverend Roy Pearson, currently President of Andover Newton Theological School, Newton Centre, Massachusetts. The sermon was published in the June, 1962, issue of *Think* magazine. It argued that the Bible should be read carefully by anyone regardless of his religious faith (including *none*) for a variety of reasons. The experimenters found a total of eight humorous items which they felt were appropriate to the sermon material in which they could be embedded.

The humorous version of the sermon began with the following anecdote:

> My sermon today is on the Bible. And whenever I decide to speak on the Bible, I am reminded of that story about the minister who left his Bible upon his pulpit, lying open to the passage he intended to quote during services. A mischievous boy, discovering the open Bible before the services, glued two pages together. The minister, then, when he came to the scripture reading, read: "When Noah was one hundred and twenty years old, he took unto himself a wife, who was . . ." Then turning the page . . . "one hundred forty cubits long, sixty cubits wide, built of gopher wood, and covered inside and out with pitch." The minister blinked, then said to his congregation: "I never came across this in the Bible before, but I accept it as evidence that we are fearfully and wonderfully made."

Three paragraphs later appears a crack about ministers, comparing them to "literary" masterpieces:

> He is very much like the poor parishioner who complained about his minister. What was wrong with his minister? He was invisible during the week, and incomprehensible on Sundays.

The next paragraph claims that even agnostics or atheists should read the Bible, and *defines* an atheist:

> Of course, we know what an atheist is. He is a man with no *invisible* means of support. Or, as a tombstone once pro-

claimed: "Here lies an atheist, all dressed up and nowhere to go!"

About one-third the way through the speech the next humorous item appears. Pointing out that an essential part of an education is knowledge of the Bible, the paragraph ends:

> And we all want to appear educated. Which can become a cause of embarrassment if it is claimed and not achieved. A minister once began a sermon by announcing that he was going to preach that day on the subject of "lying," and, therefore, was taking his text from the 17th chapter of St. Mark. Then he paused, and directly asked the members of his congregation to raise their right hands if they were familiar with the 17th chapter of Mark. Practically every right hand in the church went up. The minister then observed: "There happen to be only 16 chapters in St. Mark. Now I will proceed with my sermon on 'Lying.'"

A page later, the same theme of "knowledge of the Bible is valuable education" is still pursued, ending with this humor:

> A thorough knowledge of the Bible might even save one from possible embarrassment. Why, just the other day I saw a bumper sticker with a bit of modern graffiti that would be incomprehensible without an understanding of Biblical lore. It read: "Jesus saves. Moses invests." And not long ago I overheard two boys talking after Sunday School. One said, "Gee, before I started Sunday School and reading the Bible and all, I thought Sodom and Gomorrah were brother and sister." The other replied, "That's nothing. I thought the epistles were the wives of the apostles."

Just before a five-word admonition to heed the sermon's thesis ("Avoid embarrassment. Read your Bible."), appeared the final humorous passage:

> Such ignorance of the Bible reminds me of the story of the Sunday School teacher who asked little Johnny, "Who tore down the walls of Jericho?" Johnny replied quickly, "Honest, Teacher, I didn't do it!" Amused, the teacher later told her supervisor, "I asked Johnny who tore down the walls of Jericho, and he said he didn't do it." The supervisor answered: "I've known Johnny all his life, and if he says he didn't do it, he didn't." Amused still further, the teacher related the story later to the minister: "I asked Johnny who tore down the walls of Jericho and he said he didn't do it. I told my supervisor, Mrs. Smith, about the incident and she

said that if Johnny said he didn't do it, he didn't." The minister replied: "Mrs. Smith is a fine judge of character. If she vouches for Johnny, he probably did *not* do it."

Before actually deciding upon their use in the sermon, the senior author actually "test-marketed" the humorous items in one of his college speech classes to see if they drew laughter from students. They did, and so were used in the humorous version of the sermon. A colleague, a former minister and still practicing part-time minister, agreed to record the sermon before a live audience.

Two speech classes were brought together, and the speaker delivered the speech before them; it was tape-recorded, along with the resultant laughter. This tape-recorded speech was the "humorous" version; a nonhumorous version was completed by retaping the original electronically and editing out the humor and the recorded laughter thereto.

Speech students heard one or the other version of the sermon over earphones in the department's speech laboratory at the University of Georgia. Students were randomly chosen to hear one or the other version by alternately flicking switches keying them in to one or the other master tape in the control room. After hearing one or the other version of the sermon the students were asked to reply to a Likert-type attitude scale measuring their attitude toward Bible-reading, and to other scales rating the sermon on its humorousness and the speaker on aspects of his "image."

As with the other studies thus far reported in this chapter, the addition of the humor to the sermon cannot be said to have increased (or decreased) that sermon's persuasiveness. And this finding resulted even though the humorous version of the speech was rated obviously higher in "funniness" than was the nonhumorous version. That is, the difference in funniness was perceived, but it made no apparent persuasive impact.

The results of the ratings on speaker "image" will be considered, more appropriately, in the next chapter.

Another recent study of humor's effect in an otherwise straightforward persuasive speech was conducted by Welford.[26] He was interested in the usefulness of humor in a speech of refutation delivered immediately following an opponent's speech.

He used two tape-recorded political speeches, supposedly a "radio debate" between two anonymous candidates for the same State Senate seat. The first speech, by the incumbent, dealt with the issues of: (1) his experience; (2) his stand for better state roads; (3) his position in favor of federal revenue sharing; (4) the money he saved the state last year; (5) his opposition to wire-tapping; and (6) his assertion that he had done nothing for the state's homes for the aged because they were already doing an excellent job.

The "Senator's" opponent spoke to each of these issues. In the "serious" version, no jokes were used; in the humorous version, one joke accompanied each issue but one.

To counter the "Senator's" experience, the second speaker claimed to not even be a politician, then said:

> I'm reminded of the story of the father who wanted to know what his son was going to be when he grew up. So he put the Bible, a ten-dollar bill, and a glass of whiskey on a table, then left the room. If the boy drank the whiskey, he would be no good; if he took the money, he would be a banker; if he took the Bible, he would probably do religious work. When the boy looked around and saw no one, he drank the whiskey, put the ten-dollar bill in his pocket, tucked the Bible under his arm, and left the room. His father exclaimed, "Oh, no! He's going to be a politician!"

He agreed that the state's roads were "a nightmare," but countered;

> It's not quite as bad as the nightmare that grandpa had the other night, however. He said he dreamed that grandma and Raquel Welch were fighting over him, and grandma won!

However, the second speaker argued that the "Senator" would have to raise taxes to repair the roads, and that the "Senator's" scheme of "just putting pressure" on the highway department was a useless proposal, adding:

> Such a proposal reminds me of a plan devised by two morons I heard about. It seems that they had been in prison for some time. One day one turned to the other and said: I'm tired of this place. I've got a plan to escape. Tonight we'll sneak behind the barracks, I'll get a flashlight, turn it on and flash the beam up against the wall. You climb up the

beam and go over. The other fellow looked at him and said: "You think I'm nuts, don't you? I know what you'll do. I'll get halfway up the beam and you'll turn the light off!"

The refuter had no joke regarding federal revenue sharing, but compared the "Senator's" claim for saving the state three million dollars to something else:

> His claim reminds me of a conversation I heard the other day between two young men. One of them held out his hand and said: "See this? I'm going to give it to my girl-friend." The other one replied: "Why, there's nothing in your hand." "Oh, yes," said the first, "It's an invisible birth-control pill. If she'll swallow that, she'll swallow anything!"

He next defended wire-tapping as not mere "snooping," ending with a joke:

> Fear of such snoopings are [*sic*] kinda like a little boy I read about. The Associated Press recently carried the report of the floor nurse in a Salt Lake City hospital. She was trying to speak via the intercom to a patient in the children's ward—to a youngster who had never been hospitalized before and was unfamiliar with the electronic device. After several attempts failed to produce an answer from the child's room, the nurse spoke rather firmly, "Answer me, Jimmy. I know you're in there." A few seconds later, a tiny quivering voice responded, "Wh—wh—what do you wa—wa—want, wall?"

Refuting the "Senator's" claim that the state's nursing homes are excellent is a statement not coinciding with the facts, the second speaker told another joke:

> Speaking of not coinciding with the facts, a group of tech-nicians was trying to sell a computer to a businessman and they said: "Ask it a question—any question." He thought for a moment and said, "All right, ask the machine where my father is." After the usual spinning of wheels and flash-ing of lights the answer was typed out: "This man's father is at this moment teeing off on the golf course at the Greenbriar Country Club." "Well," the businessman said with some sarcasm, "There may be a golf course in heaven, but I doubt that they call it the Greenbriar. My father is dead." This information was typed into the computer and in a few moments another answer was typed out: "The husband of this man's mother is dead. But his father is at

this moment walking down the first fairway on the Green-
briar Golf Course!"

Then, after telling the following joke,

> A few years ago, after some bantering between the sexes in
> Congress, Margaret Chase Smith was asked: "What would
> you do if you woke up one morning and found yourself in
> the White House?" "I would go to the President's wife and
> apologize, and then leave at once!"

he demands that the "Senator" apologize for giving bad government in the past.

Subjects were tested on their attitude toward each of the
"content" issues in the debate. There were no differences in
attitude between those hearing the serious speech and those
hearing the humorous speech on any issue except those of
federal revenue sharing and wiretapping. And the evidence sup-
ports the *serious* refutational speech as being superior to the
humorous speech on these issues. Mr. Welford suggests that
whether the use of humor affects persuasion (or, refutation)
might depend upon the particular issue being argued.

The results of the ratings on speaker "image" will be considered, more appropriately, in the next chapter.

It is apparent from the review of studies in this chapter
thus far that humor has been found to have very little effect, if
any, on the persuasiveness of messages. Of course, failure to
find in an experiment of this kind a certain effect does not mean
that that effect has not occurred. It simply means that, if it *did*
occur, it was not detected with the particular experimental procedures employed. Perhaps the test measuring attitude was not
sensitive enough or reliable enough; perhaps the statistical
techniques used were not "powerful" enough; perhaps in any
one experiment there was too little, or too much, or not
germane enough humor. Persons sophisticated in the techniques of social science experimentation are quite aware that
any one of several dozen faults in experimental design, execution, or measuring devices can account for the finding of "no
significant differences."

However, here we have six studies conducted indepen-
dently, each with the same finding of "no persuasive effect from
humor." Three of these studies used live speakers, three used

recorded speeches. A variety of attitude measures was used. Different groups of student subjects were used for the various experiments. The kinds of humor used varied considerably, and so on. And still the six studies came up with the same negative finding. When an experimenter is confronted with the same negative findings from six different experiments, he begins to believe that maybe there is nothing to be found in further experiments using that hypothesis.

Theoretically, of course, there is no really good reason to think that humor *would* enhance a serious, persuasive message. Humor, especially that closest to the "humor" end of the continuum between it and "wit" discussed in the last chapter, is primarily intended to entertain, not persuade; it is more akin to poetic than to rhetoric. It is meant to delight, to please, to release one from tension. It is not meant to motivate one to believe or act in a particular way.

And if one will go back and reread the items of humor included in the speeches used in the five studies reviewed thus far in this chapter, he would, I think, have to conclude that the bulk of these humorous items more nearly fit the "humor" end of the continuum than they would the "wit" end. Some of the items, of course, have a bit of witty bite to them, but the majority are clearly jesting and "in fun."

The usual attempt at persuasion is quite a serious task. The speaker attempts to arouse emotion, but not that of laughter. He may hope to arouse indignation, pity, anger, hope, or fear; he knows that only those who are aroused out of their apathy and who become *motivated* will bother to change their minds or commit themselves to action. To bring in the emotion of laughter, of joy, may be, as Grimes has been quoted earlier, to cause an *interruption* in the process of achieving persuasion.

But what, then, of wit? Might it not be expected, theoretically, to be more useful as persuasion? Certainly, if wit is strongly related to rhetoric, it probably should aim to achieve persuasion. Certainly political satirists, whether their medium is the satirical editorial or the editorial cartoon, hope to sway and mold public opinion on both issues and personalities.

The bulk of the rest of this chapter is devoted to summarizing the experimental studies designed and executed to test the persuasive value of satire, that form of wit most usually regarded as persuasive by at least some literati.

The earliest known study of the persuasive power of what could be called satire was one done by A.D. Annis.[27] He was interested in comparing the persuasive effectiveness of editorial cartoons with that of direct editorials. He provided few details in his brief one paragraph report, but in general asserts that straight editorials seemed to have influenced more people than did editorial cartoons.

A couple of years later R. Asher and S. Sargent[28] studied the effectiveness of cartoon *caricatures*. They did not use "whole" editorial cartoons, but secured their hand-drawn caricatures *from* such cartoons. The caricatures selected were of such as "Uncle Sam, Labor, Mussolini, Pacifists, New Deal, John Bull, Private Initiative, Agitator, Business man, Alien, Politics, Liberals, Industry," and so forth.

Fifty terms were read off to student subjects, one term at a time, at five-second intervals. The subjects were asked to record on blank forms their immediate reaction to the word. Checking "LD" was to mean "like definitely," "LM" was to mean "like moderately," "?" was to mean neutral reaction or don't know, "DM" was to mean "dislike moderately," and "DD" was to mean "dislike definitely." A total of 185 students recorded their reactions to the 50 terms. Then they were shown a group of caricatures at five-second intervals and asked to record their reactions to them on fresh blank forms.

The responses of the 185 students to each term for which there was a corresponding caricature were averaged (with + 2 score for LD, + 1 for LM, 0 for ?, −1 for DM, and −2 for DD). The responses to the corresponding caricatures were also averaged. These average responses to term and corresponding caricature were compared statistically. Significant differences between average reaction to word and caricature occurred on eight concepts: Labor, Uncle Sam, Pacifists, John Bull, Industry, New Deal, Politics, and Liberals. Further analysis of responses indicated that, the more the student paid attention to the *visual* components of the caricature (rather than its *name*), the greater the change in his response to it in contrast to that of the term.

It might be argued that simply collecting marks on a

continuum from "Dislike Definitely" to "Like Definitely" and comparing these responses to a term and a caricature of the concept named by that term is not exactly a demonstrated "shift in attitude" as claimed by Asher and Sargent. However, it does seem to be a clear demonstration that a caricature can call forth an immediate emotional reaction different from that called forth by its name alone. And that is the purpose of caricature, it seems to me.

In general, Asher and Sargent's findings were somewhat supported by an experiment conducted at the University of Indiana by Del Brinkman.[29] He was interested in what various combinations of editorial cartoon and straightforward editorial would be the most effective in changing attitudes. Using two cartoons and four editorials, he exposed students, through booklets, to various combinations of cartoon and editorial. I summarize and paraphrase his findings below.

1. More opinion change occurs when an editorial cartoon is presented with a complementary editorial than occurs when either is presented alone.

2. More opinion change is produced by an editorial alone than a cartoon alone.

3. It is more effective to present the editorial and the cartoon together, rather than first one, then the other. But presenting the cartoon first and the editorial second is more effective than vice versa.

4. More opinion change occurred when both the editorial and the cartoon "argued" the same main point; if one argued the "main" point and the other argued an ancillary point, the effect on opinion was less.

It would appear that the practical advice to be drawn by newspaper editors from this study is to place the editorial cartoon arguing the same main point as the editorial close together on the page. However, this advice would only work if the cartoonist and the editorial writer cooperated closely (and often they never even meet, physically); the advice would only be worthwhile if readers would notice the cartoon, study it, and then read the accompanying editorial. Probably very few members of a paper's readership would actually take the time to do this.

A study by LeRoy Carl has even cast doubt on the belief that "editorial cartoons are easy to understand—easier than the written word," even if and when they are observed in the newspaper.[30] Carl found a very large communication gap between cartoonists and small town citizens.

He secured a large number of editorial cartoons by various cartoonists that were clearly "timely." He then secured from the creator of each cartoon exactly what thesis he, the creator, had intended to be drawn from the cartoon. These cartoons were then shown to random samples of people in two small towns. One was Candor, New York, a community used by Arthur J. Vidich and Joseph Bensman as typical of U.S. small towns in *Small Town in Mass Society.*[31] The other was Canton, Pennsylvania. If a person gave as the thesis of the cartoon exactly what the author claimed as its thesis, the response was graded "A." If the answer indicated that the respondent understood only some part of the author's meaning, it was scored "B." If the respondent failed to see the meaning of the author at all, his response was graded "C."

In these two small towns Carl found that only about 15 percent of the people were in accord with the cartoonists; another 15 percent were partly in accord; fully 70 percent completely misunderstood the cartoons!

One cartoon showed several large black birds, each labeled "Jim Crow," heading North. Instead of seeing the cartoonist's point that "bigotry is increasing in the North," most people interpreted the cartoon as meaning that "many Southern Negroes are migrating to the North." A cartoon showing then President Johnson being warmly greeted as he arrived in Manila was judged by many as a Philippine snub of the President.

On the assumption that a more literate, educated community would respond more accurately to the cartoons, the study was replicated in Ithaca, New York. Ithaca is dominated by Cornell University and contains people with a very high average educational level. The results were better, but not by much: 22 percent of the responses agreed with the cartoonist, 15 percent were in partial agreement, but still, 63 percent missed the points entirely. Carl puts part of the blame on the

general public's apparent inability to understand editorial
cartoons:

> it is believed that many forces are at work within individu-
> als "scrambling" the messages, which might not always be
> clearly "sent" by the cartoonists in the first place. One's
> ability to perceive details, his ethnic background, environ-
> ment, psychological set, knowledge of current events and
> history, ability to see analogies, knowledge of allegories,
> and so on, play a role in interpreting editorial cartoons.
>
> The simple size of an elephant may make a cartoon
> appear Republican in one woman's eyes. The angry, sad, or
> happy expression on a donkey may convey meaning to one
> man, yet go unnoticed by another.

But the cartoonists can be at fault, too:

> But the "fault" lies not only with the audience. One car-
> toonist apologized for his poor analogy, while another was
> embarrassed by the diverse, surprising, and even opposite
> meaning engendered by his creation.

Some "message" cartoons may be misunderstood by some
people simply because of prejudice. Eunice Cooper and Marie
Jahoda[32] have reported that, after a number of studies of how
prejudiced people react to antiprejudice propaganda, a number
of "defense mechanisms" are brought into play by bigots when
faced with antibigotry cartoons. Some of their studies were
done for the Department of Scientific Research of the American
Jewish Committee by the Bureau of Applied Social Research of
Columbia University.

Cooper and Jahoda point out that most prejudiced people
avoid antiprejudice messages, in cartoon or in other forms, by
the simple expedient of not exposing themselves to them. It is a
well-known fact that Republicans listen to Republican speakers,
Democrats listen to Democrats, and only the already-educated
attend to educational radio and TV programs. But: what do
bigots do when *involuntarily* confronted with antibigotry
propaganda?

> There are, theoretically, two possibilities: they may fight
> it or they may give in to it. But our research in this field has
> shown us that many people are unwilling to do either: they

prefer not to face the implications of ideas opposed to their
own so that they do not have to be forced either to defend
themselves or to admit error. What they do is to evade the
issue psychologically by *simply not understanding the message.*

For instance, they can make the message invalid, either
through distortion or by taking the propaganda as "just a
story."

> This technique was used in a broadcast dramatization,
> "The Belgian Village," presented on the CBS series, "We
> the People." In the story, a Jewish couple in an occupied
> Belgian Village are saved by the loyal support of the
> villagers who hide them from the Gestapo. The dramati-
> zation was followed by a direct appeal, spoken by Kate
> Smith, for sympathy and tolerance toward the Jews. Con-
> siderably more of the apparently prejudiced respondents
> than of the others in the test audience refused to admit the
> applicability of this dramatic story to other situations. They
> called it an "adventure story," a "war story," they dis-
> cussed the dramatic highlights with great interest, but
> treated the explicit appeal attached to the incident either as
> if it had not occurred or as an unjustified artificial addition.

A prejudiced person can transform a cartoon's meaning by
changing the frame of reference; in fact, he can change the
meaning to conform to his own beliefs. A cartoon of a crooked
congressman hiring a crook for "his new party" is interpreted
by an anti-Semite as the beginning of a "Jewish party" that will
"help the Jews get more power."

Some prejudiced people simply state that the "message is
too difficult," which is certainly one means of avoiding that
message; and often they may be correct in their assertion. But
many also see the message and instantaneously recognize its
thesis, but then "derail" their understanding by avoiding iden-
tification. For instance, one series of studies utilized a cartoon
character called Mr. Biggott. He was pictured as prudish and
ridiculous, with antiminority feelings quite exaggerated. In one
cartoon he was pictured in a hospital bed, with a doctor in
attendance, about to get a blood transfusion. He tells the doctor
that he wants only "sixth generation American blood." One
bigot "got the point" immediately, but then in discussion of the
cartoon gradually deprecated Mr. Biggott so that he was per-

ceived as quite unlike the prejudiced viewer of the cartoon. One chap drew an unfavorable comparison between himself and "Mr. Biggott" because the latter was *only* sixth generation American while he, himself, was *eighth* generation American!

Another study of cartoon recognition was recently undertaken by Dr. Kathy Kendall and one of her classes at the State University of New York college at Albany. This field study, results of which are yet unpublished, found that some editorial cartoons adequately communicate their messages (but, by no means 100% of the time), whereas one cartoon used was widely misunderstood. This latter cartoon involved George McGovern, who was often mistaken in the piece for Richard Nixon. It was considered possible that the difficulty of caricaturing Mr. McGovern was responsible for the ambiguity.

This is the spot at which seems to rest the status of research into political (which is to say, persuasive) cartoons. A definite potential seems to exist for persuasive effectiveness in the cartoon medium, (*a*) if the cartoons are encountered and understood, and (*b*) especially, if they are coupled with direct editorial propaganda advocating the same view as the cartoons. However, because of their subtlety and their ambiguity, editorial cartoons are quite likely to be misunderstood, either through ignorance, training, lack of perception or education or information, or simply through use of psychological defense mechanisms. It is obvious that a great deal of research is needed before much certainty of the persuasive role of "message" cartoons in our culture will exist.

The last group of studies considered in this chapter are those that have dealt with more verbal forms of satire. Written satire, as has been said earlier, is primarily intended to entertain, with a secondary purpose, usually, to persuade. The relative importance of these two purposes seems to be opposite those of editorial or political cartoons: the cartoons' main intent is to persuade; secondarily, they may be expected to entertain. For instance, the first study to be taken up in this section is one by David Berlo and Hideya Kumata;[33] the stimulus used was a one-hour radio drama produced by the Canadian Broadcasting Corporation. The radio program was blatantly satiric in theme and tone, but it would be hard to imagine that the CBC went to the elaborate trouble to cast their satiric message in the dramatic form unless the entertainment value of the drama were not a primary desideratum.

Transcripts of the radio program are not available, so the plot, as described by the authors of the study, is included here. As can be seen, it is primarily a satire of Senator Joe McCarthy, late junior senator from Wisconsin, and, secondarily, a satire of congressional investigations.

> Briefly, the plot of "The Investigator" concerns the activities of an investigator who, after being killed in a plane crash, is presented for entry to heaven (referred to as "Up here."). He finds that he first must pass the scrutiny of the "Head Gatekeeper" and be examined by the "Permanent Investigating Committee on Permanent Entry." Members of this Committee (Cotton Mather, Torquemada, Judge Jeffreys, and Titus Oates) conspire with the Investigator in removing the "Head Gatekeeper" from the committee by accusing him of laxness of duty in permitting the entrance of many subversives. In disposing of the Gatekeeper, the Investigator twists casual remarks into what appear to be explicit admissions of guilt.
>
> After removal of the Gatekeeper, the Investigator is appointed chairman of the committee. He suspends all new applications for entry and embarks on an investigation of the "subversive" elements in heaven. As a result of his investigations, Socrates, Thomas Jefferson, John Milton, Voltaire, John Stuart Mill, Martin Luther, Spinoza, Chopin, Wagner and others are deported "Down there." In all instances the actual writings (or other works) of these men are used as the basis of deportation. The Investigator's criteria of subversive activity are highly, and obviously, distorted. For example, Chopin is deported because he composed "The Revolutionary Etude." Finally, the Investigator decides to subpoena "The Chief" himself, and is rebuffed as "having gone too far." The inhabitants of Heaven realize that his methods are too dangerous to be permitted, and his power is stripped from him. The Investigator suffers a mental breakdown, muttering that *he* is "The Chief." He is deported "Down there" but the Devil refuses him entry, and he is returned to earth.
>
> Senator McCarthy is never mentioned by name, but as Gould has pointed out, "the voice of 'The Investigator' is so similar to the Senator's that it is hard to believe that it isn't Mr. McCarthy himself."

A recording of "The Investigator" was used in the experiment. Forty-five junior and senior journalism and advertising students at the University of Illinois were in the experimental group exposed to the recording. Thirty-seven other such students served as control subjects, and did not hear the recorded program.

All subjects filled out the pretest forms, which included:

1. Semantic differential attitude scales tapping attitude toward Socrates, Jefferson, Milton, MacKenzie, Senator McCarthy, congressional investigations, the Canadian Broadcasting Corporation, and security clearances.

2. Nine items from the California F scale found to measure a person's "authoritarianism."

3. Two other F scale items measuring what was called "Americanism;" what they actually measured was the person's evaluation of foreign people and ideas.

4. Background information, such as sex, religious preference, and political affiliation.

The post-test for the experimental subjects, conducted immediately after hearing the recorded program, consisted of the eight attitude scales again, plus six open-end questions they were to answer by writing in their replies. They were asked to identify the main character in the program, to describe the plot, write down the moral to be drawn, the intent of the program's author, and the desirability of publicly distributing the program on U.S. radio stations. The control subjects, who did not hear the program, merely responded to the attitude items for a second time.

It was determined from the pretest attitude scores on the eight concepts that the experimental group and control group did not differ in their mean attitude toward any of the eight concepts. It was felt, therefore, that these groups represented samples drawn from the same population. A positive, favorable or neutral attitude was reflected in the scales toward all concepts except "Senator McCarthy," whose ratings were unfavorable.

All forty-five experimental subjects correctly identified "The Investigator" in the drama as Senator McCarthy. Twenty-six, in answering the question of the dramatist's intent, identi-

fied it as an attack on Senator McCarthy; eight subjects identified it as an attack on congressional investigations in general;
nine subjects wrote that it showed the importance of individual
rights by attacking the dangers of excessive centralization of
power. Two subjects failed to answer this question.

Their major findings with regard to attitude change were
the following:

1. The only concept toward which the attitudes of the experimental group changed a statistically significant amount was
that of "congressional investigations." Attitude became less
favorable toward this concept.

2. Attitude became less favorable toward two other concepts, Canadian Broadcasting Corporation and "security clearances," but not to an extent that would meet the usual criteria
for statistical significance. The change for each was significant
at the 10 percent level, however.

3. Attitude toward Senator McCarthy, contrary to one
hypothesis of the experimenters, actually *improved*, though very
little and not a statistically significant amount. The experimenters indicate that this is a possible "boomerang" effect
caused by the "unfairness" of the satire and Americans' general
tendency to stand up for the underdog. My own inclination is to
dismiss the slight change as due to statistical regression; the
control group regressed the very same way.

These were the major results of concern to this chapter; the
authors of the article performed several more sophisticated
statistical analyses of their data, and make quite a few speculations about the causes for their results. The interested reader is
advised to consult Berlo and Kumata's original report.

The next study to be considered in this section is the one I
did for my doctoral dissertation, and which was later published
in article form.[34] At the time the study was conducted, the
academic year of 1962–63, there was very little published
research on the effects of humor or wit in terms of persuasion.
The Lull and Kilpela studies were completed, of course, but each
had utilized public speeches containing primarily *humor*, not
wit—and certainly no satire. The Asher and Sargent study
utilizing cartoon caricatures was published, and so was the Berlo and Kumata study just reviewed, which used a radio drama.

But up to the time of the Gruner doctoral study, no published experiments involving a purely satirical public speech as the experimental stimulus existed.

For this experiment I wrote a speech satirizing the idea of censorship. The speech urged with mock seriousness that, since they are so inherently and excessively obscene and violent, we ought to censor *nursery rhymes*. The general technique used throughout the speech was irony, a technique carefully analyzed from a rhetorical standpoint by Allan Karstetter.[35] According to his specific classification, the experimental speech would be classified as "Discrepancy between inner thought and outward expression; perception of the discrepancy intended." In other words, the speech said one thing while meaning just the opposite; and the intention was that the auditors would perceive that opposite, inner thought. The speech was entitled, "A Demure Proposal," and is included here in full.

A Demure Proposal

Ladies and Gentlemen:

As professor Harold HIll, the 'Music Man' has said (or rather, sung), 'We got trouble . . . we got a whole lot of trouble' these days, and I mean trouble with the growing problem of juvenile delinquency. It seems that the entire younger generation has lost any respect for authority it ever had. And, if you will just pay some serious attention to our mass media—our movies, television, magazines and paperback novels—I think you will find it not too difficult to see *why* our young people are what they are. The violence, obscenity, and leftist propaganda in our entertainment media these days are enough to corrupt good upbringing in any youngster.

Some well-meaning citizens would fight the problem with strict government censorship of movies, television, and printed material. This is undoubtedly an excellent idea, but I am convinced that such censorship, needed as it is, is inadequate. It does not go far enough; it does not reach deeply enough to be completely effective. For our children are brought up in an atmosphere *saturated* with fictional violence and depravity from a very early age. And they receive this corrupting influence, not from Hollywood or New York, but at their mothers' knees! I am speaking, ladies and gentlemen, of that insidious literature we innocently call *Nursery Rhymes*.

A preposterous charge, you say? You think that nursery rhymes can have nothing in common with, say *The Untouchables*? Look at some examples with me.

Take, for instance, 'Rock-a-bye, Baby'. What happens to the innocent babe of this little horror story? You know how it ends: down comes the baby, cradle and all, crashing to the ground from the treetops! Now, isn't that a lovely little ditty to croon to your pre-school child? Isn't that a pretty image with which to send him off to beddy bye!

Look at another example: 'Humpty Dumpty'. He stupidly falls from a high wall to a death gory enough to turn the stomach. But what then? Do they sweep the carcass into a rubber sack for a decent Christian burial? No! These men and horses try to paste the sticky mess back together again! Now, I ask you: just how revolting can you get? After enough of this kind of horror should we be surprised when six-year-olds occasionally dissect a playmate?

These two cases are not isolated examples either. Nursery rhymes abound in violence, sadism, and deviant behavior. There's 'Georgie Porgie', who kissed the girls against their wishes, making them cry (sound like a future sex offender?). But this Georgie is so cowardly he runs when the other boys come out to play. There's 'Tom, Tom the Piper's Son', who stole a pig and away he run. There is the brutal story of the attempt to *bake alive* four and twenty blackbirds, one of whom retaliates upon the person of an honest maid by biting off her nose in the garden. In the story of the brutal bow-and-arrow slaying of 'Cock Robin', the Fish freely admits to catching the murder victim's *blood* in a dish! Again, I ask: how long can we allow our children's minds to be poisoned by this trash?

What must little children think when they hear of the farmer's wife sadistically cutting off the tails of three defenseless, blind mice? How will they feel toward 'Little Johnny Green' who threw 'Pussy in the Well' down there in 'Ding Dong Dell'? Will they condone the crime of 'Peter', the pumpkin eater, who apparently killed his wife and stuffed her corpse into a pumpkin shell simply because he could not afford to keep her?

Perhaps you have been wondering why youngsters today seem to be so lazy, shiftless, and irresponsible? They're probably just emulating another nursery rhyme hero. 'Little Boy Blue', who slept away under a haystack while the cows and sheep he was supposed to be tending ate away at his father's corn and meadow.

I haven't the time now to discuss with you the murky Freudian implications underlying the story of 'Jack and Jill'. You remember that they went *up* a hill supposedly in search of water, when anyone knows that water is found in *low* places. But I would ask you to ponder what sort of ideals are being suggested to our kids by that mysterious woman who lives in the house shaped like a *shoe*. She apparently lives off relief and the Aid to Dependent Children handout—but you will notice there is *not one mention of a husband*!

Do you begin to see *now* the extent to which our children are exposed to objectionable material? Is it not shocking to realize that all this garbage is taught them by their mothers and nursemaids?

By now you are probably wondering what can be done about this menace.

The protection of our young people demands that we rid our nurseries of the despicable influence of so-called nursery rhymes. Nothing less than a nationwide ban on their printing, with penalties of fines and jail terms for their publication would be adequate. In addition, mothers, nursemaids, and others having intimate contact with our toddlers must be educated, then *warned* against the repetition of such trash. After a suitable time, punishment for recitation of nursery rhymes would be imposed. A motto of the John Birch Society says, 'If Mommy is a Commie, you gotta turn her in'; for mommies who tell nursery rhymes to children, our motto might well be, 'If Mother goes and "Mother Gooses", she'll pay in one of our calabooses'.

After we successfully stamp out nursery rhymes, we can forge on to the wide and fertile field of children's literature. Mrs. Thomas J. White of Indiana has shown the way for us here. Mrs. White was part of a state committee to investigate school library books. As far as I know, she is the first to decry the communistic undertones of that famous children's classic, 'Robin Hood.' The concept of robbing the rich to give to the poor is a technique for creating a classless society right out of Marx and Engels!

And while we're about it, let us take note of how far this Robin Hood lives outside of his cultural norms. He lives, you remember, not in a house, but in the woods. Not only does he scorn the solid responsibilities of home ownership, but he is a bachelor, as are all his band. And, do they work? Of course not. They make a living breaking the fish and game laws!

One of Robin's top henchmen is Friar Tuck. Although a Church cleric, you would not want your son or daughter to take him as a model of religious piety. For he would much rather bash in heads with his trusty stave than read from the Good Book. And you *know* whom he most enjoys bashing—the Sheriff!

One could go on and on with the objectionable episodes

and nuances of Robin Hood and like stories; for instance, there's the unseemly number of times the unchaperoned Maid Marian manages to slip off to see Robin Hood—*in the woods*—but I'm sure you see my point now.

Ladies and gentlemen, the time to move against these pernicious forces in our society is now. We must launch a new crusade—a crusade of the spirit. Even as we sit here, some innocent child is being twisted and warped by the horrors of 'Mother Goose'; his older brother is learning utter rebellion from Robin Hood; and Daddy sits entranced watching the blonde singer–moll caught in the machine-gun crossfire between Eliot Ness and Frank Nitti's boys.

The battle must begin. And we will not find it easy, for censorship has enemies everywhere. Those of low taste and vicious character will fight us every step. It will be an uphill battle all the way. But this is a battle we must fight; and it is a battle we must win. For, even though the corrupt are strong, their vice cannot stand against the might of our righteousness; we must blast the enemy from their entrenchments; we must engage them on the open barren ramparts; we must strike them down as they run for cover; we must *kick* and *beat* and *grind* and *stomp* them until they are defeated utterly. For only then can we sweep into oblivion the befouling influence of nursery rhymes.

Since the stimulus speech was "home-made," it became necessary to validate it *as* a piece of satire. Several full and partial definitions of "satire" were secured from a variety of dictionaries. These were mimeographed, along with definitions for some other concepts, such as "persuasion," "invective," "philippic," and "oration." Mimeographed copies of the speech and the definitions were given to the faculty members of the English department at St. Lawrence University, Canton, New York. They were asked to read the speech and then to check which definitions or partial definitions they felt, based upon their professional judgment, fit the speech. They were also asked to write, in their own words, what they thought was the thesis or central idea of the speech. The data from this procedure overwhelmingly supported the assumption that the speech was perceived by them as a satire of censorship.

I secured the services of an excellent student speaker to make the tape-recorded version of the speech to be used in the experiment. Richard Case, a member of the college's debate team and the preceding year's winner of the "best actor" award, rehearsed the speech diligently, then delivered it before one of my classes in a classroom within the campus radio station. Unknown to the audience, the speech, along with the resultant audience laughter, was tape-recorded from the radio control booth.

Fourteen second-semester freshman English classes at St. Lawrence University were involved in the study as subjects. A total of 129 students (seven classes) were in the experimental group which heard the speech, and 125 (seven other classes) were control subjects who did not hear it. Classes were picked for experimental and control conditions to balance for the time of day they met, the instructor, and whether the group was "fast" or "average." During the times when the experimental groups listened to the tape-recorded speech, I sat in the back of the room with a copy of the speech manuscript and checked those places where overt general laughter occurred. All seven classes of listeners responded with general laughter in the same identical eleven places; at least five or six of the seven so responded in eight other identical places. In nineteen other instances there were scattered laughs and smiles. This recording procedure lent credence to the supposition that the speech was, indeed, satiric—or at least entertaining in a humorous way.

Three weeks prior to the experimental subjects' exposure to the satiric speech, all subjects completed a forty-item Thurstone attitude scale, "Attitude Toward Censorship." Immediately after the experimental subjects heard the satiric speech, all subjects again responded to the attitude scale. Experimental subjects also rated the speech they had heard on perceived funniness, and the speaker they had heard on perceived intelligence. The scales used, validated for this study, appear below:

Funniness, ranking from 1 to 8

Hilarious (1)	Humorous, but not funny
Very Funny	Unfunny
Funny	Solemn
Slightly Funny	Serious, even dangerous (8)

Intelligence

____Under 90	____121–130
____91–100	____131–140
____101–110	____over 140
____111–120	

The pretest attitude scores and the post-test attitude scores were subjected to statistical analysis (t-test) soon after the data were secured. Neither the experimental nor the control group had shifted in their attitudes toward censorship.

It was originally thought that the experimental subjects' initial attitude toward censorship would determine how funny they would consider the speech to be. However, no significant correlation between original attitude score and rated funniness of the speech was discovered. It was also hypothesized that, as ratings of the "clever" satiric humor went up, so would ratings of the speaker's intelligence. In other words, there should be a positive correlation between the humor ratings of the speech and the speaker's intelligence ratings. But in actuality a negative correlation was discovered: $-.36$! And this correlation was statistically significant. As the speech was perceived as more funny, the speaker was perceived as less intelligent, and vice versa.

So: the subjects had enjoyed the speech but apparently had not been influenced by it; and their ratings of its funniness were unrelated to their attitudes toward censorship, but *were* negatively related to their ratings of the speaker's intelligence. These facts suggested that they had responded to the speech as *humor* and not as *satire*. It therefore became important to determine whether or not the subjects of the study had perceived the *serious* thesis of the speech—for if they had perceived the serious thesis, they would have been responding to *satire*; if they had not, they would have been responding to *humor*.

Part of the original design was to administer to all subjects a delayed post-test. It was planned to have the subjects complete once more the Thurstone attitude scale four weeks after exposure to the speech in order to determine if any long-term results of either increased or decreased attitude change had occurred. Because of the necessity to find out if the students had responded to the speech as humor or as satire the students were also asked on this delayed post-test to check from a list provided the one statement they felt had been the thesis or central idea of the speech they had recently heard on "censorship of nursery rhymes."

The results of that question were surprising. Only 12 of

the 129 experimental subjects checked the thesis intended by me, "The idea of censorship is ridiculous and absurd." Instead, 104 checked the statement, "Censorship can be carried to ridiculous extremes," the thesis statement I believed would be checked by those who responded to the speech strictly as *humor*. Two subjects checked, "It would be foolish to censor nursery rhymes;" five checked "It is silly to blame juvenile delinquency on nursery rhymes;" six checked "nursery rhymes should be vigorously censored."

Analysis of the delayed post-test attitude scales revealed no delayed change in attitudes one way or the other.

In general, the results of the study seemed to support the idea that the student subjects had perceived the speaker as more of a "clown" than as a "wit." They had enjoyed the humorousness of the speech, but had not perceived its serious nature. And their ratings of the speaker's intelligence went down as their appreciation of his humor went up. That negative correlation of −.36 indicates that they may have responded much as did the subjects in a study by Jacqueline Goodchilds.[36]

Goodchilds wrote fictional protocols of three-person discussions. In half of them she wrote in one of the discussants as a "clowning" wit—one "whose humor is primarily whimsical, silly, or frivolous." In the other half of her protocols she wrote in one discussant as a "sarcastic wit," one "whose jokes are predominantly of the biting, ridiculing, pointed variety." Students then read the protocols and rated the "participants" on "influence" and "popularity." The results indicated that, comparatively, the "clowning wits" were rated as *popular* but lacking in *influence*; on the other hand, the "sarcastic wits" were rated as *influential* but lacking in popularity.

It would appear that, in the Gruner study, above, the speaker was perceived more often as a "clowning wit" than as a "sarcastic wit." Apparently, one of the dangers of employing satire *or* humor in a speech is that the speaker may suffer in audience-perceived *image*; playing the wit, he may be perceived as the clown.

Because the subjects of the Gruner study had apparently not perceived the satiric intent of "A Demure Proposal," the study was partially replicated at the University of Nebraska.[37]

The original experimental question, "Does satire modify attitude?" was altered to: "Does satire *perceived as such* modify attitude?" For in this replication experiment, strong measures were
taken to ensure that the subjects *did* perceive the thesis: they
were quite bluntly *told* the serious message in their instructions
just before hearing it.

One other question was investigated: "Does the effect of
satire perceived as such depend upon the original attitudes of
the auditors?" A word of explanation is in order.

Experimental studies of persuasion in general indicate that
those who tend toward "neutrality" on an issue are those that
most respond attitudinally to persuasive messages. Those who
are strongly committed to a position contrary to that of a persuasive message are most difficult to persuade; those originally
strongly in agreement with a persuasive message can hardly be
persuaded any more. They are already at the far limit of the
scale. Also, in the original dissertation study, those subjects
classified by the Thurstone pretest as originally "neutral toward" and "mildly favoring" censorship were those that seemed
to have "changed attitude" the most (although not a statistically reliable amount).

The basic design of the study was that of the dissertation
study. The same recorded speech was used, but it was verbally
introduced as a sharp satiric attack on the concept of censorship, to show how foolish and absurd the idea of censorship
was. The attitudes of fifty-one experimental and forty-nine
control subjects, all business and professional students at the
University of Nebraska, were measured two weeks before, immediately after, and three weeks after the experimental subjects were exposed to the satiric message. Attitudes were
measured with alternate forms of the same Thurstone scale
used earlier, "Attitude Toward Censorship." In addition, the
students responded to six semantic differential scales found by
Osgood, Suci, and Tannenbaum[38] to load heavily on the *evalu-
ative* dimension; the subjects evaluated "censorship" on these six
scales. On the pretest the semantic differential scores were
found to correlate .63 with the Thurstone scores.

As in the earlier study, also, each subject rated the speech
on perceived funniness and rated the speaker on perceived
intelligence.

Experimental and control groups' pretest and post-test attitude scores were checked for significance of shift with the t-test. Each group was also divided into four subgroups based upon their Thurstone pretest scores of original attitude (those Strongly Opposed to, those Mildly Opposed to, those Neutral Toward, and those Mildly in favor of censorship), and the scores of these subgroups were checked for statistically significant attitude shift.

Neither the control group (which did not hear the speech) as a whole nor subgroups thereof shifted a significant amount as measured by either the Thurstone or the semantic differential scales. The experimental group, which heard the speech, did not shift as a whole, either. However, those members whose pretest scores classified them as Mildly Favoring censorship shifted significantly from pre- to post-test on *both* the attitude measures. Furthermore, they tended to maintain their new mean position on the delayed post-test three weeks later. These data suggest that the answer to the second of the experimental questions, above, might be affirmative. Since those originally neutral toward censorship also exhibited a definite tendency to shift in the direction advocated by the satire's thesis, my curiosity led me to combine the data for these "neutrals" with those for the subjects mildly favoring censorship. The combination produced data with differences between pre- and post-test and between pre- and delayed post-test which were all significant at the .02 level or beyond.

A dramatic difference was found in this later study in how the experimental subjects perceived the speech and the speaker. Their ratings of the speech's funniness and the speaker's intelligence were positive: +.35, significant at beyond the .02 level. This positive correlation contrasted sharply with that negative correlation found in the earlier study (−.36). In this later study, the greater the ("clever") wit, the more intelligent the speaker seemed.

The two studies using "A Demure Proposal," taken together, seem to suggest that satire can successfully persuade those moderately approving and those neutral toward the thesis of the satire, *but only if* they are made to understand the thesis of the satire. This suggestion must be tempered with one possible experimental artifact: it is generally well known that persons at the extreme end of a scale tend to regress toward the mean on subsequent testing. Therefore, the fact that some of the shift of the subjects in the later study originally classified as "Mildly Favoring" and "Neutral Toward" censorship might be partially due to this phenomenon, statistical regression.

The two studies by Gruner, summarized just above, were partially replicated in a M.A. thesis by James Zeman.[39] He used the same speech, "A Demure Proposal" used by Gruner and the same scales for rating speaker intelligence and humorousness of the speech. But there were several differences in his experimental procedures.

One difference was that Zeman used as subjects high school students in Lead, South Dakota, not college students. Another was that he used the "post-test only control group" design, which does not employ the pretest; eliminating the statistical regression from pretest to post-test, such as may have occurred in the two Gruner studies. A third major difference in the Zeman study was that he employed three groups: a control group heard no satiric message; a "naive-experimental" group heard the satiric message, but were not told beforehand what the thesis of the speech was; an "informed-experimental" group heard the satiric message after being told specifically that it was a satire of censorship (and, "satire" was defined for them, orally).

Neither experimental group differed in mean attitude from the control group. This finding argues against the persuasiveness of the satire. However, a t-test revealed that the mean attitude of the informed-experimental group was statistically lower than was that of the naive-experimental. However, this finding may have been due to sampling error, since the subjects were not matched or randomly selected.

The correlations between ratings of speaker intelligence and of speech humorousness *tended* to support the earlier findings by Gruner. In the case of the naive-experimental group the correlation was negative, as in Gruner's original dissertation study; and in the case of the informed-experimental group the correlation was positive, as in Gruner's replication study. However, in each case the correlations were not large enough to be statistically significant. Zeman attributed his subjects' relative immaturity (when compared with college students) and lesser understanding of humor to the lack of significance of his findings.

A different approach was taken by Gary Pokorny in his M.A. thesis experiment,[40] reported in modified form in an article.[41] This experiment was designed to test the effect of *adding* satirical material to an otherwise "straightforward" persuasive speech. The straightforward (anticensorship) speech had been previously validated as an effective persuasive speech. Into it was inserted a passage consisting of most of paragraphs 4 through 8 of "A Demure Proposal," those paragraphs which had previously received the most overt laughter.

The entire speech was tape recorded "live" by a speech professor before his class. Some "guests" attended class that day for what was reputed to be the sole purpose of listening to the speech. Actually, they were graduate student "claques" who were assigned to laugh at the particular satiric points in order to key additional laughter from the "naive" members of the class. The speech and resultant laughter as recorded electronically with the laughter and the satiric passage edited out, became the "experimental-direct" stimulus.

Speech students, 180 in all, took part in the experiment, hearing either the "experimental-satiric," the "experimental-direct," or a control stimulus (a five-minute poetry reading). All responded to the Thurstone scale on attitude toward censorship immediately before, immediately after, and again two weeks after hearing their respective stimulus.

For purposes of data analysis, subjects from the three groups were matched according to their pretest scores. The result of this procedure was to produce three groups of forty-six subjects each (a total loss of forty-two subjects) with practically identical original mean attitude scores.

Both experimental groups showed a mean attitude change on the post-test in the direction of the thesis of the speech they heard; these attitude shifts were statistically dependable, and held up over the two-week delayed post-test period. However, not much can be concluded from this delayed *post*-test finding, since the *control* group, although not shifting on the post-test, did evidence a shift of opinion *against* censorship after the two-week period. This latter result, it is suspected, came from the fact that, during the two weeks, other anticensorship speeches were given in the speech classes. Analysis of the data for those originally neutral toward and mildly favorable toward censorship revealed the same statistical regression toward the mean suspected in the two earlier Gruner studies. Even the control group shifted against censorship a nearly significant amount.

While each experimental speech can be said to have produced attitude shift, there was no difference in the persuasiveness of the two; that is, addition of the satire did not make the "straightforward" speech more persuasive.

At this point in our review of experimental studies, it would be fairly easy to throw up one's hand in despair. *Humor* (as differentiated from *satire*) has shown no effect in persuasion at all. The addition of humor did not enhance the appeal of Lull's speeches for and against state medicine. Kennedy's speech extolling stronger movie and other censorship did not acquire additional persuasiveness from the addition of humor to it. Kilpela's "state medicine" speech was not made more persuasive by his bon mots and wisecracks. Brandes was unable to add persuasiveness to his speech on "What Every Yale Freshman Should Know" regardless of what *type* of humor he added. Gruner and Lampton produced no change in measurable persuasiveness in a sermon by adding what was considered an optimum amount of relevant humor.

But then, *humor* can be more of a distraction than a help to persuasion. And, according to our definitions of the previous chapter, if laughter-producing stimuli are to be persuasive, as akin to rhetoric, they should probably lean toward the *witty*, as does satire, to produce persuasion. What, then, can be concluded thus far about the effect (persuasive) of satire?

The answer is marginal, and must be hedged. Berlo and Kumata found a distinct attitude change produced by a satirical radio show toward the concept of "congressional investigating committees." And Asher and Sargent found that cartoon caricatures could change perceptions of "image" of some concepts ridiculed through cartoon hyperbole. Brinkman had found that editorial cartoons added persuasive effect to editorials.

However, there is a group of studies with negative findings: Carl found that most people misunderstand even the central thought of most editorial cartoons (so: how could they be persuasive?). Two studies by Gruner, one a dissertation study and the other a partial replication of it, found little evidence that a completely satirical speech could lead to attitude change. Zeman's replication with high school subjects produced basically the same results. And Pokorny and Gruner found that, even with a basically straightforward speech, the addition of satire seemed to add no further persuasive effect.

With such mixed results as the above paragraphs indicate, some reassessment would seem essential. The two Gruner studies, the Zeman and the Pokorny-Gruner studies used what kind of satire? The kind that could be termed "home-made." The speech that was used and reused, in whole or in part, was written by a nonprofessional satirist (Gruner). Could it be that the lack of that hard-to-define attribute, professionalism, was the leading cause for failure of that message to produce persuasion? Berlo and Kumata used a professionally made broadcast; Asher and Sargent used caricatures from professional cartoons; Brinkman found his persuasion resulting from professional cartoons added to editorials. Perhaps what was needed was the "professional touch"? The next series of studies did, indeed, use satire produced by contemporary professional satirists.

In a study published in 1967, Charles Gruner[42] investigated the impact of two Art Buchwald satirical columns. One of these columns, "Win One for Hoffa," satirized labor unions by presenting what might happen should professional football teams become unionized. The other, "Is There a Red China?" satirized the idea that we had not yet extended diplomatic recognition to Red China, a country of 800 million people. Both these columns were later reproduced in Buchwald's *Son of the Great Society*. With Buchwald's permission, both are reprinted here.

Win One for Hoffa

James R. Hoffa of the Teamsters' Union has offered to organize all the professional athletes in the United States into his union. The sport that needs it the most, they say, is pro football. While there may be many advantages to having the pro football players in the Teamsters' Union, there could be some disadvantages, as you will see if you come into the locker room of the Washington Toughskins. It is half-time and the Toughskins are behind 34 to 0.

The coach is standing in front of his blackboard.

"You're playing like a bunch of bums. Higgledorf, why didn't you take out the left end on play number 31?"

"I'm not supposed to take out ends. The union contract says I only have to take out tackles. If I took out the end, I'd be taking a job away from a blocking back."

The coach, trying to keep his temper: "All right, let's forget that. Mickazinski, why did you drop that pass that was right in your arms?"

"I caught my quota for the half. If I caught another one, the guys would have thought I was trying to speed up the game."

"Well, if you drop another pass, I'm pulling you out of the game and putting Wallnicki in."

"You can't do it. I've got three years seniority over Wallnicki. If you pull me out, the entire team walks off the field."

The coach clenches his teeth. "Harrison, you're the foreman as well as the quarterback. Can't you get any more work out of the men?"

Harrison says: "You're lucky we're here at all. We're not supposed to play on Sunday."

The coach says, "But you're getting time-and-a-half."

"We want double pay, and we also want to be paid for the time we spend going to and from the locker room."

"All right, bring it up at contract time. But right now I'm concerned with winning the game. The defense has been lousy. What happened to you, Brantowski, when they made that hole through off center?"

"I was resting. It says here, 'The linebackers are entitled to take a rest after every three plays.' If I didn't take the rest, I would have been fined by the union."

The coach wheels on his defensive back.

"And where were you, Eberhardt, when they threw the screen pass?"

"Screen passes aren't in my jurisdiction. My job is to cover the flanker. If you want me to cover screen passes, you're going to have to get authorization from the local."

"Okay, okay," the coach says. "Now I wasn't going to tell you this, but it looks like I've got to. Just before Jimmy Hoffa went to the Supreme Court to appeal his jail sentence, he said to me, 'Coach, if ever things get rough, and the team is down, and they're getting the hell beat out of them, tell them——tell them to win one for The Hoffa.' "

Tears start welling in the players' eyes.

"Gee, coach," the halfback sobs. "You wouldn't be kidding us?"

The coach looks at them. "Those were the last words Jimmy Hoffa said to me. Well, what do you say, team?"

The foreman jams on his helmet and shouts, "LET'S GO OUT THERE, GUYS, AND MURDER THE BUMS!"

Is There a Red China?

One of the most astounding discoveries in history was made the other day when a group of American State Department people found a new country named Red China. For years there had been rumors that there was a country in the Far East with a population of 800 million people. Yet no one in the United States would believe it.

But an expedition of Senators led by Marco Fulbright came across it accidentally while looking for a new route to North Vietnam.

When the existence of Red China was reported, a meeting of all the top policy people in the State Department was called.

"If this is true," said one of the Assistant Secretaries, "that means the world is round."

"Hogwash," said another Secretary. "We all know there is a country called China already, so how could there be another China? Look at our maps. China is right here in the Formosa Strait."

"That's right," a Secretary said. "And our maps are all up to date."

"What's that large land mass across the water from it?" someone asked.

"It's marked 'unexplored.' "

"Perhaps that's where Red China is."

"I'm an old China hand, and I say there is no place called Red China. The only China is located on the island of Formosa."

"What proof do we have that there really is a country with 800 million people in it, except for the word of a few disgruntled Senators?" an Undersecretary demanded. "They're only trying to discredit our foreign policy anyway."

"There is no proof," a Far East expert said, "except the West Germans have announced they plan to build a $150 million steel mill there. I don't think they'd put in that kind of money if the country didn't exist."

The Secretary of State spoke up. "That is a point. The only thing I can't understand is how we could have missed it all these years."

"Perhaps there is a cloud cover over it all the time," someone suggested.

"Does the CIA have anything on it?"

"No, sir. They're as much in the dark as we are. The French, the British, and the Canadians have all reported that they believe there is a Red China, but the Russians now claim it isn't there."

The old China hand spoke up. "Mr. Secretary, I believe we're only looking for trouble by following up the rumor. We already have a China. It's *our* kind of China. Another China would only mean trouble."

"But," said one of the other men, "if the reports are true that this land mass contains 800 million people, won't we have to deal with it sooner or later? I think we should announce that we don't believe there is a Red China, but if there is, we intend to contain it, but not isolate it."

The Secretary of State said, "That's a good phrase, 'containment but not isolation.' I think I'll use it in my next press conference. Our only problem is that if we admit there is such a place, we might be forced to admit her into the United Nations."

"Precisely, sir," a Secretary spoke out. "Besides, we've told the American people for seventeen years that there is no Red China. If we admit there is a Red China now, we would only confuse them."

One of the advisers said, "Seventeen years ago, the American people didn't believe in flying saucers, either. Perhaps we could announce the existence of Red China and flying saucers at the same time."

A total of 146 students at the University of Nebraska took part in the experiment as subjects. All subjects' attitudes toward "Labor Unions" and "Our Policy (of Non-Recognition) Toward Red China" were tapped by a six-item semantic differential attitude scale. Nineteen days later the experiment took place. A group of 146 students were handed dittoed copies of the columns, above, and asked to "evaluate" their "funniness" and "literary quality" on semantic differential-type scales. They were then asked to respond to the semantic differential scales on "Labor Unions" and "Our Policy Toward Red China" once more.

One hundred of these subjects were experimental, and were supposed to test the hypothesis that readers of a satirical stimulus will be persuaded by that stimulus *if he understands the thesis of that satire.* To insure that these subjects *did* understand the theses of the satirical pieces they read, the oral instructions given to the subjects in this condition included the fact that these *were* satirical editorials written by Art Buchwald, the "nationally syndicated columnist;" furthermore, the thesis of *each column* was explained to the experimental subjects.

The subjects in the control condition, forty-six in all, were not told who wrote the columns nor what their theses were. They were introduced only as "essays" which the experimenter wished to have "evaluated." After reading and evaluating the "essays," the subjects were to write, in their own words, what they thought was the thesis of each column, and then to respond again to the attitude scales.

A comparison of pretest and post-test mean attitude scores revealed that the control group did not change in mean attitude. The experimental group, however, changed in attitude toward *both concepts* in directions advocated by the columns. These changes were rather small in actual magnitude, but were statistically significant ($p < .01$). Further examination of the attitude data revealed that those who shifted in attitude against "Our Policy Toward Red China" and "Labor Unions" were those who were initially favorable toward those concepts.

Examination of the write-in information provided by the control group confirmed the experimenter's suspicion that, unless specifically *told* the thesis of each column, many undergraduate students would "miss the point" of these satiric editorials. Here are some sample theses attributed to the "Red China" column by control subjects:

No one in the U.S. believed there was a Red China.

If we are going to keep Red China out of world affairs, why even admit that there is such a place?

Is there a Red China?

That there is no Red China.

Among the many wrong theses attributed to the "Win One For

Hoffa" column were:

> While there may be advantages to having pro football players in the union, there could be some disadvantages.

> Not to unionize professional sports.

> There are disadvantages to having a pro football team in the Teamsters Union.

> To keep pro football players from joining the union.

It would seem obvious that, unless the experimental subjects had been told the intended theses, they would probably have misunderstood them as much as did the control group, and, would thus probably have not been influenced by them. And it is a sobering fact to remember that seldom is someone told ahead of time the thesis of a piece of satire before he reads it.

But is is also important, it seems, to remember that these brief columns, only 542 and 468 words long, respectively, requiring only a couple minutes reading time each, *did* apparently produce attitude change *when the intent was understood*. It also seems important that those who were persuaded tended to be those most in disagreement with the intent of the satire; those "most in need of persuading" were those most persuaded.

The next study to be considered here, also by Gruner,[43] concerned the question of what, if any, persuasive effect occurred from satire directed against *persons* (as opposed to against *concepts*, such as "labor unions" and "government policies"). Much political satire, for instance, is against particular public figures, politicians, and candidates for office. For this experiment, columns by Art Buchwald were again used.

Two Buchwald columns ridiculing President Richard Nixon were selected. One, "Old Nixon Is Jealous of Spiro," suggested that the "New Nixon" had not changed from his originally "shady" old self. "Little Dickey Nixon's Surprise" depicts the President as an angry and spoiled brat who did not get the "tax package" he wanted for Christmas. Both editorials appear below as they were used in the study, again with the kind permission of Buchwald.

Old Nixon Is Jealous of Spiro

The old Nixon came out of the closet in the White House on Halloween just as the New Nixon was going to bed.
"Now what?" the New Nixon demanded.

"I thought you promised me that when the mud slinging started, I could do it," the Old Nixon said.

"I know I promised it, but I've got to give Spiro Agnew something to do."

"Promises, promises," the Old Nixon sneered. "I've been hanging around for 10 months waiting to sock it to the snobs and the effete intellectuals and the arrogant, reckless, inexperienced elements within our society, and the first chance I get, you turn the job over to someone whose only claim to fame is that he's a household word."

"Dick," the New Nixon said, "at the time I told you to wait in the closet, I thought I could use you. But it would be wrong for the President of the United States to say the things I really believe. That's why I decided to use Spiro.

"If I had you saying those things, everyone would say 'Aha, the Old Nixon is back.' But if Agnew says them, people will say, 'Isn't it a shame the New Nixon can't control his vice president?' "

"And let Agnew grab all the headlines."

"Dick, remember when we were vice president together, and you did all the talking for us? Eisenhower didn't get mad. He pretended he didn't know what we were saying. And that's what I'm doing. I'm letting Agnew spout off at the mouth. I'll gain the people who agree with what Agnew has to say, and I'll avoid the animosity of those who get sore. But it will only work if you stay in the closet."

"That's easy for you to say. You get to go to Key Biscayne and San Clemente. You have all the big dinners with Duke Ellington and the Shah of Iran. And what do I do? I sleep on your shoes, breathing in moth balls."

The Old Nixon pointed his finger at the New Nixon. "I'm not going to take it much longer. You're going to have to choose between Spiro or me."

"Don't get tricky with me, Dick," the New Nixon said firmly. "I'm letting you stay in the White House because of a sense of gratitude for past favors. But as President of the United States, I'll make the decisions as to who my hatchet man is going to be."

The Old Nixon dropped to his knees. "All right, so I'm begging for a chance. Look at this stuff I wrote in the closet—'Merchants of Hate,' 'Parasites of Passion,' 'Ideological Eunuchs Straddling the Philosophical Fence.' Could Agnew come up with hyperbole like that?"

"Get up, Dick. Look, I'll tell you what I'll do. I can't let you make the speeches, but I'll talk to Spiro about putting you on his speech-writing team."

The Old Nixon shrugged. "I guess anything's better than hanging around in that closet."

Little Dickey Nixon's Surprise

Little Dickey Nixon in his pajamas ran down the stairs of his big house on Christmas morning directly to the Christmas tree. There was one large package all wrapped up under the tree.

"What could it be?" he asked, as all the people who loved him gathered around and watched.

"It's your tax package," said David Kennedy.

"Oh, boy," said Dickey. "I've been waiting for this for some time. Look, there's a card with it. It says 'From your loving cousins who live on the hill.' "

Dickey started taking off all the tissue paper which was wrapped around the tax package. There were four layers of it. Suddenly his face fell with disappointment.

"This isn't the tax package I asked for," he said tearfully. "And it's all smashed up."

"It's the best one they could find," David Kennedy said nervously.

"There's things in here I didn't even ask for," Dickey stomped around.

"Your cousins on the hill wanted to surprise you, Dickey. That's why they put in all that Social Security."

"But I told you I didn't want more Social Security. I've got enough already."

"Your cousins are a bunch of effete snobs," Dickey's good friend, Spiro said, "and they've given you a Rube Goldberg toy."

"Before you get too upset, Dickey, take a look in the package. There are some good things in it. The oil depletion allowance has only been damaged a little bit and can probably be saved, and the higher income brackets haven't been hurt much, and most of depreciation items are in perfect working order."

"But look at the tax exemption they railroaded through," Dickey said, "I can't play with that. Why can't I get what I want for Christmas?" Dickey cried as everyone stood around in embarrassed silence.

"It was a good package at the beginning," his pal, Gerry Ford, said. "It must have gotten damaged in the shipping."

"I'm going to send it back."

"Please don't, Dickey," his other pal, Hugh Scott, said. "If you send it back now, you may not get another tax package this year."

"I don't care. I have to play with it, and if they're going to change everything I asked for, I don't want their old package."

"Take it, Dickey, and try to put the pieces together with glue," Gerry said.

"I'm never going to speak to anyone on the hill again.
What else is there for Christmas?" Dickey asked.
"Nothing else, Dickey. That's all your cousins decided to
give you this year."

The discerning reader can detect the difference in subtleness
between the two pieces above. "Old Nixon" makes its point slyly
and inductively; "Little Dickey" is about as subtle as a custard
pie in the face.

It was hypothesized in this study that the *amount* of personal satire a person reads might affect the amount of his attitude change. Therefore, one experimental group read both
columns, another read only one.

Three sets of dittoed booklets were prepared. Booklet A
(for experimental Group A) contained a cover page of directions, copies of both "Old Nixon" and "Little Dickey," and scales
for evaluating the humorousness of the editorials. The last page
contained a set of semantic differential scales found by James
McCroskey to reliably measure a person's perceived "authoritativeness" and "character."[44] Booklet B was identical, except
that it contained only the "Old Nixon" column. Booklet C was
identical to Booklet B except that it substituted for the "Old
Nixon" column another column written by Buchwald totally
unrelated to Nixon. It appears below, with Buchwald's permission.

The "New German" Movie

Word has come in from West Germany that many of the
German people are getting tired of being shown as heavies
in World War II. They feel it's about time motion picture
producers and writers stopped showing the Germans in a
bad light and that everyone forgot about their past
mistakes.

I couldn't agree with them more. The German people
have suffered enough at the hands of Warner Brothers and
MGM, and an effort should be made to forget the past and
give the Germans a new image.

One of the main problems in the previous war movies is
that the Nazis are played by such disagreeable types.
They're always snarling and shouting "Heil Hitler!" and
slapping pretty French Resistance girls in the face.

If we really want to do them a service, I think we should
pay more attention to casting. In the new war pictures, we
should cast Pat Boone, Pat O'Brien or Jimmy Stewart as the

SS men, and Otto Preminger, Paul Lukas, and Helmut Dantine as the American GIs.

This would be a start in conjuring up sympathy for the German side. Once you solve the casting problem, you have to think about plot. First, we must get away from the stereotyped German U-boat commander.

I see a picture where Pat Boone is commander of a German U-boat. He is out searching for prey.

His executive officer, played by Lawrence Welk, says, "Sir, I've got a target in the periscope."

Boone grabs the periscope and says, "It's the *Athenia*, a passenger ship."

Welk says, "When should we fire?"

Boone pulls the periscope down. "We can't. There are women and children aboard."

"But they've seen us. They'll radio our position."

"I'd rather risk getting sunk than torpedo a ship with civilians aboard. Hitler would want it that way."

Another image we must change is that of the role of the Gestapo in World War II.

In the *nouvelle-vogue* World War II film, we would show Gestapo headquarters in Paris with Bing Crosby playing the head of the Gestapo. They have just brought in Pierre le Loup, head of the entire French Resistance.

Crosby says, "Loup, we want the list of every Resistance fighter in France."

Pierre le Loup says, "You'll never get it out of me."

"We have ways of getting things out of people." Crosby rings a buzzer and Fred MacMurray comes in. Crosby says to Fred MacMurray, "He doesn't seem to be in the mood to talk."

MacMurray replies, "Well, there's nothing we can do about it. If we lay a finger on him we'll have to answer to Himmler for police brutality."

The other standard plot that has been showing the Germans in a bad light has to do with prisoner-of-war camps. A new version, which could be called *Stalag Hilton*, would star Henry Fonda as the camp commandant.

Doris Day would play his wife, who rolls bandages for the Jewish prisoners in the hospital.

Glenn Ford, the SS sergeant, rushes in, shouts, "The prisoners are escaping, Herr Commandant."

"Don't talk to me," Fonda says, "I'm in on the July '44 plot to kill Hitler."

And Ford says, "Aren't we all?"

The three sets of booklets were stacked A, B, C, A, B, C, A, etc. Thus, when they were handed out to the student subjects, the three sets became randomly distributed among the subjects. Originally 156 subjects at the University of Georgia participated, but the responses of six were incomplete and were discarded. This left a total of forty-eight in Group A, fifty-two in Group B, and fifty in the control Group C.

Since the anti-Nixon editorials attacked only Nixon's "character" and not his "authoritativeness," it was hypothesized that there would be no differences in the mean ratings by the three groups on his "authoritativeness." This hypothesis was sustained. The groups did *not* differ in their ratings of Nixon's authoritativeness. It was expected, though, that in mean ratings of Nixon's "character," Group C would rate him highest and Group A would rate him lowest, with Group B's rating in the middle. The ratings did occur in the expected order, but the differences were so small in magnitude that they were not statistically dependable. The one-way analysis of variance revealed an F of 2.17, with F = 3.06 required for significance at the 5 percent level.

Additional statistical evidence suggested that the subjects may have not really understood the serious thesis intended in the "Old Nixon" column but did in the case of the "Little Dickey" piece. An understanding of satire indicates that, as personal regard for a person goes up, appreciation for satire against that person should go down. The reverse should hold true, also: as regard for the person goes down, appreciation of satire directed against him should go up (we enjoy ridicule of our enemy). For this reason, correlations between the ratings of the columns' "humorousness" and ratings of Nixon's authoritativeness and character were computed.

There was only chance (that is, no real) correlation found between ratings of Nixon's character or authoritativeness and ratings of the humorousness of the "Old Nixon" piece. However, for Group A (the only group that read it), ratings of the humorousness of "Little Dickey" correlated negatively with both ratings of Nixon's character (-.277, .10>p>.05) and his authoritativeness (-.52, p<.01). The former negative correlation was nearly statistically significant and the latter one was definitely so.

The student subjects in this study may have been too young to really catch the meanings in the "Old Nixon" column; few were even out of grammar school when Nixon was President Eisenhower's "hatchet man," for instance. They may have simply enjoyed the "humor" of President Nixon having to defend Spiro Agnew to his "old self" without perceiving the serious criticism Buchwald was making of the President. This conclusion is somewhat substantiated by comparing Group A's average "humorousness" ratings of the two columns. "Old Nixon" was rated, on the average, 9.81 on the humorousness scale; "Little Dickey" was rated almost a full point lower, 8.94 on the average. This difference in average rating was found to be statistically significant ($t = 2.157$, $p > .05$).

This study failed not only to find persuasive effect in *ad hominem* satire, but failed to find increased effect from increased exposure to that satire. It might well be that exposure to *more* than two pieces of satire ridiculing the same person would produce the intended effect; but such is usually not the way persons become exposed to such satire. Buchwald's column appears only thrice weekly, for instance, as does the column of his West Coast counterpart, Arthur Hoppe, whose material was used in the next experiment that I did.[45] The object of Hoppe's satirical attack in the study considered now was Martha Mitchell, then wife of Nixon's former chief of the Justice Department, John Mitchell.

The Art Hoppe column used in the experiment first appeared in the San Francisco *Chronicle* of November 1, 1970, and was reprinted in the Atlanta *Constitution* November 6. Entitled "John and Martha and AP and UPI," it ridiculed Martha Mitchell by comparing her compulsion for telephoning newspaper and government personnel to the agonizing urge for liquor suffered by the alcoholic. She even begs her husband John, who has hidden or removed all her phones, for "one little call? As a nightcap?"

It was assumed that some college students would not understand the Hoppe column because of unfamiliarity with Martha Mitchell. Therefore one experimental condition was engineered to ensure that the subjects therein *did* know who she was. *Time* magazine had done a feature story on her in their November 30, 1970, issue. The magazine kindly gave permission for me to reprint the first four paragraphs of that story, a biographical sketch of Martha Mitchell (copyright *Time* Inc. 1970). It appears below.

Martha Mitchell's View From the Top

In Pine Bluff, Ark., Martha Mitchell was an average Middle American high school girl. In wartime Washington, or post-war Forest Hills, or more recently in establishmentarian, suburban Rye, N.Y., she was little more than part of the background—and only dimly remembered by her neighbors. Then, about a year ago, as the wife of U.S. Attorney General John Mitchell, she told a TV reporter that the November peace demonstration in Washington reminded her husband of a Russian revolution. That indiscretion made her a nine-day wonder. Instead of fading, however, the wonder has grown. This month the Gallup poll announced that fully 76% of the American population realizes who Martha Mitchell is, and establishing her as a personality who is already better known than many politicians or entertainers.

Martha's trademark is her mouth, literally and metaphorically. Agape with laughter and framed in dimples, it dominates the Washington social scene—cocktail parties, state dinners, White House functions, ladies' luncheons—and shoots off for appreciative newsmen, telling it as Martha thinks it is. Her telephonic voice has become equally familiar to editors. She calls them in the small hours of the morning with pungent advice, such as her 2 a.m. blast to the Arkansas *Gazette*: "I want you to crucify Fulbright—and that's that." She has been known to use the blue wall phone in the privacy of the bathroom "so that John won't know," enabling detractors to insinuate that she sometimes takes a drink or two too many. Martha's friends, however, insist that her midnight telephonitis is nothing but her lifetime habit of speaking her mind on the instant.

Martha-isms such as *"Anytime you get somebody marching in the streets, it's catering to revolution,"* and *"Adults like to be led. They would rather respond to a form of discipline"* have made her a pillar of rectitude and moral resurgence to much of conservative America, a figure of ridicule to liberals, and a public embarrassment to many a traditionalist Republican. But the Attorney General, who might be the most embarrassed of all, merely smiles a wan little smile and refers fondly to her as his "unguided missile." She also has an admirer in President Nixon, who has referred to her as "spunky" and told her to "give 'em hell."

Booklets were prepared and distributed to student subjects at the University of Georgia as in the previous study reported, above. Booklet A had a cover sheet containing directions, and the *Time* piece followed by the Hoppe satire. The last page contained the scales for rating both pieces on "humorousness" and "journalistic *fairness*," and scales for rating Martha Mitchell on "character" and "authoritativeness." One other scale was included for rating her, one bounded by "ridiculous" and "sensible," which had been found to be an effective measure of attitude change induced by satire.[46] Booklet B was identical to A except that the *Time* piece was omitted. Booklet C was identical to A except that the Hoppe column was omitted. Thus Group A read first the biographical sketch of Martha Mitchell, then read the satire; Group B read only the satire; and Group C (the control group) read only the biographical sketch.

Originally, 159 students responded to the stimuli used in the study. Eight failed to complete all the measures and were thus discarded. Subjects' papers were then randomly discarded until there remained the papers from twenty-two males and twenty-two females exposed to each of the three experimental conditions (A, B, and C). This was to expedite the data analysis for testing for differences in response due to sex.

It was expected, of course, that the Hoppe satire would be perceived as much more "humorous" than would be the *Time* biographical sketch. To test this expectation, the humorousness ratings given each piece by Group A were compared. The resultant statistical analysis confirmed the expectation. The satire *was* rated as being more humorous than the *Time* piece.

Satire is generally considered to be "unfair." The usual satiric technique is to select some real or imagined fault of a person and then to exaggerate it, perhaps even to the point of hyperbole. There is little defense against satire. To rail against the exaggeration, which *everyone recognizes as exaggeration already*, is to be a "poor sport." To deny the fault at all usually seems egotistical and unrealistic. One can only smile at his own lampooning. In the present study, of course, it was expected that the satire would be rated as "unfair" whereas the neutral *Time* piece would be rated as more fair.

In the case of the independent ratings of the two pieces

made by Groups B and C, this supposition about "fairness" was the clear cut case. Group B rated the Hoppe column on the "unfair" end of the scale (3.11) and the *Time* piece on the "fair" end (4.32). This difference was quite significant, statistically. The data for Group A, who read and rated both pieces on fairness, showed a difference according to sex; therefore, the data for males and females were separated for statistical analysis.

Only the ratings by the males differed in the expected direction (4.16 vs. 3.43, t = 2.29, p < .05). The mean females' ratings of the fairness of the two pieces differed hardly at all. (Can one surmise that the girls felt that Martha *deserved* the lampooning as much as she deserved the coverage in *Time*?)

To determine whether the "image" of Martha Mitchell had been affected by exposure to the messages in the experiment, her ratings on "character," "authoritativeness," and "ridiculousness" were subjected to a 3 x 2 analysis of variance. Such an analysis separates the effects due to the kind of message exposure *and* the sex of the raters (males vs. females). It was hypothesized that, if any effect occurred, Group A would provide the lowest ratings, Group B would provide the next lowest, and Group C would provide the highest ratings. The logic which dictated such order was that Group A would read the biographical sketch, learn who Martha Mitchell "is," then *understand* more fully the satire directed against the woman. Group B would read only the satire, and understand it less well and thus be affected by it less strongly. Group C, having read nothing about Martha Mitchell except a biographical sketch from a national magazine, would rate her as fairly high.

Analysis of Martha Mitchell's "authoritativeness" ratings revealed no differences at all. This was somewhat to be expected. Her "authoritativeness" was not a matter in question.

Analysis of the "character" ratings revealed a significant difference. However, the mean ratings did not rank as expected. Group B, who only read the Hoppe column, rated Martha Mitchell lowest in character; Group C, who read only the biographical sketch, rated her highest (as expected), but Group A (who read both pieces) rated her *almost as highly* as did the control group (C).

Analysis of the "ridiculous/sensible" ratings revealed a

similar pattern. Group B rated her as *most* ridiculous, with Group A rating her next in ridiculousness, and Group C rating her as *least* ridiculous. In the case of both the "character" and "ridiculous/sensible" ratings, the male means were always lower than the females, but these differences were not statistically reliable.

The data from this study tend to support the notion that a single satirical editorial ridiculing a person can influence the perceived "image" ("character" and "ridiculousness") of that person. However, the *direction* of the results was not as predicted. It was expected that fuller impact would be produced where the subjects read first the biographical sketch and *then* the satire; but the most effect seems to have occurred where the subjects read *only* the satire.

Two factors probably produced this result. First, Martha Mitchell was probably better known by the subjects than was originally believed. She had been getting considerable notice in the press and electronic media by this time. An LP record by Fannie Flag, imitating Martha Mitchell, was in release at that time, also. Thus, the subjects in Group B probably perceived Hoppe's point and were influenced by it.

Second, the reading of the *Time* piece by the subjects of Group A probably produced some "status-conferral" to the benefit of Martha Mitchell. It has long been known that exposure in the mass media produces a "status-conferral" reaction. The extra status thus conferred upon Martha Mitchell probably prevented Group A ratings of her from going as low as they did in Group B.

Before leaving "Art vs. Martha," one other point ought to be made—and this was made by Hoppe himself in a personal letter to me: it seems that his satire had some persuasive effect *even though it was perceived as pretty unfair.*

Three other studies have utilized satirical editorials written by Hoppe. These will be briefly noted next.

Mary Ann McGown[47] chose as her thesis question, "Does a satiric editorial have the same or different persuasive effect when compared with a comparable, 'serious' editorial?" The satiric editorial she chose as one experimental stimulus was Hoppe's "Sane Capital Punishment" as published in the *Daily Nebraskan*[48] of April 24, 1967. The column playfully argued the thesis that "statistics indicate that the probability of capital punishment being a deterrent to murder are slight." It depicted the plight of a Mr. Arthur T. Pettibone who, "in a paroxysm of uncontrollable rage," decides to shoot his wife. But, before he can pull the trigger, he begins a dialogue with himself on his chances of getting the gas chamber for the deed. He eventually decides that, since he is white and middle class, his chances of execution are slim. But during the time he has taken to debate with himself, his wife has packed up and left him.

To produce the "serious" or "straightforward" editorial, the Hoppe piece was rewritten to remove its satirical nature. The "serious" editorial was carefully checked to make sure it was equal to the Hoppe piece in ideas presented, in total length, and in Flesch "reading ease."

University of Nebraska students read one or the other of the two editorials and responded on several scales already mentioned. Neither editorial can be said to have produced any attitude change. Other results:

1. The two editorials were not rated differently on an "interestingness" scale.

2. The Hoppe column was rated as significantly "funnier" than was the serious editorial, thus validating the supposed difference between the two pieces.

3. There was no perceived difference in the "authoritativeness" of the writers of the two editorials.

4. There was a tendency (almost significant) between the perceived "character" of the two authors; apparently the sarcasm of the satire made for reduced ratings of Hoppe's "character." This finding might be expected in the light of Goodchilds' findings, quoted earlier, where "sarcastic" wits were perceived as influential but *unpopular*.

McGown's study was later partially replicated by Gruner[49] at Georgia. The two editorials used by McGown had argued only one proposition relative to capital punishment (It is no deterrent to murder.) whereas the attitude scale she used measured overall *global* attitude toward that concept. Could either editorial change only the belief in capital punishment's *deterrent value?*

A total of fifty-six subjects read the Hoppe piece; fifty-four read the serious editorial; a control group of fifty-six read a control editorial ("The 'New German' Movie," included above). Each subject then rated the editorial he read on scales measuring the editorial's "interestingness" and "humorousness." Each subject also responded to several Likert-type attitude scale items, including: "3. The threat of capital punishment (of being executed) is not an effective deterrent to prospective murderers," the correct thesis of the two experimental editorials. In the two experimental groups each subject was also asked to check from the following list what he felt the editorial's thesis to be:

    ____It is difficult to tell whether capital punishment is a deterrent to murder or not.
    ____Mr. Pettibone nearly talked himself into murdering his wife.
    ____Capital punishment *is* a deterrent to murder.
    ____The Committee for a Sane Capital Punishment Policy is a great American organization.
    ____Capital punishment is *not* a deterrent to murder [The correct thesis].
    ____Crime does not pay.

The results indicated that, even though the satiric editorial was rated as more "humorous" than was the serious one, there was no difference in rated "interestingness." Again, neither editorial seems to have caused any shift in overall attitude toward capital punishment *nor* in the belief that "capital punishment has a deterrent effect."

Perhaps the most disappointing results came from the subjects' responses as to what was the thesis of the anticapital punishment editorials. Of the fifty-six subjects who read the satirical editorial, only seventeen (nine males, eight females) checked its correct thesis. Of the fifty-four who read the serious version, only fourteen (eight males and six females) were correct in checking its thesis. Such inability to perceive a correct thesis might seem astounding, except for other evidence that satire's point is often missed, and the fact that Ralph Nichols could conclude that", . . . only about 25 per cent of persons listening to a formal talk are able to grasp the speaker's central idea."[50]

By now it must be pretty clearly established that the

serious point or thesis of satire is often not understood. The Cooper and Jahoda study, mentioned earlier, found that one way prejudiced people protect themselves from satiric antiprejudice propaganda is to distort or otherwise fail to perceive that thesis. It has also been determined that people tend to enjoy humor based upon what groups they belong and relate to. For instance, Democrats most enjoy jokes ridiculing Republicans, and Republicans most enjoy jokes ridiculing Democrats.[51] These observations have led to the third of the three studies extant using Art Hoppe columns for experimental stimuli. The study was based on the hypothesis that the serious point of a satiric piece attacking a political candidate would be most often understood by antagonists of that candidate; conversely, the serious point of a satiric piece attacking a political candidate would be least often understood by the partisans of that candidate. This recognition of the satiric point directed at the "enemy" candidate would, then, "reinforce" or strengthen the antagonism toward that candidate.

The study[52] was conducted in the early fall quarter of 1972, when the Presidential campaign between President Nixon and Senator McGovern was still being contested. One Art Hoppe column critical of Nixon and one critical of McGovern were used in the experiment.

The anti-Nixon editorial was entitled "Joe Against McGovern," and depicted a fictitious conversation between "Joe Sikspak, American" and his bartender Paddy. Joe says that he is going to vote Democratic because McGovern has vowed to end that "dumbhead war" in Vietnam. He is unhappy with Nixon because the President promised to end the war with his secret plan four years ago, but has reneged. During the conversation, though, Paddy the bartender talks Joe into voting for Nixon; Paddy convinces Joe that McGovern has no experience at ending the war, he says, but Nixon has had four years of experience at ending the war, and so should be able to do the best job.

The anti-McGovern Hoppe column is entitled "The George and Tom Papers," and concerns the so-called "Eagleton Affair." George calls Tom into his office, where he puts him under a spotlight for "grilling." He winds up trying to persuade Tom to

go down in a unique place of American history "as the only candidate for that office [vice president] who ever withdrew from
the race."

Two sets of dittoed booklets were prepared. The front page
contained directions and places for the student subject to check
his sex, his class, and his Presidential candidate preference "if
the Presidential election were held today." The second page presented either "Joe Against McGovern" or "The George and Tom
Papers." The last page of the booklet asked him to check from a
list of six statements that one which he thought was the thesis
of the columnist. He was to also rate the column on "funniness" and "fairness," much the same as in previous studies. The
booklets were passed out randomly for completion by the
subjects.

A total of 162 booklets completed and usable for data analysis were finished and returned by the subjects, speech students at the University of Georgia. A total of 126 of these were
pro-Nixon, only thirty-six were pro-McGovern. Eighty-one of
these had read the "Joe Sikspak" (anti-Nixon) editorial, and 81
had read the "George and Tom" (anti-McGovern) editorial.

The total number of subjects in each condition and how
many of each correctly picked the intended thesis for the editorial they read were subjected to chi square analysis. The results appear in Table 2, below.

Table 2: X^2 Results of Correct and Incorrect
Choices of Hoppe Column Theses

Columns:	Pro-Nixon Ss		*Columns:*	Pro-McGovern Ss	
	Correct	Incorrect		Correct	Incorrect
Anti-Nixon	16	48	Anti-Nixon	7	10
Anti-McGovern	33	29	Anti-McGovern	12	7

$X^2 = 10.56$, p < .01 $X^2 = 1.74$, NS ($X^2 = 3.84$ needed for p < .05)

A statistically significant chi-square was found for only the
pro-Nixon people ($X^2 = 10.56$, p <.01). Note that for the anti-
Nixon editorial ("Joe Sikspak"), only sixteen (nine males, seven
females) out of sixty-four picked the correct thesis, whereas for
the anti-McGovern editorial, thirty-three (sixteen males,
seventeen females) out of sixty-two picked the correct thesis.
The size of the chi-square is largely due to the pro-Nixon females' inability (or unwillingness?) to check as the thesis of "Joe

Sikspak": "Nixon has failed to make good his 1968 campaign promise to end the war." Only seven of the forty-one girls did so check that correct thesis, whereas seventeen of the pro-Nixon girls out of thirty-two checked the correct thesis of the anti-McGovern editorial. On the other hand, the pro-McGovern subjects differed in their ability to select the correct thesis of the two editorials to no more than a chance degree.

The relatively small number of McGovern supporters in this study mitigates against any sweeping generalizations in drawing conclusions. However, what seemingly is suggested here is that the Nixon supporters, especially the females in that group, were either unable or unwilling to perceive the slam at Nixon's failure to live up to his previous campaign pledge. Might it be that these Nixon supporters tend to have a less broad "sense of humor"? It has been suggested, after all, that one would *have* to have had a good sense of humor in order to *be* a McGovern supporter.

The next seven experiments on the value of humor in persuasion to be discussed were done by Dorothy Markiewicz for her doctoral dissertation at Ohio State.[53] For convenience, they will be referred to as Experiment 1 through Experiment 7.

Experiment 1 involved the reading by junior high English class students of either a "serious" or a humorous essay arguing that school should run year-round, including summer. The two essays were "similar in arguments presented, approximate length . . ., and concluding paragraph." The humorous essay is presented here in full, with the permission of D. Markiewicz.

Tell It Like It Should Be—School in Summer

No one ever stops fish from going to school during the summer. Students today should demand their rights. They should have a sit-in demonstrating their protest against no school during the summer.

The reasons for closing school during the summer are out-dated. Children used to be excused from school during the summer months so that they could help harvest the crops on the farm. Today, most students spend their summers harvesting baseballs, or sunrays, or tie-dyed hot pants, or "the blahs." Sometimes they help their families, but usually they would not need the entire summer to cut the lawn a few times or to water the tomato plant, even if it *is* a large plant. Besides, housework or baby-sitting can be worse than geography.

During the summer it's tough to get around. For example, before your mother will drive you to a friend's house, you might have to do some of these things: wash the grimy kitchen floor four times, talk your three-year-old sister into watching "Sesame Street" at the neighbors', and worst of all, move your frisbee, your bullet belts, and other favorite objects from their usual spots on the floor and bed. If school were in session you would be able to groove with your friends more easily.

Summer would be a good time to study those things which are common during that season—like insects: If students would continue to make insect collections during the summer, they would lessen the chance that the insects will conquer the earth. "Bug the bug!" "Collect insects!" "Step on mosquitoes!" could be the student battle cries. They could make studies of plants and animals in their natural homes, since they could take many more field trips (not drugs). In fact they could even plant seeds as part of "Plant Parenthood."

Teachers could hold classes outside when the weather is good, and it's good more often in the summer. They could use objects outdoors, such as caterpillars, cars, and cops, as an aid to their teaching. Instead of counting their fingers and toes when adding, students might count leaves or blades of grass. It's easier to discover scientific facts outdoors than indoors. Do you think Newton could have discovered the law of gravity if he had to wait for an apple to drop on his head while sitting inside his classroom during the winter? He was probably in a class held outside when he was hit with the apple.

School should be held all year, including in the summer, for all these reasons. Children are not needed to help on the farm, since most of them don't live on farms. Students could get together more easily than when there is no school in session. Students could study things common in summer. Teachers could use things that are outdoors to help in teaching.

After reading either the humorous or the serious essay, the students responded to two questions measuring their attitude toward "school all year," and "school in the summer." Each student was also asked to write down whether the author of the essay believed school should be held during summer. And, they were asked to write down in a list "as many reasons as you remember" that the author gave. Finally, they were asked to list any other ideas they had about the author's ideas as they read the essay. They also rated the essays on scales measuring "interestingness" and "humorousness." A final question asked them if they would like to read other articles by the same author.

Results showed that the humorous essay was perceived as humorous, the serious essay as serious. No significant effects on the attitude item responses were found. However, those who had read the humorous essay wrote down more "thoughts" in agreement with summer school than did those who had read the serious essay. According to the logic of D.H. Cullen's method of determining attitude by the number of consonant thoughts listed,[54] this would indicate that the humorous essay had more persuasive effect. The humorous essay was rated as more "interesting" than was the serious essay, too; and the humorous essay elicited more positive response indicating desire for other articles by the same author. In general, it would appear that the humorous essay had a somewhat greater impact upon the English students than did the serious essay.

Markiewicz's Experiment 2 involved use of an Art Buchwald column critical of antigun control lobbyists and a "serious" message "similar in main arguments and length." Since the perceived credibility of the source was thought to be a possible factor in the persuasiveness of each, to half of the subjects reading each essay the author was described as high in credibility and to the other half the author was described as low in credibility. In the high credibility description, the author was alleged to be "a highly regarded political scientist at Stanford University." In the low credibility condition he was described as "a little-known journalist" who had "not previously considered the question and was uninformed about the issue."

The Buchwald column used in the study is presented here, by permission.

Gun Lovers on the Defensive

Wallaby Cartridge, the president of the National Gun Lovers of America and Bugle Corps, was enraged when I saw him in a restaurant one day spoon-feeding an Old-Fashioned into the mouth of a U.S. Senator.

"Americans are behaving like children," Wallaby said, "parroting nonsense, and trying to bring pressure on Congress to pass antigun legislation."

"But that's lobbying," I said in a shocked voice.

"You're damn right it's lobbying, and the National Gun Lovers of America through its lobby is officially protesting. There's a conspiracy going on to take guns away from the American people, and we won't stand for it—not after all the money and time we've spent preventing it. Senator, can I order you some caviar?"

The Senator nodded his head.

"What I don't understand, Wallaby, is why the American people just won't take your word that guns don't kill people, people kill people."

"Because the American people are being brainwashed. They think they can prevent crime and keep guns out of the hands of criminals and adolescents and disturbed people by making Americans register their guns. But at the same time they don't realize how much inconvenience they would be causing the sincere hunter and marksman."

"Nobody wants to inconvenience people who hunt," I agreed.

"How about a nice steak, Senator?" Wallaby said.

He then continued. "Do you know one of the things they want to do? They want to pass a law forbidding the sale of long guns and shotguns through the mail. Do you realize what this would do to hunters? They'd have to go down to a store and buy the gun over the counter and give their names to the sales clerk."

"But that's outrageous. Hunters shouldn't be forced to go to a store to buy their guns. They've got too much to do, getting up at three in the morning and sitting in a duck blind for four hours in the mud, to find time to go to a store."

"I'm glad you understand it," Wallaby said. "But there's more to it than that. They want to take our guns away from us."

"Who does?"

"*They* do," Wallaby said ominously.

"Then it's a conspiracy," I cried.

"Of course it's a conspiracy," Wallaby said. "Who do you think is behind all those letters being sent to Congressmen and Senators this week?"

"The American people?"

"You fool. The conspiracy's behind it. They know if they can get a list of the people in the United States who own guns, *They*'ll be able to take over."

"And the only thing standing between *they* and us is *you*."

I thought Wallaby was going to burst into tears.

"Everything was going so well. We had Congress in our pocket. Our mail campaign for guns outnumbered the anti-gun mail by six to none. We had the thing in the bag. But now the mail is running against us, and everyone's blaming me. I've been a good lobbyist, a loyal lobbyist, a free-spending lobbyist. If they pass a strong antigun law, who will have me?"

My heart was breaking. "Maybe people will stop writing letters against guns," I said hopefully. Wallaby shook his head. "Then why are you entertaining this Senator?" I asked. "I can't help it. It's the only thing I know how to do." Wallaby shoved a cigar in the Senator's mouth and started to pour some brandy down his throat.

In this study, results indicated that the humor and credibility manipulations were both weak. The Buchwald piece was rated as only marginally more funny than was the serious piece, and the credibility of the author in the "high credibility" source only slightly higher than was the low credibility source.

There was no difference in persuasive effect between the high and low credibility conditions, nor in the humorous vs. serious condition. The weakness in the manipulation of these variables may have mitigated against significant differences in response.

The results of how the student subjects did, comparatively, on recall tests over the material of the essays are included in Chapter 7.

Experiment 3 by Markiewicz involved the mailing out of 400 letters to students at Ohio State University. In each case the letter argued that a recycling center should be established at the university. One hundred of the letters contained only a "low persuasion" appeal, while another 100 contained the "low persuasion letter" accompanied by a humorous cartoon (See Plate 2). Another 100 contained the "high persuasion" appeal (an extra paragraph added to the "low persuasion" appeal) with the cartoon, and another 100 letters contained the high persuasion appeal minus the cartoon. The letters contained a stamped, self-addressed postal card containing questions about recycling. Subjects were asked to answer the questions and to return the cards. The magnitude of the return of each of the four conditions was to be the measure of persuasive success.

The results indicated that addition of the cartoon did not have noticeable effect on the "high persuasion" appeal, but slightly increased the return of postal cards when included in the low persuasion letters. One problem may have been that the cartoon was perceived only as moderately funny by those reacting to it. Also, the cartoon effect may have been confounded with the effect of any picture at all that might have been added to the letters.

Experiment 4 attempted to measure the effectiveness of filmed introductions to a persuasive message. Four groups of student subjects participated in the study. One group heard a tape-recorded speech advocating a law requiring use of safety belts after a filmed *humorous* introduction. Another group heard the same taped message after viewing a *serious* filmed introduction. A control group responded to the criterion measures but did not hear the taped persuasive message.

There were no significant differences in attitude among the four groups, *including* the control group. This result indicated that the "persuasive" message could not be considered effective as persuasion at all, with or without filmed introductions. The students had also rated the sources of the filmed introductions and the taped message (it was alleged that, in each case, the source of both the message and the film were the same). The film-message source of the *serious* condition was rated as significantly better "informed." Because of the lack of effect from the persuasive message, little can be concluded from Experiment 4.

Experiment 5 attempted to determine whether initial opinion affected the persuadability of humorous messages v. that of serious messages.

The opinions of student subjects were experimentally manipulated on the question of whether OSU campus policemen should carry guns. One group was made to become in favor of it, a second group was made to become opposed to it, and a third group was left neither in favor of nor opposed to campus policemen carrying guns. Then one third of each group was exposed to a humorous message advocating the carrying of guns by campus cops, another one third of each group read a serious message advocating the same thesis, and another third of each group (control subjects) read no message.

The humorous and serious messages were alike in arguments, order of arguments, summaries in the middle and end, length, and format. The humorous essay, pretested for funniness, appears below, through permission from Markiewicz.

Should Campus Police Carry Guns?

Reputable social scientists who have recently completed a number of studies on the issue have found that campus police should carry guns. Other authorities, such as Liberace, Lawrence Welk, and Racquel Welch have argued that campus police should be stripped (of their guns). Let's set the issue straight by accompanying a young campus policeman, Kop Kelley, on a typical day.

8:04 A.M. Kop Kelley arrives at the campus police station together with four other campus policemen.
8:07 A.M. The order is given to "hand in the guns."
8:08 A.M. Five guns and four badges are handed in.
8:09 A.M. Kop Kelley practices drawing his official police long stem rose from his holster.
8:10 A.M. "Goddam pricked myself again."
8:11 A.M. "Goddam drew blood this time."
8:25 A.M. A message warning that a prowler is robbing Arps Hall comes in on the teletype.
8:30 A.M. Kop Kelley pummels the crook into submission with vicious lashes from his long stem, prize-fighting American Beauty Rose.
8:32 A.M. "Let this rose warn would-be meanies that the long stem of the law will ferret them out everywhere."
9:18 A.M. Kop Kelley stops a student for jay-walking. Is talked back to.
9:34 A.M. Kop Kelley gives a student a parking ticket. Is talked back to.
9:57 A.M. Kop Kelley fines a student for writing graffiti in a female bathroom. Is talked back to.
10:31 A.M. BULLETIN: "Jay-walker, illegal parker, and creative writer suffering from severe pummeling from a prize-fighting American Beauty Rose are rushed to the emergency room of University Hospital."
11:06 A.M. Kop Kelley reports to his supervisor "Gee Chief, playing cops and robbers is more fun now. When I had a gun no one played with me."
12:03 P.M. Kop Kelley breaks for lunch . . . "Hamburger, fries, shake, and a large glass of water with an aspirin for my rose here, please."

By now it must be clear that guns are necessary to campus policemen. Without them the campus police forces would be very undermanned, their efficiency greatly impaired, and their ability to act as a deterrent to criminals virtually eliminated. But for you skeptics, consider these facts.

Training policemen would be far more expensive and complicated than it is now. For example, in order to neutralize gun-wielding criminals at a distance, an officer must be trained in long-distance hypnosis, the ancient Japanese art of making oneself a small target, or the equally ancient art of falling on one's knees and begging for mercy.

In some situations we agree with Welch and Welk that guns are not necessary. For example a large, burly officer sneaking up on a rabid dog to immobilize it in hand-to-paw combat. Imagine Woody coaching the dog. . . Three mouthfuls and a cloud of dust!

Obviously the quality of law enforcement would be poorer. Sniveling cops on their knees deter only runny criminals. At least by-standers would not be in danger of being accidentally shot by police. Only by criminals, which is altogether less accidental.

Therefore it is clear that campus police should continue to be armed. Taking away their guns would greatly reduce the size, effectiveness, and efficiency of the campus police force.

All subjects reacted to two types of attitude questionnaires regarding gun-carrying by campus policemen, after the experimental groups had read one or the other message. In addition, the experimental subjects reacted to several scales evaluating the message on several factors and the author of the essay on "trustworthiness." In a partial replication of the study, thirty-eight students read either the humorous or serious message and responded to a test of information contained in the essays.

Data from two other sources were used by Markiewicz to explain the possible reasons for the serious message being the more persuasive. First, the information comprehension indicated that more was learned and retained from the serious than from the humorous message. Second, the source of the serious message was perceived as more "trustworthy" than was that of the humorous message. (Apparently, the author was considered more "clownish" than "sarcastic" in the use of wit?). Wither reason (or both) would explain the greater persuasiveness of the serious message: we are persuaded both by what we remember best and by what comes from what we consider a trustworthy source.

Experiment 6 was designed to overcome the possibility that subjects might learn and remember more from one or the other stimulus, as apparently occurred in Experiment 5. For this reason, short (sixty-second) films, previously used on television, were used. A series of pretestings determined that two short films, one humorous and one serious, on the subject of seat belt use, could be used. The two films were validated in the pretestings as differing in "humor," but alike in arguments, "mood productions," interest, cleverness, and believableness.

Subjects' initial opinion on the topic were secured in a pretest, then they were exposed two or five days later to one of the films. The results indicated that the serious message appeared to be more persuasive in the case of subjects already favoring or neutral toward the message thesis, but the humorous message was more effective for those opposed to the message thesis.

However, contrary to the results of Experiment 6, the humorous film's source was rated by the subjects in the experiment as more "trustworthy" (and, in addition, more "interesting") than was the serious film.

Experiment 7 was actually three separate but similar experiments; and they were conducted in such a way that the results of each could be examined individually and, in addition, the results of all three could be combined for analysis in a factorial design. This series of studies, instead of testing the effects of serious vs. humorous messages per se, were concerned with the effectiveness of "straightforward" persuasive messages "embedded in a humorous or a serious context."

Each study used five short messages validated in pretests as effective persuasion. These messages were played to students, but messages were separated by the "context:" either three-to-six minute segments of Bill Cosby routines (humorous context) or segments of like length from recorded speeches of Martin Luther King, Jr. The overall analysis of the data revealed that no real advantage in producing attitude change can be claimed by embedding persuasive arguments in either serious or humorous (distracting) contexts.

None of the previously mentioned studies concerned itself

with personality or attitudinal variables in connection with persuasion by satire. On the assumption that how much a person is
ego-involved with an issue would determine one's reaction to
persuasion, both satiric and non-satiric, Larry Powell[55] conducted a study to determine:

> 1. Whether a satiric or comparable non-satiric message
> would be more persuasive on a topic in which persons were
> either highly ego-involved or not, and

> 2. Whether a satiric or comparable non-satiric message
> would better "immunize" persons against a subsequent
> counter-persuasive message on a topic in which persons
> are either highly ego-involved or not.

Powell exposed subjects to an Art Buchwald written satire crit-
icizing Congressional politicians, or to a non-satirical written
message using the same arguments as the Buchwald column, or
to no message (control group). Five days later all subjects were
exposed to a speech designed to counter the persuasion of the
other experimental messages. The subjects filled out attitude
questionnaires before and after exposure to the experimental
message and after the counter-persuasion message. Powell concluded, in part:

> The results indicated that the level of ego-involvement is
> a factor in subjects' responses to written satirical mes-
> sages. Satire appears to be an effective means of changing
> attitudes in low ego-involved subjects, but this effect is not
> maintained in the presence of counter arguments. More
> importantly, satire would appear to be a definite means of
> reinforcing the beliefs of high ego-involved receivers, and
> it is significantly better than a direct message.

Powell used a more complicated experimental design to
further explore the role of satire as an immunizor to later counter-persuasion.[56] He used the same messages of his previous
study, this time presented orally by an actor via video-tape.
Subjects were classified as being either high or low in salience
(belief in the importance of the message topic) and either positive or negative in attitude toward the topic of the message.

Some results were similar to the previous Powell study.
The non-satiric message was the more persuasive, initially, but
the satiric speech seemed to immunize against the later counter-persuasion better. An interesting "boomerang" effect oc-

curred among those believing the message topic to be highly important. Their attitudes changed in the direction opposite that of the satiric message. Powell theorizes that they probably were disappointed in hearing a message dealing in a somewhat trivial manner with a topic of importance (high salience) to them, and thus reacted negatively.

Larry Powell's two studies seem to indicate that satire has the effect more of a reinforcing of one's attitudes than a changing of them (unless, of course, there is the boomerang effect). Such a conclusion also is supported by a few field studies of how satiric and/or humorous television programs affect viewers selectively.

Stuart Surlin[57] studied the reactions of people to viewing "All In The Family," the television series that ridicules Archie Bunker for his bigotry. He found, in general, that viewers who initially agreed with Archie's ideas felt that Archie tended to get the better of the arguments he got into over prejudice. Also, he found that even those viewers who *dis*agreed with Archie's views of life tended to "like" him despite his offensive attitudes toward those of another race or religion.

Neil Vidmar and Milton Rokeach[58] also studied the reactions of "All In The Family" viewers in both Canada and the United States, with very much the same conclusions as Surlin. The last paragraph of their article begins with, "On balance the study seems to support more the critics who have argued that 'All In The Family' has harmful effects."

A later study by Stuart Surlin[59] tapped the responses of viewers to the television program "The Jeffersons." This is a spin-off from the older "All In The Family," and details the lives of George Jefferson, a black, and his family; they have prospered with George's dry cleaning business and have moved from Archie's old neighborhood to the fashionable East Side of New York. George's caustic remarks are often directed against a racially mixed couple (white husband, black wife) who live on their floor. This racially mixed couple, by the way, offended more whites than blacks. Surlin concludes:

> The reinforcement of one's social reality is a rewarding result of viewing [this program]. Thus, if viewing is rewarded in this manner then the viewing is deemed more pleasurable and it occurs at greater frequency. In this par-

ticular instance, open-minded blacks want to see that
blacks are making it into the white middle-class society, and
enjoy seeing the closer integration of the races as epito-
mized by the racially integrated married couple on "The
Jeffersons."

It is not an easy task to summarize the research reviews in
this chapter. In the first place, even though the reader may, after plowing through this far, believe he has covered an almost
interminable number of individual studies, the actual amount of
research done on humor/wit as persuasion is quite small. In fact,
a book reviewer has pointed out:

> Humour [sic] is a commonplace human characteristic of
> some complexity that has been largely ignored by main-
> stream psychology. As Chapman and Foot remind us,
> psychology suffers from a "tenderness tabu", shunning the
> investigation of pleasant emotions in favor of dismal
> negatives.[60]

For another thing, the studies reported here have differed
widely in technique. They have not proceeded from the same
experimenter, or group of experimenters working closely together. Thus they do not follow a logical pattern of development. The kinds of stimuli, subjects, message topics, criterion
measuring devices, even statistical techniques of evaluating
data have varied markedly.

However, despite the real and present danger of overgen-
eralizing, it seems that some tentative conclusions can here be
set forth. The tentativeness of these conclusions cannot be
overstressed; these generalizations, in fact, should be considered more as "suggestions" than as conclusions.

Perhaps the one conclusion that can be drawn with the
most certainty of any in this list is that humor fails to increase
persuasiveness of argumentative messages. Sprinkling jokes,
wisecracks, puns, sarcasm, or even satire throughout a speech
seems to add nothing to that speech. Adding humor which is
germane to the particular message seems to heighten its entertainment (amusement) value, but that is about all. Not one
study reviewed here, with the exception of the one Markiewicz
experiment, has shown that humor adds persuasiveness to a

message. And Markiewicz's one experiment merely resulted in a higher number of prepaid postal card returns as the result of a cartoon added to a low-persuasion letter.

On the other hand, no study thus far has found that the addition of humor to a message will *detract* from that message's persuasiveness. This conclusion seems to be limited to three conditions, however. The original message must be an effective, persuasive message with *or* without the humor. And the humor added to the message must be appropriate to the audience and germane to the message portion into which it is inserted. And the humor used must apparently be of a kind and nature that will not cause the source of the message (the writer or speaker) to be perceived by his audience as "clownish."

Cartoonlike caricaturing of concepts may produce the results they intend: lowered esteem and evaluation of the ridiculed concepts. Extending this point to editorial cartoons seems mildly warranted, also, especially if the editorial cartoon is encountered concomitantly with an editorial of the same thesis. However, it must be remembered that much editorial cartooning (and, presumably, *some* caricaturing) is not understood, and is even misunderstood, by the general public. It seems that inability (or unwillingness) to understand satirical messages, whether they be cartoons or other forms of satire, can result from lack of the necessary intellectual equipment as well as from prejudice (bigotry or reference group membership). Gerald Miller and Paula Bacon[61] have even determined that general "close-mindedness" as measured by the Rokeach Dogmatism Scale decreases ability to perceive some kind of humor.

It is apparent that much satire is completely misunderstood. Gruner has found that part of the cause of such misunderstanding can be attributed to dogmatism.[62] He had student subjects read each of three editorial satires and then select from a list of statements which was the editorialist's central idea for each satire. Subjects also responded to a short-form dogmatism measure. Dogmatism scores were divided into four groups, those of subjects correctly identifying all three editorial theses, those identifying only two, those identifying only one, and those identifying none. Their mean dogmatism scores were found to differ systematically, going up as fewer theses were identified.

Of course, much misunderstanding is due to ignorance or stupidity, and some must also be due to perceptual difficulties created by goal- and group-oriented emotion. But the great diversity with which individuals react to humor and satire can only be imagined. In a study of joke-telling at Indiana University, Thomas Burns was forced by his data to conclude that: "Tellers were found to view the content of the joke quite differently, to be involved in different aspects of the joke's content, to gain from the joke quite different benefits, and to gain these benefits at different levels."[63]

The writer or speaker who wishes to be "perfectly clear" as well as persuasive should probably eschew satire completely and stick to the straightforward rhetorical message. An extensive (and still growing) accumulation of research upholds the notion, for instance, that a speaker who can and will follow the prescriptions of speech content, organization, and delivery which are advocated by almost any speech textbook will produce *some* measurable persuasion. As this chapter shows, the track record for satire is not nearly so clear. It may be that more innovative research in the future will discover ways in which satire affects attitude formation and change, ways that perhaps have not even been thought of yet.

It must be remembered, of course, that the experiments showing that both "traditional" and satirical attempts at persuasion can be successful were conducted primarily with captive (thus attentive) student audiences. Whether the use of humor in persuasion or the casting of one's persuasive message in the more entertaining satirical form will increase *attention to* one's message is an issue not yet resolved. Common sense would indicate that, if one speaker or writer is known to be entertaining as well as persuasive, he would draw the audience whereas the persuasive but nonentertaining speaker or writer would not. Both Roy Wilkins and Dick Gregory have just about the same message for the public: that the American black man wants his rights and must have them. But, of the two, it is Gregory, after all, the comedian-cum-civil-rights-activist, who draws the crowds.

It does seem that, where satire is perceived as such, and its serious message is understood, some persuasion seems to result. Those *strongly* opposed to its message may distort it to the point where it cannot be effective with these most-prejudiced. But the people the message may most affect are those mildly opposed or neutral toward the satire's thesis. And those already favoring the satire's main point may have their belief reinforced.

One other encouraging note might be added here for "fans" of humor—from the field of advertising. Although experiments, such as that done by Perreault,[64] generally show that humorous ads are no more persuasive than are serious, straightforward ads, there can be little doubt that the current trend toward using more and more humor in advertising indicates that advertising men have found humor to be successful in moving the merchandise.

7

What Else Happens When You Tell Jokes?

The previous chapter was concerned with wit and humor as *persuasion*, and perhaps rightly so, since the goal of most communication is the changing of attitudes or motivating others to action. But much communication, even public speaking, is for other purposes, as to inform or entertain. It is common to find students enrolled in speech communication courses assigned classroom speeches to persuade, to inform and to entertain.

Modern communication theory holds, also, that the range of effects sought can vary even further. David Berlo's highly influential text declares, for instance, that

> Our basic purpose in communication is to become an affecting agent, to affect others, our physical environment, and ourselves, to become a determining agent, to have a vote in how things are. *In short, we communicate to influence—to affect with intent.*[1]

Further, on page 16 he states that:

> Purpose and audience are not separable. All communication behavior has as its purpose the eliciting of a specific response from a specific person (or group of persons).

This more modern approach to communication *purposes* allows for *any* effect sought by communicators.

It is further recognized by modern theorists and researchers that much of what we would call speech has no really
"communicative" purpose—that is, it does not seek some particular effect in some particular person or group. Jon Eisenson, J.J.
Auer, and John Irwin, in their *The Psychology of Communication*[2] list
simple "oral pleasure" and "verbal contact" as "noncommunica-
tive" speech purposes. They go on to list other "communicative" purposes of speech. "Social gesture" is one of these, the
greetings of "Good morning, how are you?" or "See you in
court," being examples. Other such speech purposes are to
"disarm hostility," "speech as aggression," and "speech for con-
cealment."

The review of research presented in Chapter 6 could not
conclude that humor and/or wit can be regularly counted on to
produce persuasion *itself* or even to enhance the persuadability
of a communication. In the present chapter we will be concerned
with research and theory that seek to determine what other communicative *effects* may be produced by the use of humorous and/or
witty communication material.

Although it appears, as evidenced by the last chapter, that
communication experts are far from unanimous in their opinions as to the role, if any, that humor does or should play in
communication, it is probable that considerable agreement
exists on the value of humor for *attention* or *interest*. Milton
Dickens' speech textbook discusses the uses of humor in his
chapter, "Gaining Audience Attention."[3] The late William Nor-
wood Brigance, one of the most popular textbook-writers in the
field, has noted: ". . . remember that apt anecdotes and brief
humorous stories heighten interest, and also reinforce serious
points."[4]

Other authors of public speaking textbooks concur that humor is an apt source for attention and interest. John Wilson and
Carroll Arnold include humor, which they define as "introduction of exaggeration, incongruity, irony, word play, unexpected turns of thought or phrase," as one of nine "factors of attention." They explain as the basis for humor's influence the
following:

> The nature of response to humor is not fully understood,
> but the attractions of the *novel* or unexpected and satisfac-

tion derived from safely regaining reality—the *familiar*—after having expectations built up, then reversed, appear to be involved.[5]

Robert Oliver, Harold Zelko, and Paul Holtzman argue that, "Humor is a special kind of change and suspense which, when effective, is interesting to everyone—even to those who habitually groan or complain at an unexpected pun."[6] They also provide a warning that is echoed by other writers in the field:

> In our earlier discussion of humor as a factor of initial interest, the point was made that humorous material must focus listeners on the speaker's idea—not divert them from it. This is no less true in maintaining interest through the use of humor.

Allan Monroe and Douglas Ehninger show enthusiasm for the use of humor for attention, and offer some advice for its use.

> Few things hold attention as well as humor judiciously used. Quips and stories provide relaxation from the tensions created by some of the other factors of attention and prepare listeners to consider the more serious ideas that may follow. Wherever appropriate, introduce amusing anecdotes or allusions to lighten a talk; but . . . follow these two guiding principles for the effective use of humor: *(a) Relevance*—be sure your story or reference contributes directly to the point being discussed. *(b) Good taste*— avoid any quip or anecdote that would offend the audience; do not use jokes about race or religion which would make your listeners uncomfortable or would detract from your credibility.[7]

Arthur Kruger claims that, "The theory behind using humor is that it helps an audience to relax and get into a frame of mind favorable for listening."[8] Waldo Braden proclaims that, "Speakers have long realized the advantages of humor in speechmaking," in his section "Use Humor to Create and Hold Interest."[9] And Kenneth Andersen asserts that, "Humor also functions as an attention factor and may have direct motivational effects."[10]

There is a small collection of experimental studies bearing on the question of whether the inclusion of humor in a speech actually does produce better attention or heightened interest.

The rest of this section is devoted to an explication of these research studies.

The speaker rarely seeks "attention" and/or "interest" from his audience for the mere sake of obtaining those audience attributes. Rather, he seeks to arouse his audience's attention and interest as a means to another end: to cause them to listen more carefully and more energetically. If he can cause his audience to listen more carefully and more energetically, the speaker increases the probability of achieving his *real* purpose—that of informing or persuading his audience.

I have noted that Donald Kilpela's study failed to find a greater persuasive impact for a persuasive speech containing humor than for the same speech without the humor.[11] If greater attention were paid by his subjects to the humorous speech, that heightened interest did not seem to translate into greater persuasive effect. However, Kilpela's study contained a feature unmentioned until now. In addition to testing his subjects for attitude change as a result of hearing either the humorous or nonhumorous speech, he also had them reply to an objective examination over the factual contents of the speech. Here the theory is that, if the humor heightened interest and, therefore, listening, the students might have learned more of the speech's content regardless of how much they were or were not persuaded.

But, again, if the humor produced greater audience interest, it cannot be said to have translated into greater learning as measured by the objective test. One group did not learn significantly more from the speech than the other.

Let it be suggested here only in passing (and taken up in some detail later in this section) that it may be that Kilpela's nonhumorous speech was already quite interesting and that, therefore, the addition of the humor could not raise the interest level significantly (the so-called "ceiling effect"). If it were already interesting enough to maintain a high level of audience attention, the addition of further "interest material" in the form of humor may have been superfluous. But a more serious misgiving about this negative result in terms of learning factual material from the speeches might be that, after all, this was a *persuasive* speech, not an *informative* one. Would not different results be likely if one were to use a nonpersuasive speech to *instruct*, to *inform*?

The first known study to test the hypothesis that humor has an effect on an informative speech was done by Pat Taylor.[12] He prepared two seven-minute speeches explaining how an eighteenth century minister affected the thinking of contemporary people. One of these speeches contained humor, the other did not. The two were otherwise identical, and were tape-recorded by an experienced public speaker. Taylor played these speeches to high school summer institute students in 1963. One group heard the humorous version of the speech, the other heard the nonhumorous version.

Taylor had had each group take an objective examination over the contents of the speeches before hearing it. A comparison of the two groups' pretest average scores showed that they did not differ. He again administered the examination *after* they had heard one or the other version of the speech. A statistical analysis of the results revealed that, as with the pretest, there was no significant difference in average factual retention. Taylor had to conclude that he had not proven the value of humor to produce greater interest and, therefore, greater learning.

Despite the negative and discouraging results of his study, Taylor persevered. He was later able to persuade his doctoral committee at the University of Indiana to let him try again. Thus we have one doctoral dissertation in the field of speech communication tackling the question of what effect, if any, does the inclusion of humor in speeches to inform have upon the retention of information.[13]

This time Taylor prepared a nonhumorous and a humorous version for each of two speeches. One speech was entitled, "What is Totalitarianism," and the other was called "An Explanation of the Whorf Hypothesis."

Correspondence with Taylor produced the information that copies of the speeches he used in his earlier study are no longer in existence. However, the humorous versions of both speeches in the doctoral study *are* available. The humorous contents of each will be specified so that the reader may judge for himself the humorousness of the items.

The second sentence of the "totalitarianism" speech contains the first wisecrack. Of the thirties, the speaker says, "As you know, this was a time when they developed the art of making deep noises from the chest sound like important messages from the brain." Later in the same opening paragraphs the speaker cracks:

> In the American press, for example, the term *totalitarianism* is applied to virtually anything that doesn't reek of democracy. Dictators, communists, strong military leaders—even an organization called the Bird Watchers of America—have been labelled totalitarian.

The second paragraph begins with a crack about Lyndon Johnson using a capital D when spelling "democracy." A couple sentences later he exemplifies a point by saying, " . . . even though your parents may tell you when to jump, they don't tell you how high." In the next paragraph he mentions a professor who "expands a two sentence idea into a fifty page monograph." That same paragraph ends by mentioning that some students probably have felt that some teachers have maintained total and comprehensive control over them, the students.

The next paragraph (the fourth) begins by comparing the power of totalitarian government to the swinger's quest for girls. Both are unlimited. Later in that same paragraph he exemplifies how a totalitarian uses a particular *means* to achieve his single-minded ideology: "An example of this might be a wife's control of her husband by knowing his favorite foods and what restaurants serve them."

The fifth paragraph contains an old anecdote, this one applied to Winston Churchill, who strolled into Parliament one afternoon slightly inebriated.

> A woman came up to him and said, "Sir, you're drunk." Churchill replied, "And you, madam, are ugly. —But tomorrow I'll be sober."

The next paragraph compares the Jesuits' treatment of Paraguayan natives as high class apes with "the genesis of the popular Indiana statement referring to animals." Supposedly, "the farmers send their cattle to market and their pigs to Indiana University."

The sixth paragraph contains a pun on the late Mayor

Daley of Chicago. Totalitarians attempt "to achieve a unity through the absolutization of the state, thereby hoping to achieve a unity of thought and purpose." Supposedly, "This is what the poor of Chicago accuse their mayor of doing by making them beg for their *Daley* bread."

The seventh paragraph of the speech contends that modern communication technology actually can aid the cause of totalitarianism. The complete second half of that paragraph is reported here, as it seems to contain three distinct jibes:

> An excellent example of this might be the college sorority. The girls certainly have an all-embracing means of communication and their high speed transmission of commands and reports is unequaled. It is, in fact, at this point that some political scientists distinguish between a totalitarian state and the absolute monarchy. According to one theorist, "It isn't that Louis the Fourteenth didn't try, he just didn't have the means available." Indeed this dependence on technology seems to be what Alexander Herzen, a nineteenth-century Russian liberal, foreboded when he wrote, "Some day Genghis Khan will return with the telegraph"; or as a modern version "be careful what you promise her, the olive in the martini might be a microphone."

Paragraph eight contains an old spoonerism by a disc jockey: "There's an Empty Bunk in the Cat House Tonight." However, the last two paragraphs seem to lack humor.

Taylor's speech on the Whorf hypothesis begins with what could be interpreted as a wisecrack: "It's popularly believed, except by those advocating women's liberation, that reality is present in much the same form to all men of sound mind." The next humorous item appears to be a crack at philosophers, defining one as "a lunatic who can analyze his own delusions." The next couple of sentences refer to the Whorf hypothesis as "exotic," but "not stirring in the same way as exotic dancers," which allusion might be considered humorous.

The second sentence of the third paragraph contains another contemporary wisecrack. After stating that, according to Whorf, language acts as molds into which minds are poured, thus determining how they will think, he wonders "if he were looking into the future at this point and commenting upon former Vice President Spiro Agnew's brand of Communication."

Most of the next (fourth) paragraph is a humorous explanation by example of the "literal translation argument." It is:

> . . . the French translation of our phrase, "How are You?" The French phrase, translated literally means "How go you?" After I translated it that way one time in French class, my teacher told me where to go. At this point Whorf would ask, does this mean that the French are more kinetic and the speakers of French more sedentary?

The fifth paragraph contains no humor. The sixth, explaining Whorf's "name and lack of name" hypothesis, utilized this bit of humor:

> I'm still searching for a name for the pilot I recently flew with. As we landed he said, "Ladies and gentlemen, we're now arriving in Indianapolis. Please set your watches back sixty years."

The rest of that paragraph was also classified as humor:

> . . . the Eskimos have three different words for snow, we have only one word—that we use in polite company.

The last sentence of paragraph 6 is intended to be humorous, an example of Doob's hypothesis that the longer the description, the less precise that description. "The longer we take to explain why we were two hours late for a date, the less precise we become."

Paragraph 7 lacks humor. Paragraph 8 ends with a jibe that Whorf's and competing theories on explanation-length vs. familiarity with phenomena being named "does nothing to explain why one has more and more trouble explaining being two hours late, the more frequently it occurs."

Paragraph 9 points out that the Iakuti language has but one word to describe both "blue" and "green" and, that the speaker "once tried to explain to a traffic cop who ticketed [him] for [his] inability to tell green from red." Paragraph 10, regarding "etymology," a word look-alike for "entomology," comes into play for punning purposes: "Although some do consider all of Whorf as being capable of *bugging* a person, this shouldn't be confused with entymology."

Paragraph 11 is concerned with Whorf's argument on "unlike etymology." The speaker concludes that, "Were he alive today, I'm sure Whorf would analyze the college radical's favorite term of endearment, fascist pig, . . . by saying the two cultures concentrate on different attributes of the same thing."

The next paragraph contains one throwaway wisecrack. The speaker admits that "we normally don't consider nouns to have gender—and some rock singers are doubtful . . . ." The last two paragraphs seem to lack humor, except for the last two sentences of the speech. After commenting upon the difficulties inherent in understanding the Whorf hypothesis, the speaker states:

> It is, as a matter of fact, this very question that leads so many professors to quit teaching and go into industry. Why not mention it to *your* favorite professor?

It should be stated here and now that the humorous items Taylor included in his speeches were pretested to ensure that subjects like those to be in his study actually perceived them as humorous. Also, ratings of the completed speeches indicated that the humorous and nonhumorous speech on each topic did, in fact, differ from each other only on the humorous dimension.

So, what happened to learning? On the totalitarian speech, there appeared to be no differences in learning. But on the Whorf hypothesis speech, a significant difference in learning occurred—but it favored the group which heard the *non*humorous version. These findings, especially with the Whorf speech, contradict what one would expect from the theory of "humor causes interest and attention." Unless, of course, the humor may have had some sort of function that, in the case of the Whorf speech, detracted from the informational points covered by the objective examination.

The one study which *does* tend to support the notion that the addition of humor to informative speaking increases attention and thus heightens learning is a master's thesis done by John D. Gibb at the University of Utah in 1964.[14] Gibb used a speech concerned with biology, with one version containing eight humorous passages.

After the introductory sentence of the humorous version, the audience was regaled with:

> There is an old perennial joke about the curious little boy who went wading with the little daughter of the family next door. Pretty soon they decided that the only way they

could keep their clothing dry was to take them off. The small boy stopped to look the little girl over. "Gosh," he remarked, "I didn't know there was that much difference between Catholics and Mormons."

Two paragraphs later the audience of the humorous version heard:

Two people were walking down the street and one said to the other, "Look at that youngster with her short hair, sweat shirt, pedal pushers and gym shoes. You can't tell if she is a girl or a boy." "I can," said the other, "because she is my daughter." "Oh, I'm sorry. I would never have said that if I had known you were her father." "I'm not her father. I'm her mother."

The next paragraph was fairly long, ending with this unusual joke:

One man spent his life turning cucumber seeds inside out before he planted them so when grown they would have dimples instead of warts.

The next paragraph was even longer, ending with:

Speaking of comparing animals with us, a teacher had taken her small-fry class to the zoo. Pointing to a deer, she asked one of the small boys, "What is that?" The boy looked hard, but said, "I don't know." "Come, come," said the teacher, "you know what that is. What does your mother call your father?" The boy looked again, then said, "Don't tell me that's a louse!"

The next paragraph is a long one, about cell division. The middle of the paragraph contains a joke, related to the subject of cell division:

A drunk, standing in the middle of the sidewalk, saw two nuns coming toward him. As they got near him they parted. He staggered between them and then they came back together again and continued walking down the street. The drunk, taking it all in, said, "How did she do that?"

The text of the speech continues on a serious vein for a full typewritten page. Then a serious point is made about early biologists and it is "reinforced" with a joke:

Although the early naturalists knew of thousands of plants

and animals, there was no system for naming and classifying them. One biologist would say to another biologist,
"What is that you have?" "Why, that's a chrysanthemum,"
said the other. "It looks like a rose to me." "Spell it."
"K–r–i–s– . . . by golly, that is a rose!" Thus, confusions
arise.

The next paragraph, about more recent developments in biology, mentions that several biologists paid special attention to
researching bacteria. That topic calls up these jokes:

Did you know that thousands of bacteria can live on the
point of a needle? What a strange diet!

Did you know that cigar smoke kills bacteria? But it's hard
to get 'em to smoke.

More than a full typewritten page of serious text follows. Just
before the concluding two sentences the last joke appears:

The announcement of the biochemistry professor's new
book and his wife's new baby appeared almost together in
the paper. The professor, when he was congratulated by a
friend upon that proud event in his family, naturally
thought of that achievement which had cost him the
greater effort and modestly replied: "Well, I couldn't have
done it without the help of two graduate students."

Gibb exposed two groups of University of Utah students to
the biology lecture containing the humor, above. Two other
groups heard the same lecture, but without the humor. Another "control" group heard the control (nonhumorous) lecture, but with additional information included in it to make it as
long as the lecture containing the humor.

As will be noted later, Gibb's is the *only* study of this kind
which tends to support the thesis that humor aids in the retention of knowledge. I believe that there are two reasons for
Gibb's finding success where others have failed.

The first reason, a fundamental difference between Gibb's
study and others (some yet to be reported here), is that he went
about constructing his lecture backwards. He began with his
test of the information and worked back from there. The test he
began with was a standardized biology examination used at
Utah. From this he constructed a lecture which included the
answer to each question in the test; and, apart from the humor

he added, the lecture seems to contain little more than the answers to his questions. The lecture seems remarkably "compact," containing no asides, no nuances, no conjectures—just factual information that can be the basis for objective test questions.

Ordinarily a teacher will prepare a lecture first, including conjecture, nuance, reasons for various statements, and so on, and *then* write up an examination on the lecture. And, if the teacher writes up an objective-scored examination, he will stick very close to only the *factual* data of his lecture.

The second major reason why I feel that Gibb's humorous speeches produced better recall is that, in his experiment, there was no satisfactory control over the time of day the students heard the speeches. One group of control students who heard the "regular" control speech did so at 7:45 in the morning, a time not noted in academic circles for producing the most bright-eyed and intellectually aware students. The other "regular" control group met at 12:00 noon, when students are either already sleepily digesting an early lunch or else hungrily anticipating a later lunch. The larger control group who heard the "extended" speech met at the "decent" hour of 9:55 A.M., but the extra information in the "extended" speech may very well have produced in the students hearing it what psychologists call "retroactive inhibition" of learning, or what communication theorists call "overloading the channel"; that is, giving them too much to learn so that learning efficiency is lowered.

When did the experimental subjects hear the humorous speeches? At the quite decent academic hours of 8:50 and 11:00.

One other possible reason must be considered, this being another possibly uncontrolled variable: what I call "practical intelligence."

My several years of experience in the field of higher education have convinced me that there is a kind of "practical intelligence" which immensely aids one in the day-to-day tasks, activities, and actions that constitute the process of "going to college." This practical intelligence is made up of several factors. "Test-wiseness," that ability to take tests well, to spot in a book or lecture an item of information that will make a good answer to a multiple-choice question, is one factor. Another is a kind of gritty stick-to-itiveness that causes one student to follow through on a project while another leaves the open book and heads for a beer or sandwich. A kind of shrewdness, part native intelligence and part a learned knowledge of how human nature and the college bureaucracy works, plays a part. And there are obviously others.

This practical intelligence of "how to go to college," in my experience, seems to be especially useful to college students in the practical game of getting a good schedule of courses at registration. The shrewd and the gifted get themselves in to see their advisors early, and thus get into the more desirable 9, 10, and 11 o'clock classes; the less shrewd and the more leisurely wind up getting the 7:45 A.M. and the noon-time class hours, both usually anathema to the average college undergraduate.

So what I am suggesting is that the two "regular" control sections in Gibb's study may have averaged something below what the experimental groups would in the "how to go to college" practical intelligence.

Either of these two reasons would adequately explain Gibb's success, the "intelligence" factor depending upon the schedule factor, or his technique of creating his test of the dependent variable first and the stimulus last. But some feature of the design must be at fault, for no one has been able to replicate Gibb's superiority of recall for a humorous over a nonhumorous message.

In fact, in two of the experiments conducted for Markiewicz's dissertation reported in the preceding chapter, recall produced by serious messages was superior to that produced by similar but humorous messages. And in two studies by Gruner to be reported next, humor was again found to not aid retention of factual material.

I became interested in the connection between use of humor and retention of information from an informative speech as a result of reading the above two studies by Taylor and Gibb. Consequently I performed an experiment at the University of Nebraska in 1966[15] to further study the phenomenon. In addition to testing again the hypothesis of humor aiding in learning from informative discourse, the study investigated another question: Does the use of humor affect the speaker's "image" in terms of audience ratings?

Male upperclassmen in a beginning speech course at Nebraska served as subjects. On each of two days, Tuesday and Thursday, a large lecture class was separated by shuffling and then randomly stacking the class cards of the two lecture section students into two piles, "experimental" and "control." After dividing, then, one group was sent to another room for the experimental or control procedures. Such random selection controlled for most factors, including "practical intelligence," age, class standing, and so on.

Each group of students was told they would hear a tape-recorded speech on "listening" that was being evaluated for use in the course the next semester. They were told that they would take a test over the material later, as well as respond to several evaluation measures.

After the tape-recorded speech was played, the students were handed the test and the evaluation measures. They answered the questions, responded to the evaluation measures, and then were dismissed.

The basic speech used was one on the process of "listening" developed for the doctoral dissertation of Robert J. Kibler.[16] It contained mostly research results of studies of the listening process. The test used was a twenty-five item exam shortened from the original thirty-six item test Kibler also developed for his dissertation. Each question in the test had been previously validated as being answered in the speech.

The evaluation measures the students responded to were: the twelve semantic differential scales which McCroskey's factor analysis[17] had found to reliably measure a speaker's "character" and "authoritativeness," the two major aspects or factors of a speaker's "ethos" or "image"; two semantic differential scales measuring the speech's funniness":[18] and a semantic differential scale bounded by "highly interesting" and "uninteresting."

The humor added to the basic speech was considered appropriate to the content in which it was imbedded, and came from my stock of "tested" material and anthologies of humorous material. Four of the humor items appeared early in the speech introduction, with three more in the first paragraph of the speech body. Six more were scattered throughout the rest of the speech. This arrangement was used for the reason that the concentration of humor at the beginning, it was expected, would build up in the subjects an expectation of humor (inducing attention), and this expectation would be reinforced occasionally throughout the speech. Also, the relevancy issue had to be settled satisfactorily: each humor item needed to be contiguous with material to which it was relevant. The scattering of the humorous items seemed to fit that issue.

Below is the opening paragraph of the introduction; only that in italics was included in the "serious" or nonhumorous version:

> It has been said that the human brain is a wonderful and remarkable thing. It starts to function the instant you are born and doesn't stop until the moment you stand up to give a speech. Most of you in speech class can appreciate this remark because *you have experienced some anxiety in this speech class. But how many of you function effectively when you're not speaking—when you're listening?*
>
> Listening, for instance, to a lecture. Some say, you know, that: "Lecturing is the process of conveying information from the notebook of the professor to the notebook of the student—without going through the minds of either." This is due partly to poor listening. And partly due to poor lecturing. I suppose you've all heard about the professor who dreamed he was lecturing to his classes—and when he woke up, he was?
>
> *We're going to spend about ten minutes together today trying to understand the listening process.*

The body of the speech began with the paragraph below. Again, only that part in italics appeared in the nonhumorous version of the speech.

> *But you still want to know, "Why study listening?" Your grades are based on tests over lectures. Studies reveal training increases comprehension and understanding . . .* of lectures. And I'm sure we've all sat through some lectures that needed all the comprehension and understanding they could get! You've probably already heard my favorite definition of a lecture: "Something that makes you feel numb on one end and

dumb on the other." Which reminds me of a philosophy class I was in once. The professor looked up from his yellowed notes, peered toward the back of the room, and asked: "Who's smoking back there?" One student yelled back: "No one. That's just the fog we're in."

The other six items, scattered through the rest of the speech, appear below:

> So, you see—the next time you get a low grade on an hour exam, you have a ready-made alibi for your instructor. Just tell him that your problem is you never had training in listening. He might not believe you, but at least he'll appreciate hearing a new and rather creative excuse.

> One pilot who apparently did not get such listening training was that one Shelley Berman told us about. Remember, he came on the intercom with something like, "Hello Ladies and Gentlemen. This is the Captain speaking. Welcome to Flight 207, nonstop to-uh —— uh —— uh——

> Or, to paraphrase one wag's description of a colossal bore: "His dull conversation is occasionally highlighted by one of his brilliant flashes of silence."

> To put it analogically, to say that reading or hearing is the same as listening is like saying that there is no difference between calling your girl friend a "vision" and calling her a "sight."

> Keep your head. After all, if you can keep your head when all those about you are losing theirs—you're either a man, my son, or else you don't understand the seriousness of the situation.

> Then, why take notes? You may be mistaken for a "grind," you know. You all know what happens when an instructor walks in and says, "Good morning, class." The C students say "good morning" back—the A students write it down in their notes.

As the comments on the study by John Gibb earlier revealed, the addition of humor to the speech on listening did not aid learning of its factual material. Each group averaged just barely more than fourteen correct test items each.

Did the students perceive the humor in the so-called humorous version of the speech? The answer is yes. On the "funniness" ratings, the humorous version averaged over eight "points," whereas the nonhumorous version averaged only a fraction above four "points." Differences this large, statistical tests showed, would happen less than once in a hundred times by sheer chance alone.

Did the humor affect the speaker's "image?" The answer is yes, partially. There was no difference in the speakers' average "authoritativeness" scores; but, then, none was really expected. The telling of jokes does not (and perhaps should not) cause a speaker to be perceived as more "expert," "knowledgeable," and so on. But there *was* a significant difference in how the humorous and nonhumorous speakers were perceived on the "character" dimension of image. The humorous speaker was perceived as from over two to almost four points "higher" in character.

This last finding tends to support the common-sense notion that we "like" better the fellow who uses in his lectures apt, relevant humor that pleases and entertains us somewhat more than we "like" the fellow who only informs us.

The results of the "interestingness" ratings of the speeches were initially (but not eventually) surprising. Both the humorous and the nonhumorous speeches were rated highly interesting, on the average; and there was practically *no* difference in their average ratings of interestingness. This finding suggested that the humor added to the speech did *not* increase the speech's interestingness.

Some careful thought and a rereading of Kibler's dissertation, which first used that speech, revealed why the addition of humor probably failed to add to its initial interestingness. The original speech was already interesting to a maximum, or at least optimal, degree.

Kibler's speech had been carefully written and rewritten to conform to what Rudolf Flesch's research shows is what heightens prose in both "reading ease" and "human interest." To achieve the ease, a message must be composed of both short sentences and short, easy words. To score high in human interest, according to the Flesch formula, a message must be high in what he calls "personal words" and "personal sentences."[19] Kibler's experimental speech was found to score quite high on both criteria.

If a speech is already so interesting that the addition of humor will not increase interest (the "ceiling effect"), the next question to occur to me was: would such addition of humor aid the interestingness (and, thus learning from) an *un*interesting speech? The only way to try to answer that question was to conduct another study, which I did in 1968.[20]

For this study, the experimental design, the test over the speech's information, and the criterion measures the students completed were much the same as in the earlier experiment. What was different is that an additional level of *interestingness* of speech was employed, plus the fact that some additional humor was added to the humorous version.

In all, four versions of the speech were used: a humorous/interesting, a nonhumorous/interesting, a humorous/dull, and a nonhumorous/dull speech.

The same speech developed by Kibler and used earlier by Gruner served again as the nonhumorous/interesting speech. To create the nonhumorous/dull speech, the original speech was rewritten to make it score quite low on the Flesch "human interest" scale and somewhat lower on the Flesch "reading ease" scale. Practically all *personal words* were removed; all "personal sentences" were depersonalized; most sentences were rewritten to make use of an inactive rather than an active verb, etc. For example, the following paragraph in the "interesting" version,

> What's the point? Simple! Most students benefit from listening training. Reducing wide differences in listening ability produces more effective communication.

was rewritten to read

> The relevant point behind these experimental conclusions is relatively elemental: listening training is beneficial to most students. More effective communication is produced by reduction of wide differences in listening ability.

To create a "humorous" version of each of these speeches, the same items of humor used in the earlier study by Gruner were added, plus some other items that had become available to him since the earlier experiment. Two more items were added to the introduction. One was:

> And I'm keeping this [speech] short . . . After all, a speaker who can't strike oil in ten minutes should stop boring.

The introduction concluded with:

> Stay awake, now. I have heard, you know, that if all the people who have ever sat through a lecture like this were laid end to end, they would still stretch and yawn.

Added to the first paragraph of the body of the speech was one more crack:

> Of course you know what a philosopher is . . . . He's a man who talks about stuff he doesn't understand, and makes his audience think it's *their* fault.

After the crack about "no listening training" as an excuse for a poor exam grade, professors are punned-at: "After all, what is a professor? He is a man who got that way by degrees." Two items were added just before the crack about the dull conversation of a colossal bore:

> As a great man once said, silence is the only message that can't be misquoted.

> Of course, silence has also been called the only real substitute for brains. Remember the old saying—"Better to remain silent and be *thought* a fool than to speak up and remove all doubt?"

Four paragraphs later were added two more items, with some little nonhumorous lecture between them:

> Yogi Berra once remarked that you can see an awful lot just by observin'. One can also hear an awful lot just by listenin'.

> For instance, don't think of after dinner speeches as "The highest possible longitude and the lowest possible platitude." And don't consider public speaking simply as "The art of making loud noise seem like deep thought," or think of oratory as "the art of making deep noises from the chest sound like important messages from the brain."

I tape-recorded the "humorous/interesting" speech, using an optimum amount of vocal delivery features which research tells us tends to add interest to a speech. That is, the speech was recorded using pleasing amounts of vocal variety in pitch, rate, and intensity. The conversational mode predominated. On the other hand, in order to make the "humorous/dull" speech less interesting, it was tape-recorded in a dull, listless, monotonous voice. As in the previous study, nonhumorous versions were made by rerecording each humorous version electronically, and then editing out the humorous passages. Thus four speeches were created: a "humorous/interesting," a "humorous/dull," a "serious/interesting," and a "serious/dull."

The student subjects in the study were exposed to one of the four speeches during regularly scheduled laboratory periods. They accepted the task with no especial unwillingness; in fact, the assignment came just one period after they had taken a standardized "listening test." They were told they would hear a speech on "the listening process," and then take a test over the material and also respond to some measures that would reveal their evaluations of the speech and speaker.

A total of 220 students originally took part in the experiment, but the total number used in the data analysis was reduced to 144 because of the necessity of "matching" the subjects. Since these students heard one of the speeches with their regular classroom groups, they could not be said to be selected for exposure to a particular speech on a totally *random* basis. So more students than would be actually needed were included in the study originally; and the matching variable used was that of their "listening test" score they had made in the previous laboratory period.

The listening test scores for the students who had been included in the study were secured. Note was made as to which of the four experimental speeches each had been exposed to. Then one person was chosen from each of the four experimental speech groups with listening test scores identical or near-identical. The result was one group of thirty-six people from each of the four experimental conditions with average listening abilities which were practically identical. This subject selection process ensured that any results that occurred would not be due to the fact that one group was, on the average, better listeners than any other group.

The students heard one of the speeches, took an exam over its content, and responded to the criterion measures as they had done in the previous experiment. Results:

1. Both of the two "interesting" speeches were rated significantly higher on "interestingness" than were the "dull" speeches. That is, the supposition that the "interesting" speeches were interesting and the "dull" speeches were dull was upheld.

2. Both of the "humorous" speeches were rated significantly higher on "humorousness" than were the two "serious" speeches. That is, the supposition that the "humorous" speeches contained humor and the "serious" ones did not was upheld.

3. The "humorous/dull" speech was rated significantly higher in "interestingness" than was the "serious/dull" speech. However, in the case of the "interesting" speeches, the "serious" version was rated slightly (and insignificantly) higher than was the "humorous" version. These two facts lead to the conclusion that the addition of humor to the "dull" speech added to its interestingness, but that adding the humor to the already-interesting speech did not significantly increase its interestingness; this, of course, was a basic assumption underlying the study in the first place.

4. As in the previous study, the addition of humor resulted in higher ratings of the speaker's "character." In the present study, this occurred in both the "interesting" and the "dull" versions. In other words, it was again confirmed that audiences "like" the speaker who entertains *and* informs better than the one who merely "informs."

5. In the case of the "dull" speeches, addition of the humor also enhanced ratings of the speaker's "authoritativeness." The humor added to the "interesting" speech did not affect ratings of speaker authoritativeness.

6. The "interestingness" quality produced higher ratings of both speaker character and speaker authoritativeness.

7. Even though it seems clear that the addition of humor to the dull speech made it more interesting (even though it did not add interest to the already interesting speech) as was hypothesized, there were no significant differences among the groups on the amount of information they retained from the speeches.

So, once again, an attempt to establish humor as an

enhancement to learning from an oral message failed. But, again also, humor *does* seem to add favorably to the informative speaker's "image."

But, although the two Gruner studies summarized above both lead to the conclusion that using humor is apt to enhance one's "image," especially the "character" aspect, it must be remembered that there are several conditions in the experiment that must limit this conclusion. For instance, the subjects were students, not representative of the general population. The question arises: would a wider range of people react the same? Also, they heard the speeches by tape-recorder, not radio or television or in person; and the messages were heard, not read. Would hearing the speeches by television or in person, or reading the speeches as opposed to hearing them, make for different responses? Since the recorded speeches were presented in a classroom setting, would the audience members be especially "set" to listen, as to a teacher's lecture? Also: the speeches were heard by individuals gathered together in fairly large groups. Would it make a difference in their responses had they heard the messages as single individuals?

Three other recent studies indicate that one can*not* be sure that his use of humor will enhance his "image." By using different experimental procedures, different results were obtained by both John Kenneth Reid[21] and by David Mettee, Edward Hrelec, Paul Wilkens,[22] and Pat Taylor.[23]

Reid began by "test-marketing" the jokes as presented in the earlier (1967) study by Gruner. He had groups of students read the printed speeches and rate each joke therein on a five-point "funniness" scale. In another pilot study, he used the same speech, but with all the "original" jokes removed and twelve others he had found inserted. These twelve jokes were also rated on the same five-point scale of "funniness." As a result of these two pretesting procedures, he was able to come up with the funniest of the jokes and to construct a "high-humor" speech and a "low-humor" speech with different numbers of jokes which, however, were equally funny, on the average. His "low-humor" speech on the listening process contained *five* jokes averaging 2.08 in "funniness" rating; his "high-humor" speech on listening contained *ten* jokes averaging 2.08 in "funniness." A third speech, the "serious" version, contained none of the jokes.

Reid's "low-humor" speech contained the following jokes:

> I suppose you've all heard about the professor who dreamed he was lecturing to his class and when he woke up, he was!
>
> And I'm keeping this short, I'm like the politician who discontinued long speeches because of his throat. Too many people threatened to cut it.
>
> One pilot who wouldn't have been much aided by this [listening] training, however, was once approached by an old New Englander and his wife who wanted to take a plane ride. "$10? Too much!" they said.
>> The pilot made a proposition. He would take them free if they did not say a single word during the trip. If they spoke, they would pay the $10.
>> Trip over and not a word spoken. Once landed, the pilot said he didn't think they'd do it.
>> "Well," said the old man," you almost won—sure felt like hollering when mama fell out."
>
> You might prefer an answer offered by W.C. Fields—"If at first you don't succeed, try, try again. Then quit. There's no use making a fool of yourself."
>
> Then why take notes? You may be mistaken for a "grind," you know. You all know what happens when an instructor walks in and says, "Good morning, class." The C students say "Good morning" back—and A students write it down in their notes.

Reid's "high-humor" speech contained the above five jokes, and, in addition, these five:

> Besides, I've always had a great deal of respect for men who didn't need an overabundance of words to get their message across. You may have heard the story of Calvin Coolidge who, upon his return from church one Sunday, was asked by his wife what the minister spoke about.
>> "Sin," said Coolidge.
>> "What did he say about it?" asked Mrs. Coolidge.
>> "He was against it."
>
> Which reminds me of a philosophy class I was in once. The professor looked up from his yellowed notes, peered toward the back of the room, and asked: "Who's smoking back there?" One student yelled back: "No one. That's just the fog we're in."
>
> And I'm sure we've all sat through some lectures that

needed all the comprehension and understanding they could get. I remember one philosophy class in which the professor wanted to make a point in logic, so he said, "The United States is bound on the East by the Atlantic Ocean, and on the West by the Pacific Ocean. Now, how old am I?"

"You are forty-eight," called out one of the students.

"How did you arrive at that?" asked the surprised professor.

"It was easy," said the student. "My twenty-four-year-old brother is only *half* crazy."

Speaking of problems with remembering, I know a young woman schoolteacher who boarded a city bus, noticed a familiar face across the aisle, and nodded at him. He stared at her blankly, giving no sign of recognition. Flustered, the girl called out, "I'm sorry. I thought you were the father of one of my children."

Don't be like the coed on her way to a political rally who said, "I'm going with an open mind, a complete lack of prejudice, and a cool, rational approach to listen to what I'm convinced is pure rubbish."

Reid's experimental procedures differed from those of Gruner's two studies in two important ways. First, the speeches were recorded and presented on *video*-tape, not just audio-tape. Secondly, the student subjects viewed one of the three video-taped speeches alone, with no other audience members present. The same skilled speaker presented each of the three speeches (nonhumorous, low-humor, high-humor) for video recording.

After each person in the experiment had observed one of the three speeches on the listening process, he filled out the same semantic differential scales rating the speech's funniness and the speaker's character and authoritativeness scales as used in the Gruner studies.

Statistical analysis of the ratings of the speeches' humorousness revealed that manipulation of the humor variable was successful. The nonhumorous speech was rated lowest in humor, the low-humor speech was rated significantly higher, and the high-humor speech was rated significantly higher than was the low-humor speech.

The results from the ratings of speaker image, however, did not show statistically significant increments in speaker image with greater increases in humor. Reid reports that the differences are "in the hypothesized directions," however; but the differences simply were not large enough to be termed statistically reliable.

Reid attempts to explain the difference between his negative findings of humor-enhanced speaker image with those of Gruner's positive findings in two ways. First, he notes that in his study the subjects were exposed to an experimental message *alone*, without anyone else even in the room, whereas Gruner's subjects heard the speeches in large groups. And he notes, rightly so, that jokes seem to be enjoyed more in groups than in solitude. Leslie Malpass and Eugene Fitzpatrick[24] established this conclusion in an experiment. They exposed students singly and in groups to either "jokes" presented orally or to cartoons, and measured their overt reactions (laughter, smiles) to them, as well as had them rate the jokes and/or cartoons. By both measures, overt reactions and ratings, it was determined that the jokes were better enjoyed in groups, but that cartoons were better enjoyed in solitude. Malpass and Fitzpatrick ascribed the greater enjoyment of jokes in groups to the fact that laughter of *some* in a large group "socially facilitates" the laughter (and, thus, enjoyment) of others.

The other difference between the Gruner studies and his own which may have contributed to the difference in "image" findings, according to Reid, is the fact that his speeches were *seen* as well as *heard*, whereas Gruner's speeches were only heard. It is quite possible, of course, that the visual image of the speaker produced a kind of "anchoring" effect. And, it is quite true that one is apt to react to a visual/auditory message differently than one would to an auditory-only one. Ota Reynolds reports one such example occurring during the first 1960 Nixon-Kennedy television debate:

> John Crosby, who was then the TV and radio critic for the New York *Herald Tribune* and no stranger to the strengths and weaknesses of the media, listened to the debate on radio. A few days later he watched a videotape replay, and in his column he reported amazement at the difference in impact provided by the two experiences. As he listened to the radio he felt that Nixon clearly had the better of the argument, and he was surprised at the general agreement in the press that the laurels went to Kennedy. But after he

viewed the tape, visual effect was so powerful that he could clearly understand the basis for the consensus.[25]

Aside from the differences in individual vs. group and audio vs. audio-visual presentation, I can think of one other reason for the difference between his and Reid's findings on speaker image. It is a well-known fact that one factor affecting whether or not a difference is statistically reliable, or significant, is the number of scores, or subject responses, you are dealing with. It takes a very small difference (if that difference is *regular*) to be statistically significant if your number of responses is large (that is, in groups as large as thirty or more). For a difference to be statistically significant with *small* groups, that difference must be quite a bit larger. In Reid's study, as mentioned above, the differences in speaker image scores were in the hypothesized, or expected direction. However, he was dealing with only thirty subjects, which meant only ten in each of the experimental conditions. Both of Gruner's studies dealt with groups of over thirty in each condition. Perhaps if Reid's study had included more subjects he would have found the "differences in the hypothesized direction" to be statistically reliable. On the other hand, more subjects might have introduced more variance, thus still precluding statistically significant results.

My own tendency is to suspect that Reid's findings failed to reach significance because of his small number of responses, to feel that his failure to replicate the earlier Gruner findings on image enhancement is mostly a statistical artifact. The suspicion is bolstered by the strength of the earlier findings, by "common sense" reasoning, and some of the findings of a study, previously mentioned, by Mettee and associates.

In the Mettee, Hrelec, and Wilkens study, students at Yale were told that an experiment was in progress to determine if Yale students could successfully aid in the process of selecting new faculty members to be hired at their university. Seventy-two Yale undergraduates were paid to participate in the study. It involved watching a brief portion of a video-taped lecture by the "prospective faculty member," followed by a set of questions evaluating that lecturer.

One variable manipulated in the study was that of the *reputation* of the man they were to judge. In one condition the prospective faculty member was reputed to be "aloof," and in the other condition he was "clownish." In both conditions, the lecturer was introduced thusly:

> Mr. _____ is an excellent scholar and knows his field thoroughly. He is imaginative, resourceful, and an asset to any English department. His lecture material is always well-organized and instructive and he is able to make his lectures interesting.

For the "aloof" condition, the introduction ended thusly:

> My only criticism is that sometimes he is too aloof and cold or austere; this personal "detachment" is often the result of his humorless approach to most things in life. This unfortunate trait sometimes detracts from his effectiveness as a lecturer.

For the "clownish" condition, the ending of the introduction was changed to this:

> My only criticism is that sometimes he tries too hard to be interesting and funny, with the result that his humor is often feeble and used in situations where humor is inappropriate and unnecessary. This unfortunate trait sometimes detracts from his effectiveness as a lecturer.

The "lecture" by the "faculty member" was actually videotaped by a graduate student in psychology. A "successful humor attempt" version was made, as well as a "no humor attempt" version.[26] The "successful humor attempt" included the following anecdote:

> As a matter of fact, there is a story which I think is very humorous that shows he [G.B. Shaw] didn't *always* get the last word, or laugh, so to speak. Shaw sent Winston Churchill two tickets to his latest play with an accompanying note that read: "Dear Sir Winston. Here are two tickets to the opening night of my latest play, for you and a friend, if you have one." Churchill sent back the tickets with the following reply: "Dear Mr. Shaw. Unfortunately I am unable to attend the opening night; however, I would appreciate two tickets to the second night performance, if there is one!"

In the "no humor attempt" version a nonhumorous paragraph on the Shaw-Churchill quarrels was substituted for the above anecdote.

Statistical analysis of the competence ratings made by the students of the lecturer indicated that, for the "aloof" condition, the addition of the humor added to or enhanced the lecturer's perceived competence. But the same addition of successful humor *detracted* from the perceived competence of the lecturer in the "clownish" condition. The explanation would seem to be that, where no humor is expected from a "cold, aloof, austere" communicator, the sudden appearance of successful humor enhances his image, whereas the same kind of humor detracts from the image when one is already expecting "clownish behavior." It is even possible that the humor used in the two conditions may have been perceived as different "kinds" of humor. In the "aloof" condition, the humor may have been perceived as brilliant wit; in the "clown" condition the humor may have been perceived as low comedy thrown in as a cheap attempt to enhance the lecturer's popularity. At least this explanation seems compatible with the Goodchild study, mentioned in the preceding chapter, where "sarcastic" wits were perceived as influential but unpopular and "clowning wits" were perceived as popular but *not* influential.

In his study, already mentioned, Pat Taylor also tested for speaker image as a result of using humor in informative discourse. Instead of finding that the use of humor enhanced the speaker's image, he actually found that the humorous speaker was rated *lower* in ethos. However, even Taylor seems to believe that the level of humor used was excessive, and that the humorous speaker was perceived as "clownish" as in the Mettee study. Taylor reports that verbatim reports from his subjects indicate that they thought the speaker was more a "frustrated comedian" than a serious-minded communicator.

The level of humor used by Allan Kennedy in his study reported earlier, was more suitable, probably. Although Kennedy was mostly interested in the enhancement of the speech's persuasiveness through the addition of humor, he also measured for both speaker image and audience recall of factual material. His subjects rated the speakers on scales measuring "dynamism," "expertise," and "trustworthiness." Their comprehension was measured by a twenty-item multiple-choice test.

The humor enhanced only the speaker's perceived "dynamism" on the immediate post-test; however, on the delayed post-test four weeks later, the data revealed higher ratings on all three aspects of "image" for the humorous speaker.

As with most previous studies, no difference occurred in recall scores, either immediately after or four weeks after exposure to the speeches.

Up to this point all the studies reviewed here which used humor in otherwise informative or persuasive messages used humor that was relevant, or germane to the content of the message in which it was imbedded. The only study utilizing humor *not* germane to the material in which it appeared was done by Robert Youngman for his master's thesis.[27] He used an adaptation of the speech, "What Every Yale Freshman Should Know," the same one used later by Brandes in the study already reported. Student subjects heard the speech "straight," or else with either germane or non-germane humor added.

The speech argued that students have a responsibility in college to (1) become curious, and, thus, discover knowledge, and (2) to communicate that knowledge. In other words, the speech urges college students to become *scholars*. The humor items used that were pre-judged to be germane to these ideas were the following:

> Very often questions and answers that are elusive at the moment become increasingly important in later investigations. When a baby rabbit asked his mother, "Where did I come from?" she answered, "A magician pulled you out of a hat, so stop asking so many questions!" The baby rabbit accepted its mother's meaningless answer without question. However, unlike the rabbit, the scholar must continue to ask questions and to seek the truth.
>
> Therefore, if someone had interrupted Adam in the middle of the process of producing Eve, Adam's excuse for his research might have been: "That he and the Lord were taking some spare parts and making the first LOUDSPEAKER." But Adam and the Lord may have been prompted by nothing more than curiosity. I wonder if Adam would have explained his behavior in terms of utility.
>
> In fact, the scientist who doesn't have his head in the clouds these days may be working on the wrong project.
>
> In the scholar's search for truth he has come to learn and

accept his responsibility for communicating it as well. The scholar, unlike the typical convention speaker who suggested to his audience, "Gentlemen, these are not my figures I am quoting; they are the figures of someone who knows what he is talking about." The scholar, unlike this speaker, is driven by a force as strong as curiosity that impels him to tell what he knows.

So failures in learning to communicate effectively are serious failures. As one freshman diligently and anxiously prepared for his first oral report, he chanced to ask one of his fellow classmates, "Do you know what it is to go before an audience?" Whereupon his classmate replied, "No! I spoke before an audience once, but most of it went before I did." If you don't learn to communicate effectively in college, if your audience leaves when you begin to speak, you have failed to find a proving ground where you may test your findings against criticism.

One college roommate asked another, "What is your brother in college?" "A half-back." "No, I mean in studies." "Oh, he's away back." It is all right to have various purposes for coming to college, and you may fulfill them. You can play football as part of your education, but we do not want you away back.

The non-germane humor added to the other version of the speech appears below:

As one politician said to his opponent: "There are many ways, my friends, of making money. But there's only one honest way." Opponent: "What's that?" Politician: "I was pretty sure you wouldn't know."

Mrs. Jones opened her refrigerator and to her surprise found a rabbit sitting inside. "What are you doing here?" she asked the rabbit. "Isn't this a Westinghouse?" asked he. "Yes," said Mrs. Jones. "Well, I'm just westing."

A Chicago newspaper points out that the government prints and distributes the speeches made by congressmen without the slightest profit. It might also be added that they are read the same way.

A funeral director spied an elderly lady attending the wake of a friend. He immediately approached her and said, "Madam, may I ask how old you are?" Whereupon the old lady proudly replied, "Of course, I will be 106 on my next birthday." The undertaker quipped, "It's hardly worth going home."

> This reminds me of one college graduate who was over-
> heard talking to another. Grad: "This university certainly
> takes an interest in a fellow, doesn't it?" A friend: "Why?"
> Grad: "Well, I read in the graduate magazine that they will
> be very glad to hear of the death of any of their alumni."

> This brings me to a woman who was famous for being a
> great talker and who came down with an ailment and de-
> cided to see a doctor. She babbled on and on about her
> symptoms. Finally the doctor said, "Stick out your tongue,
> please." The woman did. "Now," said the doctor, "keep it
> there till I've told you what to do in order to get well."

Each of Youngman's subjects responded to the version of
the speech he heard on nine-point scales tapping several attitudinal variables and evaluations of that speech. Statistical analysis of the results indicated that both humorous versions of the
speech were perceived as more humorous than the "straight"
version; furthermore, the germane humor was perceived as
germane to the subject matter whereas the non-germane humor was not. The speech using germane humor was perceived
as more "worthwhile" than the one using non-germane humor, but was not perceived as superior on any other dimension. There seemed to be no difference among the three
speeches' effect upon the subjects' attitudes toward scholarship.

In addition to the attitudinal and evaluation items, the subjects took a test over the information in the speech. As in all
other studies (with the exception of Gibb's), the addition of humor, whether germane or not, did not add to the subjects' retention of information.

The bulk of experimental evidence to date tends to support
the notion that the proper—and emphasis is placed here on the
word *proper*—use of humor can enhance the image of a speaker,
even though it may not add the kind of interest that can increase learning from an informative message. Of course, what
is "proper" at one time or in one situation may not be "proper"
in another, so no definition of "proper" use of humor is attempted. Human beings and human interactions are highly
complicated and extremely diverse phenomena.

It is obvious to the most casual observer that the uses of
laughter and laughter-producing stimuli as communication far
outnumber those of attempting persuasion, improving learning,

and enhancing speaker image. Laughter, jokes, puns, etc. are used for a host of interpersonal communication situations and effects. However, little really careful research has been done on humor used as communication other than the studies mentioned above and in Chapter 6. As Jay Davis and Amerigo Farina put it,

> And while many writers recognize the social nature of humor . . . little research has been done along these lines . . . and probably no research attention has been paid to the communication function of humor [sic]. Yet common experience indicates that the presence and degree of laughter is very often a function of what people wish to communicate. Consider, for example, the situation where a new member of a group offers his first (but, alas, poor) joke. If he is liked, his joke is apt to meet with laughter from his listeners. In this situation, the laughter implied acceptance of his offering and by extension—acceptance of him—the individual who laughs at a racially biased joke while in racially mixed company may be viewed as communicating agreement with the derogatory implications of the jest.[28]

For their own study Davis and Farina hypothesized that male undergraduates would use interest in sexual cartoons to communicate their sexual interest in a sexually attractive female experimenter. Scholars who regularly must plow through the oftentimes pedantic, unreadable accounts of extremely technical investigations of irrelevant, uninteresting minutiae in scholarly journals occasionally find and delight in studies such as Davis and Farina's. It is to find a lily among the thorns.

The writers hired a highly attractive female, Sherry Friedman to conduct their experiment under four separate conditions.

In one condition, called the "arousal/communication," she asked each young man who entered the lab for the experiment to view some cartoons and rate them on a funniness scale. In this condition she was "dressed in such a way as to maximize her (considerable) sexual attractiveness." Also, "she behaved in a flirtatious manner—a routine which was practiced and standardized as much as possible." Friedman's dress and flirtatious manner established the "arousal" part of the "arousal/communication" condition.

For the "communication" part of the condition, each subject was handed the cartoons and was asked to verbally give Friedman his ratings—thus he would be directly communicating to *her*—whereupon she would record them on a form. Each subject judged and rated a total of twenty-four cartoons, eight of which were blatantly sexual in nature.

In the "arousal/noncommunication" condition Friedman's behavior and dress were as above, but each subject was to record his ratings of the cartoons on a standardized form and turn it in to the departmental secretary as he left. Friedman remained in the room, but, apparently no longer interested in the young man or the experimental procedures, busied herself with a book. Thus, the subject was aware that his judgments of the cartoons would *not* be communicated to the lady.

The other two conditions for the subjects' ratings of the twenty-four cartoons were the "nonarousal/communication" and the "nonarousal/noncommunication." In the first the subject communicated his evaluations to Friedman, who recorded them, as above, and in the other he recorded his own to be turned in, unsigned, to the departmental secretary, also as above. For the "nonarousal" part of these conditions Friedman's "manner and dress were proper, polite, and formal."

From their data, Davis and Farina were able to conclude positively that "sexual arousal does have a clearly measurable impact upon [sexual] humor appreciation." Further, they concluded that, "As predicted, providing an opportunity to communicate [with this attractive girl] through [sexual] humor has a striking influence on [sexual] humor appreciation . . . ." In other words, both the feigned seductiveness of the girl and the opportunity to communicate their humor ratings to her, whether she was feigning seductiveness or not, contributed to higher ratings (and, presumably, higher appreciation) of the *sexual* humor. This conclusion from an experimental study seems to bolster the validity of G. Legman's claim that the telling of "dirty jokes" by men around females can be interpreted as initial attempts at seduction.[29]

In discussing their study, Davis and Farina point out that "in the usual course of social interaction, both the offering of humor and the response thereto provide a potent sub rosa means of communication." For instance, they ask that we consider the problem of defining the limits one should respect regarding acceptable social intercourse.

> A number of strategies may be used to cope with this problem, the most common of which appears to be the selection of obviously banal and inoffensive topics. Another strategy, it is suggested, is to broach the potentially taboo subjects by incorporating them within the fabric of a joke. The listener, by providing or withholding laughter, may then indicate whether the topic falls outside the range of topics acceptable to him. This indirect method clearly smooths the process of designating limits, since in this way the listener may reject the offered jest on the pretext that it is simply a poor joke. Had the taboo remark been made openly, it would have been more difficult for the listener to reject the remark without rejecting the speaker at the same time.

A study by Rose L. Coser indicates the diverse purposes to which people can put humor in a hospital setting.[30] Coser, while not performing an experimental or even a quantitative study, for three months did carefully study, through personal observation, the social structures linking patients in a large hospital. She offers several hypotheses about how these patients use "jocular talk" among themselves for clearly interactional and communicative ends.

She notes, for instance, that hospital patients are the people of the lowest prestige and esteem in the hospital hierarchy; as a result, they suffer from insecurity. They therefore use humor ridiculing the staff of the hospital (those in higher position) through jocular talk among themselves. Further, they relate potentially dangerous incidents of hospital routine in a jocular fashion, thereby stripping such events of their threatening aspects. This, it is felt, makes them feel less insecure.

Coser also points out that the "jocular gripe" is used as a mechanism for transforming a personal experience into one that can be shared by all. An individual, Coser points out, is much more apt to make a *personal complaint* ("I can't eat the food in this place") *to another single individual.* But, when addressing a *group* of peers (fellow patients), the patient is more likely to use a jocular gripe ("Those hamburgers today were hard as rocks, if I'd bounced them against the wall they'd come right back").

The consensual laughter resulting from such a jocular gripe is likely to produce in the laughing patients another source of pleasure: by laughing together at the common "enemy," they share, however briefly, a kind of group consensus, something which Alfred S. Stanton and Morris S. Schwartz have pointed out in their book, *The Mental Hospital*[31], is an enjoyable experience to patients in and of itself. The jocular gripe, in addition, is simply and purely an invitation for others to join in with their own jocular gripes. In short, it is an invitation to communicate, to interact with one's poor fellows, all caught in the same insecure boat of a hospital. Coser concludes her study with the following summary:

> . . . humor allows the participants, in a brief span of time and with a minimum of effort, mutually to reinterpret their experiences, to entertain, reassure, and communicate; to convey their interest in one another, to pull the group together by transforming what is individual into collective experience, and to strengthen the social structure within which the group functions. Whereas Freud has pointed to the *psychic economy* that humor makes possible for the individual, the contribution it makes to *social economy* should be stressed—a contribution that should not be underestimated in groups whose membership is continuously changing, and especially in the transient little subgroups that are formed for short spans of time each day in wards and sitting-rooms. In such a shifting and threatening milieu, a story well told, which, in a few minutes, entertains, reassures, conveys information, releases tension, and draws people more closely together, may have more to contribute than carefully planned lectures and discussions toward the security of the frightened sick.

As with the experimental methodology for investigating humorous and/or witty material as persuasion, the techniques of studying other communicative effects of humor have yet to be perfected. It is this imperfection of experimental methodology, plus the obvious *recency* of experimentation with humorous stimuli as communication, that has limited the findings in the field to those few detailed here.

We can say that humor in persuasion apparently makes for no increase in persuasion, but that satire, under some conditions, can be persuasive with some kinds of people. About the use of humor in informative discourse, we can probably conclude that its inclusion does not aid in learning factual material; that it adds interest to dull messages but not to already-interesting ones; that the addition of humor to informative messages may, under some conditions, enhance the "image" of the message's source. However, we cannot specify under what conditions these various effects are most or least likely to take place.

I noted earlier that the study of humor seems to have been neglected by psychologists in favor of studying the less pleasurable emotions. A natural result of this neglect is a paucity of research on wit and humor *as communication*.

But the future for humor research may be brightening. A very good sign of the change in climate is the July, 1976 International Conference on Humor and Laughter held in Cardiff, Wales.[32] It is my hope that such conferences as this, and this book which I now conclude, will encourage such research.

Epilogue

Keeping up to date on research in an area, while a book on it is in production, is very much like trying to count baby spiders while the house is on fire. As the manuscript would pass across my desk at various stages of production, I would add to Chapters 6 and 7 what I had found since the last cut and paste job. After going into page proofs, several studies came to light which deserves mention here.

Stuart Surlin and Eugene D. Tate ("*All in the Family*: Is Archie Funny?" *Journal of Communication*, 26, 61–68) had American and Canadian TV viewers reading transcripts of specific, brief vignettes from TV's *All in the Family*. They then rated the vignettes for funniness and responded to a short-form authoritarianism scale. People's ratings of the vignettes varied according to their culture (Canadian or American), their sex, whether high or low in authoritarianism, and which vignette was being rated. Two interesting conclusions emerged: (1) greater appreciation of Archie's humor came from the high authoritarian males and the *low* authoritarian females, and (2) how TV comedy is rated depends explicitly upon the particular comedy vignette in question.

For his master's thesis (to which I lent a hand) at National Chengchi University in Taipei, Scott L.S. Wang exposed Taiwanese students to either an Art Buchwald column or one by a Taiwanese satirist (HO-fan) on the same topic. He varied the credibility of the writers by his introduction of them and divided his subjects according to whether they scored, on a scale by Rotter, as "internal-control" or "external control" personality types. Attitudes toward the satirized topic were measured by semantic differential scales. No statistically significant results emerged to indicate that either message had been effective; however, that is not so surprising. For again, only 35 percent of the Ss (subjects) understood the thesis of the Buchwald piece and only 56 percent caught the gist of Mr. HO-fan's piece.

Larry Powell, in a study still unpublished at this time, exposed subjects to a video-taped satirical or comparable direct attack on congressional politicians (described on p. 201). Ss rated the topic of congressional politicians on "salience" ("importance to them") and attitude valence (pro/con). After viewing one or the other message, they rated the speaker on "sociability," "extroversion," "composure," and "character-competence." Ss generally rated the satirical speaker higher in "sociability" and "extroversion." On the other dimensions of source credibility, the interaction effects suggest that the satirical speaker was only rated higher on "composure" and "character-competence" by those subjects for whom the topic was very important (high salience) and who disagreed with the thesis of the message. It would seem that the satirical approach was a "softer" one and thus less distasteful to those not in agreement with the message and who thought the topic important.

Another researcher has found that short humorous stimuli do not enhance short-term learning, but that the "novelty effect," the effect of having a new teacher with or without humor, is enough to overshadow the interest of the humor. Ann Davies ("Humor as a Facilitator of Learning in Primary School Children," In *It's a Funny Thing, Humor*, edited by Chapman and Foot, New York: Pergamon Press, 1977) has been experimenting with children eight to eleven years old. But she now reports:

> Studies are now in progress in which children are shown four, twenty-minute slide-type programmes during

one school day (either humorous or nonhumorous). The
effects of showing programmes on four consecutive days
are also being examined. . . .

Perhaps looking for longer-range results is the more fruitful
technique. For in a recent study (the original report of which I
have not yet found) described in *Family Weekly* (February 19, 1978,
p. 22) a humorous lecture improved test scores in San Diego
State University psychology classes. The students heard either a
nonhumorous lecture or one of three containing humor. On a
quiz immediately after the lectures there was no difference in
scores. But a retest six weeks later showed higher scores for
those who heard the humorous lecture. Apparently the lecture
contained both germane and nongermane humorous material. It
was reported that humor that was not related to the lecture
material was not conducive to learning. But it did get a better
evaluation of the lecturer. *Family Weekly* concludes that those
witty professors know what is good for college students after all.

Well, we try, anyway.

Notes

Chapter 1

[1]Ernest Harms, "The Development of Humor," *Journal of Abnormal and Social Psychology*, 38 (July, 1943), 356.

[2]In *Children's Humor: A Psychological Analysis* (Glencoe, Ill.: The Free Press, 1954), p. 11.

[3]As quoted in Lewis C. Henry, ed., *Best Quotations for All Occasions* (New York: Fawcett Publications, 1945), p. 127.

[4]Ibid.

[5]Edwin A. Weinstein and Morris B. Bender, "Integrated Facial Patterns Elicited by Stimulation of the Brain Stem," *Archives of Neurology and Psychiatry*, 50 (1943), 34–42.

[6]Personal letter from Desmond Morris dated November 27, 1970.

[7]Greer Williams, "What We Can Learn from the Apes," *Saturday Evening Post* (August 2, 1947), 26–27.

[8]Personal letter from Charles H. Heossle dated June 21, 1971.

[9]Clarence Leuba, *The Natural Man* (Garden City, N.Y.: Doubleday and Co., 1954), p. 30.

[10]Baroness Jane Van Lawick-Goodall, "New Discoveries

among Africa's Chimpanzees," *National Geographic,* 128 (December, 1965), 817.

[11]Katharine Hull Kappas, "A Study of Humor in Children's Books," M.A. thesis, University of Chicago, 1965, pp. 53–56.

[12]New York: McGraw-Hill, 1957.

[13]New York: Bramhall House, 1952.

[14]Louis Untermeyer, ed., *A Treasury of Laughter* (New York: Simon and Schuster, 1946), p. 300.

[15]Ibid., p. 301.

Chapter 2

[1]Calvin S. Hall and Gardner Lindzey, *Theories of Personality* (New York: John Wiley and Sons, 1957), p. 10ff.

[2]Ibid., p. 14.

[3]W.E. Blatz, K.D. Allen, and D.A. Millichamps, *A Study of Laughter in the Nursery School Child* (Toronto: University of Toronto Press, 1936).

[4]J.Y.T. Greig, *The Psychology of Laughter and Comedy* (New York: Dodd, Mead, and Co., 1923).

[5]Edmund Bergler, M.D., *Laughter and the Sense of Humor* (New York: International Medical Book Co., 1956).

[6]Ibid., p. 57.

[7](London: Constable and Co., 1932).

[8]As quoted in Carolyn Wells, ed., *An Outline of Humor* (New York: G.P. Putnam's Sons, 1923), p. 7.

[9]As quoted in the Atlanta *Journal,* April 17, 1971, p. 10.

[10]H.F. Gollob and J. Levine, "Distraction as a Factor in the Enjoyment of Aggressive Humor," *Journal of Personality and Social Psychology,* 5 (1967), 368–72.

[11]D.L. Singer, H.F. Gollob, and J. Levine, "Mobilization of Inhibitions and the Enjoyment of Aggressive Humor," *Journal of Personality,* 35 (1967), 562–69.

[12]Ibid., 569.

[13]"The Relation of Drive Discharge to the Enjoyment of Humor," in Jacob Levine, ed., *Motivation in Humor* (New York: Atherton Press, 1969), p. 54.

[14]Personal letter to me dated November 23, 1970.

Chapter 3

[1]Rapp's phylogenetic theory first appeared in "A Phylogenetic Theory of Wit and Humor," *Journal of Social Psychology*, 30 (1949), 81–96, and later in book form: *The Origins of Wit and Humor* (New York: E.P. Dutton and Co., 1951).

Chapter 4

[1]Max Eastman, *The Sense of Humor* (New York: Scribner, 1921), p. 6.

[2]Calvin S. Hall and Gardner Lindzey, *Theories of Personality* (New York: John Wiley and Sons, 1927), p. 82.

[3]Ibid.

[4]Carl G. Jung, *Psychological Reflections* (Princeton, N.J.: Princeton University Press, 1970), pp. 38–9.

[5]Ibid., pp. 14–15.

[6]Ursula Vils, "Children's Jokes Mostly Hostile?" Atlanta *Journal*, Oct. 3, 1971, 3-B.

[7]Hall and Lindzey, *op. cit.*, p. 85.

[8]George C. Thompson, *Child Psychology* (New York: Houghton Mifflin Co., 1952), p. 328.

[9]Horace B. English and Ava C. English, *A Comprehensive Dictionary of Psychological and Psychoanalytical Terms* (New York: Longmans, Green and Co., 1958), p. 222.

[10]Ibid.

[11]Ibid.

[12]Ibid., p. 158.

[13]Ibid., p. 466.

[14]John E. Pfeiffer, "The Apish Origins of Human Tensions," *Harpers Magazine*, 227 (July, 1963), 55–60.

[15]*Athens* (Ga.) *Daily News*, May 10, 1972. Reprinted by permission of Sydney J. Harris and Publishers-Hall Syndicate.

[16]Ernest Harms, "The Development of Humor," *Journal of Abnormal and Social Psychology*, 38 (July, 1943), 351–69.

[17]The idea that "the development of the individual (from zygote to adult) repeats in miniature the development of the race" is not a new one.

[18]*Encyclopedia Britannica, 1971 edition*, vol. 15, p. 1125.

[19]Ibid.

²⁰Albert Rapp, "A Phylogenetic Theory of Wit and Humor," *Journal of Social Psychology*, 30 (1949), 89.

²¹Ibid.

²²See her *Children's Humor* (Glencoe, Ill.: The Free Press, 1954).

²³Jose A. Benavent Oltra, "Genesis de la Risa Infantil [Origin of Laughter in Children]," *Anuario de Psicologia* I (1970), 107–114.

²⁴*Psychological Abstracts*, 45, (1971) 863.

²⁵Alexander Laing, "The Sense of Humour in Childhood and Adolescence" (thesis abstract), *British Journal of Educational Psychology*, 9 (1939), 201.

²⁶Rapp, *op. cit.,* p. 93.

²⁷U.P.I., "Anti-Nazi Jokes Flowered but Good One Could Kill," *Atlanta Journal*, April 22, 1971.

²⁸Richard Hanser, "Wit as a Weapon," *Saturday Review*, Nov. 8, 1952, p. 51.

²⁹Ibid.

³⁰See R.F. Priest and J. Abrahams, "Candidate Preferences and Hostile Humor in the 1968 Elections," *Psychological Reports*, 26 (1970), 779–83 and R.F. Priest, "Election Jokes: The Effects of Reference Group Membership," *Psychological Reports*, 18 (1966), 600–602.

³¹*Athens* (Ga.) *Daily News*, August 27, 1971.

³²Katharine H. Kappas, "A Developmental Analysis of Children's Responses to Humor," *The Library Quarterly*, 37 (1967) 72.

³³(Los Angeles: Nash Publishers, 1971).

³⁴Ibid., p. 237.

³⁵"A Two Stage Model for the Appreciation of Jokes and Cartoons: An Information-Processing Analysis," Chapter 4 in Jeffrey H. Goldstein and Paul E. McGhee, eds., *The Psychology of Humor* (New York: Academic Press, 1972).

³⁶Goldstein and McGhee, *op. cit.*, p. 248.

Chapter 5

¹Albert Rapp, *The Origins of Wit and Humor* (New York: E.P. Dutton & Co., 1951), p. 150.

²In *Phylon*, 29 (1968), 339–46.

[3]Rapp, *op. cit., p. 150.*

[4]Albert Rapp, "A Phylogenetic Theory of Wit and Humor," *Journal of Social Psychology,* 30 (1949), 82.

[5]Vivian Mercier, "Truth and Laughter; A Theory of Wit and Humor," *The Nation,* 191 (Aug. 6, 1960), 74.

[6]Ibid.

[7]Ibid.

[8]Ibid.

[9]See his *The Irish Comic Tradition* (London: Oxford University Press, 1962).

[10]Mercier, *op. cit.*

[11](Palo Alto, Calif.: Pacific Books, 1963).

[12]For a complete development of Rapp's position see the items in footnotes 1 and 3, above, esp. pp. 152–53 of *Origins of Wit.*

[13]For instance, see Donald C. Bryant, ed., *Rhetoric and Poetic* (Ames, Iowa: University of Iowa Monograph, 1965).

[14]In *Southern Speech Journal,* 29, (December, 1953), 83–97.

[15]See Hoyt Hudson, "Rhetoric and Poetry," *Quarterly Journal of Speech (Education),* 10 (April, 1924), 143–54, and Bower Aly, "Rhetoric and Poetic," *Dictionary of World Literature,* Joseph Shipley, ed., (New York: 1943), pp. 480–81.

[16]The general position argued in this section first appeared in Charles R. Gruner, "Is Wit to Humor What Rhetoric Is to Poetic?" *Central States Speech Journal,* 16 (February, 1965), 17–22.

[17]*Op. cit.,* 88–89.

[18]Edgar Johnson, *A Treasury of Satire* (New York: Simon and Schuster, 1945), p. 18.

[19]Ibid., p. 37.

[20]Gilbert Highet, *The Anatomy of Satire,* (Princeton University Press, 1962), p. 156.

[21]Marie Collins Swabey, *Comic Laughter: A Philosophical Essay* (Yale University Press, 1962), 59–60.

[22]*Time,* Sept, 21, 1962, p. 76.

[23]Cited by James Riedel, "Politics in the Comics," *Symposium,* a publication of Union College, New York (Summer, 1962), p. 8.

[24]Clayton Fritchey, "A Politician Must Watch His Wit," *The New York Times Magazine,* July 3, 1960, p. 8.

252 Notes

²⁵Ibid.

²⁶Leonard Feinberg, *Introduction to Satire* (Ames, Iowa: Iowa State University Press, 1967), 254.

²⁷Ibid., p. 261.

²⁸Bigelow, *op. cit.*, p. 88.

²⁹G. Legman, *Rationale of the Dirty Joke: An Analysis of Sexual Humor* (New York: Grove Press, 1968), p. 217 ff., esp.

³⁰Highet, *op. cit.*, p. 238.

³¹In *The Art of Satire* (Harvard University Press, 1940), p. 37.

³²Bigelow, *op. cit.*, 94–95.

³³Feinberg, *op. cit.*, p. 258.

³⁴Johnson, *op. cit.*, pp. 9 and 16.

³⁵Ibid., pp. 32–33.

³⁶*Christian Century*, August 16, 1961, p. 991.

³⁷"The Unrocked Boat," in "Satire: A Symposium," *Nation*, April 26, 1958, p. 370.

³⁸Bigelow, *op. cit.*, 92–93.

³⁹Johnson, *op. cit.*, p. 32.

⁴⁰Bigelow, *op. cit.*, 90–91.

⁴¹Hudson, *op. cit.*, p. 145.

⁴²Ibid., p. 144.

⁴³Bigelow, *op. cit.*, 90–91.

⁴⁴*Enjoyment of Laughter* (New York: Simon and Schuster, 1936), p. 3.

⁴⁵Examples quoted from Feinberg, *op. cit.*, pp. 136–38.

Chapter 6

¹Elliot Carlson, "Wanted: A Bit of Campaign Humor," *Wall Street Journal*, September 18, 1972, p. 10.

²Wilma H. Grimes, "A Theory of Humor for Public Address," Ph.D. dissertation, University of Illinois, 1953, p. 77a.

³Ibid., 228–29.

⁴Ibid., p. 230.

⁵Ibid., p. 231.

⁶Ibid., p. 232.

⁷William S. White, "Humor in Politics," *Harpers*, 220 (February, 1960), 101.

⁸Clayton Fritchey, "A Politician Must Watch His Wit," *New*

York Times Magazine, July 3, 1960, p. 8.

[9]White, *op. cit.*

[10]"State of the Nation's Humor: A Symposium," *New York Times Magazine,* December 7, 1959, p. 27.

[11]Gilbert Cannan, *Satire* (London: G.H. Doran, 1914), p. 13.

[12]Edgar Johnson, *A Treasury of Satire* (New York: Simon and Schuster, 1945), pp. 7–8, 16.

[13]Marie Collins Swabey, *Comic Laughter: A Philosophical Essay* (New Haven: Yale University Press, 1961), p. 60.

[14]Gilbert Highet, *The Anatomy of Satire* (Princeton, N.J.: Princeton University Press, 1962), p. 156.

[15]"Milestones," *Time,* 80 (September 21, 1962), 65.

[16]"Krokodil Criticisms," *New York Times Magazine,* October 28, 1962, p. 30.

[17]*Congressional Record,* 108 (May 17, 1962), No. 79, A3728.

[18]Leonard Feinberg, *Introduction to Satire* (Ames, Iowa: Iowa University Press, 1967), p. 255.

[19]Ibid., pp. 258, 261.

[20]Ibid., pp. 264–72.

[21]P.E. Lull, "The Effects of Humor in Persuasive Speech," *Speech Monographs,* 7 (1940), 26–40.

[22]Donald E. Kilpela, "An Experimental Study of the Effects of Humor on Persuasion," M.A. thesis, Wayne State University, 1961.

[23]Allan J. Kennedy, "An Experimental Study of the Effect of Humorous Message Content Upon Ethos and Persuasiveness," Ph.D. dissertation, University of Michigan, 1972.

[24]Paul D. Brandes, "The Persuasiveness of Varying Types of Humor," paper presented at the Speech Communication Association Convention, December, 1970, New Orleans.

[25]Charles R. Gruner and William E. Lampton, "Effects of Including Humorous Material in a Persuasive Sermon," *Southern Speech Communication Journal,* 38 (Winter, 1972), 188–96.

[26]Thomas W. Welford, "An Experimental Study of the Effectiveness of Humor Used as a Refutational Device," Ph.D. dissertation, Louisiana State U., 1971.

[27]A.D. Annis, "The Relative Effectiveness of Cartoons and Editorials as Propaganda Media," *Psychological Bulletin,* 36 (1939), 628.

[28]R. Asher, and S. Sargent, "Shifts in Attitude Caused by Cartoon Caricatures," *Journal of General Psychology*, 24 (1941), 451–55.

[29]Del Brinkman, "Do Editorial Cartoons and Editorials Change Opinions?" *Journalism Quarterly*, 45 (Winter, 1968), 724–26.

[30]LeRoy M. Carl, "Editorial Cartoons Fail to Reach Many Readers," *Journalism Quarterly*, 45 (Summer, 1968), 633–35.

[31](Garden City, N.Y.: Doubleday and Co., 1960).

[32]Eunice Cooper and Marie Jahoda, "The Evasion of Propaganda: How Prejudiced People Respond to Anti-Prejudice Propaganda," *Journal of Psychology*, 23 (1947), 15–25.

[33]David K. Berlo and Hideya Kumata, "The Investigator: The Impact of a Satirical Radio Drama," *Journalism Quarterly*, 33 (1956), 287–98.

[34]Charles R. Gruner, "An Experimental Study of Satire as Persuasion," *Speech Monographs*, 32 (June, 1965), 149–53.

[35]See his "Toward a Theory of Rhetorical Irony," *Speech Monographs*, 31 (June, 1964), 162–78.

[36]Jacqueline D. Goodchilds, "Effects of Being Witty on Position in the Social Structure of a Small Group," *Sociometry*, 22 (September, 1959), 261–71.

[37]Charles R. Gruner, "A Further Experimental Study of Satire as Persuasion," *Speech Monographs*, 33 (June, 1966), 184–85.

[38]Charles E. Osgood, George J. Suci, and Percy H. Tannenbaum, *The Measurement of Meaning* (Urbana, Ill.: University of Illinois Press, 1967).

[39]James V. Zeman, "An Experimental Study of the Persuasive Effects of Satire in a Speech Presented to a High School Audience," M.A. thesis, University of Nebraska, 1967.

[40]Gary F. Pokorny, "An Experimental Study of the Impact of Satiric Material Included in an Argumentative Speech," M.A. thesis, University of Nebraska, 1965.

[41]Gary F. Pokorny and Charles R. Gruner, "An Experimental Study of the Effect of Satire Used as Support in a Persuasive Speech," *Western Speech*, 33 (Summer, 1969), 204–11.

[42]Charles R. Gruner, "Editorial Satire as Persuasion: An Experiment," *Journalism Quarterly*, 44 (1967), 727–30.

[43]Charles R. Gruner, "Ad Hominem Satire as a Persuader:

An Experiment," *Journalism Quarterly*, 48 (Spring, 1971), 128–31.

44James C. McCroskey, "Scales for the Measurement of Ethos," *Speech Monographs*, 33 (March, 1966), 65–72.

45Charles R. Gruner, "An Experimental Study of Ad Hominem Editorial Satire: Art Hoppe *Vs.* Martha Mitchell," paper presented at the Speech Communication Association Convention, December 29, 1971, San Francisco. Biographical information on Mrs. Mitchell reprinted by permission from *Time*, the Weekly Newsmagazine; copyright Time, Inc., 1970.

46Charles R. Gruner, "Research Report #84: Semantic Differential and Thurstone Measures of Attitude Toward Censorship," *Central States Speech Journal*, 17 (August, 1966), 179–80.

47Mary Ann McGown, "An Experimental Study of the Persuasive Impact of a Satiric Editorial and That of a Comparable Direct Editorial," M.A. thesis, University of Nebraska, 1968.

48Student newspaper published at the University of Nebraska, Lincoln.

49Charles R. Gruner, "Art Hoppe *vs.* Capital Punishment: An Experiment," paper presented at the Southern Speech Communication Association, April 6, 1972, San Antonio.

50Ralph G. Nichols, "Do We Know How to Listen? Practical Helps in a Modern Age," in J. Jeffery Auer (ed.), *The Rhetoric of Our Times* (New York: Appleton-Century-Crofts, 1969), p. 232.

51See R.F. Priest, "Election Jokes: the Effects of Reference Group Membership," *Psychological Reports* 18 (1966), 600–02; and R.F. Priest and J. Abrahams, "Candidate Preference and Hostile Humor in the 1968 Elections," *Psychological Reports*, 26 (1970), 779–83.

52Charles R. Gruner, "Satire as a Reinforcer of Attitudes," paper presented at the SCA convention, December 28, 1972, Chicago.

53Dorothy Markiewicz, "The Effects of Humor on Persuasion," Ph.D. dissertation, The Ohio State University, 1972.

54D.H. Cullen, "Attitude Measurement by Cognitive Sampling," Ph.D. dissertation, The Ohio State University, 1968.

55Larry Powell, "The Effects of Ego Involvement on Responses to Editorial Satire," *Central States Speech Journal*, 26 (Spring, 1975), 34–38.

56Larry Powell, "Satirical Persuasion and Topic Salience,"

256 Notes

Southern Speech Communication Journal, 42 (Winter, 1977), 151–62.

[57]Stuart H. Surlin, "The Evaluation of Dogmatic Television Characters by Dogmatic Viewers: 'Is Archie Bunker a Credible Source?' " Paper presented at the International Communication Association's Annual Convention, April, 1973, Montreal.

[58]Neil Vidmar and Milton Rokeach, "Archie Bunker's Bigotry: A Study in Selective Perception and Exposure," *Journal of Communication*, 24 (Winter, 1974), 36–47.

[59]Stuart H. Surlin, "A Prosocial Message for Blacks: 'The Jeffersons,' " *Georgia Speech Communication Journal*, 8 (Fall, 1976), 28–40.

[60]Ray Brown, "Out of Humour," a review of Antony Chapman and Hugh Foot, *Humour and Laughter: Theory, Research and Applications* (New York: John Wiley & Sons, 1976).

[61]Gerald R. Miller and Paula Bacon, "Open- and Closed-Mindedness and Recognition of Visual Humor," *Journal of Communications*, 21, (June, 1971), 150–59.

[62]Charles R. Gruner, "Dogmatism: A Factor in the Understanding and Appreciation of Editorial Satire?" paper presented at the SCA convention, December 29, 1974, Chicago.

[63]Thomas A. Burns, "A Joke and Its Tellers: A Study of the Functional Variations of a Folklore Item at the Psychological Level," Ph.D. dissertation, Indiana University, 1972. Quote is from Burns' abstract.

[64]Richard M. Perreault, "A Study of the Effects of Humor in Advertising as Can Be Measured by Product Recall Tests," M.A. thesis, University of Georgia, 1972.

Chapter 7

[1]David K. Berlo, *The Process of Communication* (New York: Holt, Rinehart, and Winston, 1960), pp. 11–12.

[2](New York: Appleton-Century-Crofts, 1963).

[3]*Speech: Dynamic Communication* (New York: Harcourt, Brace and World, 1963), 255–58.

[4]*Speech: Its Techniques and Disciplines in a Free Society* (New York: Appleton-Century-Crofts, 1961), p. 446.

[5]John F. Wilson and Carroll C. Arnold, *Public Speaking as a Liberal Art*, 2nd ed. (Boston: Allyn and Bacon, 1966), p. 100.

[6]Robert T. Oliver, Harold P. Zelko, and Paul D. Holtzman,

Communication Speaking and Listening, 4th ed. (New York: Holt, Rinehart, and Winston, 1968), p. 165.

[7]Allan H. Monroe and Douglas Ehninger, *Principles of Speech Communication*, 6th brief ed. (Chicago: Scott, Foresman and Co., 1969), p. 232.

[8]Arthur N. Kruger, *Effective Speaking: A Complete Course*. (New York: Van Nostrand Reinhold Co., 1970), p. 329.

[9]Waldo N. Braden, *Public Speaking: The Essentials* (New York: Harper and Row, 1966), p. 161.

[10]Kenneth E. Andersen, *Persuasion: Theory and Practice*. (Boston: Allyn and Bacon, 1971), p. 185.

[11]Donald E. Kilpela, "An Experimental Study of Effects of Humor on Persuasion," M.A. thesis, Wayne State University, 1962.

[12]Pat M. Taylor, "Research Reports: The Effectiveness of Humor in Informative Speaking," *Central States Speech Journal*, 15 (November, 1964), 295–96.

[13]Pat M. Taylor, "The Role of Listener-Defined Supportive Humor in Speeches of Information," Ph.D. dissertation, University of Indiana, 1971.

[14]Entitled, "An Experimental Comparison of the Humorous Lecture and the Nonhumorous Lecture in Informative Speaking."

[15]Charles R. Gruner, "Effect of Humor on Speaker Ethos and Audience Information Gain," *Journal of Communication*, 17 (September, 1967), 228–33.

[16]Robert J. Kibler, "The Impact of Message Style and Channel in Communication," Ph.D. dissertation, Ohio State University, 1962.

[17]James C. McCroskey, "Scales for the Measurement of Ethos," *Speech Monographs*, 33 (March, 1966), 65–72.

[18]See Raymond G. Smith, "Development of a Semantic Differential for Use with Speech Related Concepts," *Speech Monographs*, 24 (November, 1959), 263–72.

[19]See Rudolph Flesch, *How to Test Readability* (New York: Harper and Brothers, 1951).

[20]Charles R. Gruner, "The Effect of Humor in Dull and Interesting Informative Speeches," *Central States Speech Journal*, 21 (Fall, 1970), 160–66.

[21]John Kenneth Reid, "The Effect of Humor on Perceived

Attractiveness of a Speaker," M.S. thesis, Oklahoma State University, 1971.

22David R. Mettee, Edward S. Hrelec, and Paul C. Wilkens, "Humor as an Interpersonal Asset and Liability," *The Journal of Social Psychology*, 85 (1971), 51–64.

23Taylor, *op. cit.*

24Leslie F. Malpass and Eugene D. Fitzpatrick, "Social Facilitation as a Factor in Reaction to Humor," *Journal of Social Psychology*, 50 (1959), 295–303.

25Ota Thomas Reynolds, "American Public Address and the Mass Media," in J. Jeffery Auer, ed., *The Rhetoric of Our Times* (New York: Appleton Century Crofts, 1969), p. 173.

26They used one other version of the lecture, with an "unsuccessful humor attempt," discussion of which is not germane to the point made here.

27R.C. Youngman, "An Experimental Investigation of the Effect of Germane Humor Versus Non-germane Humor in an Informative, Communication," Master's thesis, Ohio University, 1966.

28Jay M. Davis and Amerigo Farina, "Humor Appreciation as Social Communication," *Journal of Personality and Social Psychology*, 15 (1970), 175–78.

29G. Legman, *Rationale of the Dirty Joke: An Analysis of Sexual Humor*, First Series (New York: Grove Press, 1968). See especially Chapter 4, "The Male Approach," pp. 217ff.

30Rose L. Coser, "Some Social Functions of Laughter: A Study of Humor in a Hospital Setting," *Human Relations*, 12 (1959), 171–82.

31(New York: Basic Books, 1954).

32The proceedings of that conference are published as Antony J. Chapman and Hugh Foot, eds., *It's a Funny Thing, Humour* (New York: Permagon Press, 1977).

Name
Index

259

Name Index

Subject
Index